Blade Runners, Deer Hunters & Blowing the Bloody Doors Off

Blade Runners,
Deer Hunters & Blowing the
Bloody Doors Off

My Life In Cult Movies

Michael Deeley

with Matthew Field

faber and faber

First published in 2008
by Faber and Faber Limited
3 Queen Square London WC1N 3AU

Typeset by Faber and Faber
Printed and bound in the UK by CPI Mackays, Chatham ME5 8TD

A CIP record for this book
is available from the British Library

ISBN 978-0-571-23919-1

2 4 6 8 10 9 7 5 3 1

Contents

Illustrations

Foreword

Michael and I partnered to make *Blade Runner* in the late 1970s. It was to be my first actual experience making a film in Hollywood. It was a bumpy ride but one I wouldn't have missed – for anything . . .

Michael's sense of humour and wit prevails in his book, making it an accurate and entertaining read. A producer's life is not for the faint-hearted.

Sir Ridley Scott

Overture

'And the Winner Is . . .'?

It is 9 April 1979, 'Oscar Night' at the Dorothy Chandler Pavilion on Grand Avenue in downtown Los Angeles. Inimitable master of ceremonies Johnny Carson announces the presenter of the last and most important award category, Best Picture – and the audience is astonished to see John Wayne mount the stage.

'The Duke', seventy-one years old and terribly afflicted by stomach cancer, has made an extraordinary effort to be here. In the course of the previous year's ceremony MC Bob Hope sent a get-well to Wayne from the podium, inviting him to amble down in person next year. And now here he is. The audience's ovation is prolonged, and all the more moving because Wayne's obvious and uncharacteristic frailty suggest that he is losing his well-documented battle with the disease. (In fact, this would be his last appearance in public: two months later he was gone.)

I was among that audience – an English film producer and Academy member of ten years' standing, yet this was the first time I had ever attended the Oscar ceremony. I was nominated for a picture called *The Deer Hunter*, and had spent the last five hours waiting nervously to learn the names in the sealed envelope between Wayne's shaky fingers. Robert De Niro, the star of our film and fellow nominee, wasn't in the audience, such was the state of his own nerves. He had asked the Academy if he could sit out the show backstage, but no permission was forthcoming, and so De Niro chose to stay at home in New York.

I

From my place in the stalls I had slowly come round to the view that De Niro had spared himself a good deal of grief.

An Oscar nomination can be a life-changing marvel for a film-maker, but if your nomination is for Best Picture then you must accept that you are in for an interminable evening. The Academy demands that attendees be seated by 5:30 p.m., but you are unlikely to hear your fate any time before eleven o'clock. This comes, moreover, at the end of a peculiarly long day. A limo arrives to fetch you at 2:30 p.m. and off you go in full evening dress on a bright sunny afternoon – an object of curiosity to everyone in your neighbourhood. Faces peer through the window as your limo creeps along the line towards the theatre entrance, awash with press, TV cameras and avid movie fans. But it's all worth it, no question, for the glitziest event in the Hollywood calendar. And yet the actual making of the film for which I was nominated had been one of the more unpleasant experiences of my career.

The adventure had begun when I bought a first-draft script called *The Man Who Came to Play* for the modest sum of $19,000. By the time I produced it as *The Deer Hunter* I was president of EMI Films Inc., but before then I had taken the project to every studio in Hollywood, all of whom decided to pass. The standard response was that 'no American would want to see a picture about Vietnam'. I was constantly amazed by this argument, because the film that became *The Deer Hunter* was never a 'Vietnam movie'. (In the completed film the depiction of combat runs to about thirty seconds of screen time, and that is that.) But in the early days the illusion around the project persisted. Still, no producer worth their salt can afford to take 'No' for an answer. But even after I found financing, I had then to battle the antics of the film's director, amid the complications of what turned out to be an arduous post-production. I had worked with such famously taxing temperaments as Sam Peckinpah and Lindsay Anderson, and lived to tell the tale. I hired Michael Cimino, firstly to work on the script of *The Man Who Came to Play* and then, if that experience worked out, to direct the picture. In hindsight I was naïve, failing to realise until too late the depths of malice and dishonesty lurking in this soft-spoken little man.

In short, the picture had been a travail. I thought it just possible, though, that a golden statuette might compensate me for the whole experience. But the competition posed by our fellow nominees was tough. Perhaps my most immediate concern was David Puttnam's production of Alan Parker's *Midnight Express*. (Years later Puttnam would tell me that he and Parker had very nearly decided not to attend, such was their opinion of their chances. Still, I thought they could win.) In the spirit of good sport David and I made a deal that we would each take $500 to the ceremony, and if one of us won he would hand over the cash to the other, so that the loser might at least drown his sorrows in style. But in truth David was probably not the chief threat to *The Deer Hunter*'s chances – not if I had got my calculations right about how the voting might tend.

Academy membership is by invitation and covers the full spectrum of people working in film, from producers and directors to wardrobe and make-up. There is a myth which floats around the Academy that there are four bases upon which the average member decides his vote. His first cast will always be for any picture with which he is connected, however remotely. If there is no such picture, then he will vote in a way to spoil the chances of any enemy he may have. Category three is that he will vote for a friend, irrespective of the quality of the work. The fourth category – not that it usually gets this far – is that he will vote exactly as his judgement tells him about the standard of the year's pictures. My view was that the 3,500 or so members were sensible judges, no doubt, but easily put off by any irregularity, which was clearly what arch-plotter Warren Beatty was counting on.

In the weeks leading up to the event, orchestrated lobbying against *The Deer Hunter* took place, led by Beatty, whose own picture *Heaven Can Wait* had multiple nominations. It seemed that

Beatty had rustled up the services of his legion of ex-girlfriends. Julie Christie, serving on the jury at the Berlin Film Festival where *The Deer Hunter* was screened, had joined a walkout of the film by Russian jury members on account of its negative portrayal of North Vietnamese combatants. That atmosphere of political protest would persist: even on this night of the Oscar ceremony, when all the votes had already been cast, police fought to hold back protestors thrusting pamphlets berating *The Deer Hunter* through the windows of the long line of limousines. Jane Fonda's campaigning on behalf of the North Vietnamese cause had seen her nicknamed 'Hanoi Jane', and she too had fiercely criticised *The Deer Hunter* in public. It hardly seemed coincidental that *Coming Home*, Hal Ashby's anti-war 'Vietnam movie' starring Fonda, was vying with *The Deer Hunter* for Best Picture. In the event I had managed to plant a friend of mine in the special Oscar press area behind the stage, and when Fonda was ushered in as newly crowned Best Actress for her performance in Ashby's film, my accomplice asked her if she had actually *seen* this *Deer Hunter* that she so castigated? Her snapped response was something along the lines of 'No, I don't have to. I know what it's about . . .'

Inside the Chandler Pavilion I watched De Niro's co-star Christopher Walken collect the Supporting Actor Oscar, followed by further *Deer Hunter* wins for Sound and Editing (though in fact Cimino had got rid of our editor Peter Zinner for the sin of agreeing with me that the picture was too long). My suspicion remained that we were being compensated with technical prizes prior to being denied Best Picture. And then Cimino scooped Best Director. It is rare that the Best Picture and Best Director awards are split. *The Deer Hunter*'s odds had dramatically improved, which only increased the suspense leading to the final prize. I wasn't breathing so easily as Wayne carefully opened the envelope to reveal the winner. But it was *The Deer Hunter*.

My ex-colleague Barry Spikings and I took to the stage, joined by Cimino, who emerged from behind a curtain where he had been regaling the press after his earlier victory. By this point in the evening the audience wants to go home – nobody wants to hear you thank your grandmother or pets. My speech was brief: I thanked the agent Bobby Littman who had introduced me to the original script, and Harry Ufland, Robert De Niro's agent, a first-class professional who had smoothed the path for me to cast his esteemed client.

So it had proved a suspenseful yet triumphant night, the kind which few people get to experience, and rarely see repeated. The gamble of *The Deer Hunter* and of EMI's foray into Hollywood had proved profitable, and now it was crowned as an artistic success too. After twenty-five years in movies I had officially 'made it' – an Englishman ahead of the game in the rat race of Hollywood. It was now time for the Governor's Ball, the first in a roundabout of extravagant Oscar Night parties, routinely attended by all nominees – winners and losers both. I duly handed over to David Puttnam a cheque for $500 that had been burning the proverbial hole in my top pocket all night. Congratulations from other fellow Best Picture nominees were not much in evidence: the majority, I supposed, had been actively opposed to us. But then that ball was also the last time I saw Michael Cimino, and the moment couldn't have come too soon. To this day the only flaw I find in my Oscar is that Cimino's name is also engraved on it. I keep it on a very high shelf, so that I can see the award but not the unpleasantness minutely chiselled there.

In January 2005 I watched a special-edition DVD of *The Deer Hunter* which was never distributed in America. To be precise, I sat and listened to Michael Cimino lying through his teeth. He told the interviewer how he had created the idea for *The Deer Hunter* – thus ignoring Louis Garfinkle's and Quinn K. Redeker's original story. He claimed to have pitched the idea to Lew Wasserman at Universal, though I doubt he ever met that legendary patrician head of the movie industry. He said he had originally pitched the idea to Lord Delfont at EMI, an amusing notion had it been true. He said that Joann Carelli had really produced the movie. Ms Carelli had been credited as Associate Producer (an old joke has it that this functionary is so called because he/she is the only person willing to associate with the producer). My memory of Joann Carelli's function was that she had provided Cimino with admiration and support, and confirmed that his every decision was the correct one. Such capacities did not qualify her as the 'real' producer of *The Deer Hunter*.

As I carried on watching and listening to Cimino's fantastic account, it seemed to me that his dyed blond hair and dark sunglasses only added to the falsehood of his image. The only sensible thing he said referred to 'the morons at EMI, those so-called "producers"'. He was right. We must have been morons to have dealt with Michael Cimino.

Whatever I felt about Cimino's behaviour, I had the satisfaction of knowing that *The Deer Hunter* had been made because I had caused it to be made. I found the script, I hired the writer, I hired the director, I hired the star and I sold the package to a major US distributor. However some individuals may seek to rewrite history, I know what I did and I am proud – *The Deer Hunter* was my invention. But when you come right down to it, a producer doesn't really make films: to reiterate, he *causes* them to be made, and this I find a better definition of the job than any that has yet appeared.

People sometimes ask me why I don't keep copies of the films I have produced. The answer is because each one carries with it a measure of regret: sometimes, that I let a director persuade me to waste money on some sequence that added nothing to – perhaps even subtracted from – the drama; or, sometimes, that I denied some spending over the budget for a certain aspect that, in retrospect, I realise probably would have improved the result. Directors aren't perfect and nor are producers. I don't want mentally to remake my pictures every time I look back at them. But for the purpose of this book I have had to look again at as many of them as could be found. A nudist film that was one of my earliest efforts has, understandably and thankfully, disappeared – as have a few B-pictures. Films rarely disappear completely, but some of mine have faded away. Does anyone remember *One-Way Pendulum*, directed by Peter Yates in 1964? And yet when we made it we had such high hopes . . .

The subtitle of this book is *My Life In Cult Movies* – but aren't 'cult movies' little films that have been largely ignored by the general public, yet defended vigorously by a few aficionados? I would propose that it is really a question of the degree of devotion a movie inspires. One could argue that the mega-grossing *Star Wars* is also a 'cult movie'. But one can say the same of *The Wicker Man*, which barely saw the light of day back in 1973 when I was MD of British Lion Films. Or consider *The Man Who Fell to Earth*, which I produced in 1975 – a film that Paramount Pictures effectively disowned at that time, but which is treasured by discerning movie-goers to this day on the strength of its inimitable leading man, David Bowie, and its brilliant director, the visionary Nicolas Roeg.

Cult movies are often works later reckoned to be 'ahead of their time', and I think I can claim to have produced a few of those. There are others whose time has yet to come, and I'm not holding my breath for *One-Way Pendulum*. But it is a real joy when those 'mistimed' pictures grow up and find the public appreciation they always merited. When *The Italian Job* was in production in 1969 I naturally had no idea that it would become a 'cult classic'. But every year, two hundred or so Minis make a drive for charity from London to Turin, the birthplace of the movie. *The Italian Job*, nearly forty years after its release, is rooted in the affections of the British public and, as far as that public are concerned, is probably better loved and respected than the two heavyweight contenders of my career – *The Deer Hunter* and *Blade Runner*. *The Deer Hunter* ought really to be my personal favourite, since it delivered me that Oscar. A certain unpleasantness surrounded the conclusion of *Blade*

Runner, and its subsequent release was slow and perhaps ill-timed, banging heads with Spielberg's *E.T.* rather than slipping into the marketplace in December, in time for Oscar consideration. But these matters were essentially superficial and did nothing to diminish my delight in the picture. In 2007, twenty-five years after it first came and went from screens, *Blade Runner* returned to theatres and on DVD in a 'Final Cut', and was acclaimed as Ridley Scott's masterpiece. Set in 2019 – now barely a decade hence – *Blade Runner* managed to forecast drastic climate change, rampant immigration, urban decay and genetic advances scarcely imagined at the time, and there are still a few years to go. (Look out, humans.) All told, *Blade Runner* is – yes, by far – my favourite among the films I produced. *The Deer Hunter*, I think, is impressive still, and its creation began happily and optimistically. If I don't love it, this is because of the unpleasantness I will describe in the pages ahead.

But perhaps you have begun to wonder: how did this man come to be associated with so many pictures that have inspired such passionate followings? Was he drawn to – did he seek out – 'difficult' subject matter and volatile directors? Or is his curriculum vitae just a string of happy (or not-so-happy) accidents?

I should say from the outset that I never, ever wanted to be a director of movies. And when I embarked on a film career I had no conception of what kind of picture I wanted to produce, either: I was just focused on making pictures. As such, my first forays into the field didn't seem to have any great importance or unifying purpose. And yet, when I look back . . . the very first film on which I worked, as a humble assistant editor, was Jacques Tati's *Les Vacances de Monsieur Hulot* (1953). Tati's film was completely off the wall: a unique – one might say ridiculously unique – piece of work. A little later, the first film that I personally produced – *The Case of the Mukkinese Battlehorn* (1956), starring Peter Sellers and his then-fellow Goons – was also quite unclassifiable. So, in a sense, I started out from an anomalous position: these were two films that could

8

have been said to lead one in the direction of madness.

I would say that once I reached a point in my career of having a *choice* of pictures to make – then it was always about doing something different, something that wasn't instantly recognisable, not a cross between Blockbuster A and Blockbuster B, as people forever propose when they're pitching in Hollywood ('It's *Star Wars* meets *Titanic*', et cetera). I didn't want to do remakes – I hate the idea of them, much as I hate the idea of sequels now (though at the time I would have been grateful of an *Italian Job* sequel.) I did make one or two pretty bland films, but above all the intention was to be completely original – to do things that hadn't been done before.

Perhaps the simplest way for me to underscore my proposition is to look at the directors with whom I worked. Sam Peckinpah, my director on *Convoy* (1978), was nobody's idea of an easy way to make a living. And any project undertaken with Nicolas Roeg is bound to be an adventure. Ridley Scott is not 'easy', but as the wise old saying has it, 'Easy-going goes nowhere': I had such huge respect for Ridley that it was certainly an easy decision for me to take the journey with him, inevitable difficulties and all. In general, as I went along I found that the directors got more and more talented and more and more difficult. They usually had their own *idée fixe*, and they didn't always share it with me – rather, it would emerge. But I went in knowing they might be hard work, and I never kidded myself otherwise. Even if they're trouble, they're talented: for example, the famously prickly Lindsay Anderson, with whom I clashed early in my career, nevertheless taught me a major lesson about the mechanics of getting films made.

I didn't anticipate that Michael Cimino would be much bother – his CV had a bland look to me – but I was wrong. Such experiences are the least savoury aspect of the producer's lot. The moviegoing public might be more inclined to sympathise if they had a better understanding of what a producer actually *does* in the first place. Or they might not.

★ ★ ★

There is an old Hollywood adage about Roger Corman, producer of over three hundred pictures and always on the tightest of budgets. It is said that Corman could negotiate a film deal on a payphone, shoot said film in the booth, and cover the entire cost with the money in the change slot. If this procedure sounds a tad parsimonious, it offers at least a hands-on model of how to produce a movie that anyone in or out of the business could comprehend.

And yet modern Hollywood productions can have up to a dozen confusing 'producer' credits – executive producers, co-producers, associate producers, line producers et cetera. On *Blade Runner*, Brian Kelly and Hampton Fancher were executive producers because of their early investment in the screenplay, long before I became involved in the enterprise. Sometimes agents who package the talent for a movie can wangle themselves associate producer credits, but these are not highly valued at large. It's widely known that packagers and financiers of movies are not prone to spending large amounts of time on set or location, and this is where the line producer comes in. He is on the picture every hour of the day wherever it is being shot – the ramrod figure who concentrates on supervising the day-to-day management of the production. He will not exercise much creative input, but that too may be appreciated. (Occasionally a good screenwriter gets his first directing job and, being keen to retain creative control, seeks not a real partnership with a producer but rather a reliable line producer who will busy himself entirely with logistics.)

But being a producer is an activity which requires no exam passes and no specific training. You don't even have to join a union, and the title can be self-awarded: a lot of young men and women with or without a script to peddle are 'producers'. There are almost too many routes into the job. Quite a few actors' and writers' agents step up to become producers. The profession can be a sort of sanctuary for fired movie executives. Actors can become powerful enough to produce, as can directors, though it is usually a mistake for the latter group, whose natural delight in the material they have shot often needs an independent restraining hand.

An agent may be best placed to become the consummate deal-making producer, but if your ambition is to become a full-service producer – creative, managerial and financially acute – the best background must lie within the ranks of almost any of the crafts and technical grades which make up a film unit. Not having worked on a production unit is a negative when it comes to the task of understanding and managing the more than a hundred people routinely employed on a motion picture. I would argue that the best training is to have come through the cutting room. Film editing brings the photographed material down to its essence, and while it is tremendous training for directors (consider the example of David Lean) it can also be very valuable to a producer when the crunch comes at the final stage of preparing a film for public presentation.

But then I would say this, wouldn't I? It was as a young man fresh out of the cutting rooms that I learned the business, working for Woodfall Films which turned out *Saturday Night and Sunday Morning*, *A Taste of Honey*, *The Knack* and the multiple Oscar winner *Tom Jones*. I admit that when I entered the film industry I had no idea what the functions of a producer were – nor did I particularly care. It was only when I managed – with Harry Booth, my editing partner – to cut a day's work in the space two hours that he and I decided there must be further profitable ways to make money in the industry. Camera crews all have to be on the set constantly but editors have their own studio office – the cutting room – a telephone and, in some cases, plenty of spare time. We decided it wouldn't be bad to start at the top. We produced our first three pictures while still holding down our editing jobs. Those were the days . . . but it wasn't long before I learned that producing for a living would be rather more time consuming.

For instance, I shudder to think how much of my working life has been wasted on fruitless pursuits of saleable movie ideas. Still, an independent producer cannot function in Hollywood or anywhere else without a property to sell, and so the ability to identify and snap up promising material is an essential skill. Where do movies come from? Sometimes it's a book or a play, a magazine article, a news story, an historical event. One of my pictures, *Convoy*, began life as a hit song. But winning the auction for the rights to anything that's already been a smash in another medium is simply beyond the means of the tyro producer. Instead he or she must become a detective, scavenging the bookshelves or the press clippings for neglected stories that might yet snare the attention of millions.

This raw material must then be converted into the first draft of a screenplay. Good screenwriters tend to have good agents who like to earn good money, so it's not a bad idea to stay in the good books of any talented writers you happen to meet: down the line, they may be prepared to do some initial work in exchange for love – and a profit percentage – rather than hard cash.

When a screenplay is as good as the producer and his friend the writer can get it, he starts putting together his package – the director and stars. On the surface this sounds like the fun part, but of course one very rarely has one's pick of the available talent. Then comes financing – most often dependent on the star-rating of one's talent, and the part that many a novice would assume to be the most tiresome chore. True, this stage is not nearly so fascinating as being on a set with Robert De Niro, nor will you ever get to regale dinner-party gatherings with tales of how you managed to pull off a great multi-territory pre-sale (as opposed to your best anecdote of what it was like working with 'Bob'). But all I can say is that the sooner a producer gets his head around the multifarious means of raising funds for a picture, be it territory by territory or medium by medium, the quicker he will come to earn a reasonable living and so secure his future happiness.

And then, at last, the making of the movie: at this crucial stage the producer's job becomes above all a matter of providing everything necessary for the director to perform his own function, which is directing actors and photographing their performances. Directors, be they good, bad, or mediocre, all tend toward the fastidious; and, short of agreeing to move the Taj Mahal two inches to the left, the producer must deliver. Sometimes conflict occurs when the director either comes to a different vision of the project – perhaps one which is much more expensive – or because he always had other intentions, and simply didn't deign to mention these to the producer. On two separate pictures I found myself in just such a slippery situation, and unhappily both were at the same time – with the directors of *Convoy* and *The Deer Hunter*.

But whatever has been the state of on-set relations, once shooting is over the producer must give the director complete freedom for at least two months to edit the film the way he wants. Ideally he will see the picture in a form that is reasonably near to what the financing studio contracted. If he has other grander or more eccentric ideas, then the air can start to fill with rancour. Quite often this is when the director complains that the producer or studio are butchering his elegant and gently paced masterpiece, while the studio execs are shuffling contracts, pointing out that they agreed to finance what was on the page rather than all the imaginary flourishes the director has inserted. I have been there too, several times over . . .

Why, then, did I ever decide to take up this apparently thankless profession? What possessed me to stick at it? In order to answer, I should first rewind the spool back to the start.

1

Robin Hood, the Goons and the Nudist Boom

Everybody wants to be in the movies. This has been the case since the earliest moving pictures, and it's liable to remain so for the foreseeable future. In spite of all one could say to disabuse young people of their dreams, the film world retains an incredible allure and remains a vital aspiration for far more individuals than the industry could ever hope to employ gainfully.

So I hope it won't sound cavalier if I say that I was someone who stumbled into the film business, more or less by accident. My father was in advertising, a director of the McCann-Erickson agency. As for myself, after a respectable boarding-school education at Stowe, and some military adventures in the Far East, I thought of law or the diplomatic service as my future. That said, it's undeniably the case that my mother Anne had worked as a PA to certain film producers, and so my school holidays were often spent hanging around on movie sets. One such was *Caesar and Cleopatra*, made in 1944 when I was twelve years old. I remember watching Claude Rains and Vivien Leigh chatting as they leaned against a Sphinx on an elaborate set constructed at Denham Studios, Buckinghamshire. Gabriel Pascal, as mad as any movie director before or since, had insisted on shipping tons of sand from Egypt, for apparently the local British sand 'didn't look the same' – and this during wartime, with Britain under siege. Come 1949, I spent my school holidays as the clapper-boy on a picture called *The Girl Is Mine* starring Patrick Macnee, still some years away from perfecting his exportable brand of dapper Pierre Cardin-clad charm in the role of *The Avengers'* John Steed.

The British film industry immediately after the war was dominated by gentlemanly directors (from Anthony 'Puffin' Asquith to David Lean and Carol Reed), all making very posh films mostly derived from books or plays. But by the early 1950s their influence was fading. Sir Michael Balcon's Ealing Studios was producing *The Lavender Hill Mob* and *The Man in the White Suit*. Powell and Pressberger were still working on the lavish scale of *The Red Shoes* but British film was very much a cottage industry. The only major productions were Hollywood costume dramas shot in England, a tradition which had existed under Sir Alexander Korda and Michael Balcon when he was head of MGM-British in the late 1930s. (By the 1970s Mick Balcon had become a great friend and something of a mentor to me.)

But in 1950 I was called up for my obligatory National Service. An eighteen-year-old junior officer, I was sent to Malaya, ostensibly to help combat the communists who were said to be gradually taking over South East Asia. Really it was part of a strategy to protect Britain's important rubber and tin-mining activities on the Malay Peninsula. It *was* a war – we shot people and they shot some of us – but it was labelled 'an emergency' in order to protect the British companies in Malaya from having their insurance cancelled, which would certainly have happened had the conflict been given its true name.

I arrived back in London in November 1952 with no plans other than to attend university, but a phone call was about to change my life for ever. My mother happened to be working on a picture in Switzerland and while I was staying in her house in London I took a phone call from the film editor Joe Sterling, whom I had known for some years. 'What are you up to?' Joe asked. I told him I supposed I should get a job for the next ten months. '*I'll* give you a job,' he said.

Joe was employed by Douglas Fairbanks Jr, son of the legendary movie actor who co-founded the United Artists studio in Hollywood. Fairbanks Jr had had a distinguished naval career during the war, albeit not so much aboard ship as in the drawing rooms of London society, where his charm and good looks were a valuable bridge between British and American allies. Though an American citizen, he was awarded an honorary knighthood by King George VI in recognition of those diplomatic skills. And while he would never have insisted on the observance of such dignities, the telephonists at Elstree's National Studios invariably referred to him as Sir Douglas.

I began work for Joe as an assistant editor on the modest wage of £7.50 a week: exactly what I had been paid for the last year I had spent in the jungle ambushing – and being ambushed by – the guerrillas of the Malayan Races Liberation Army. Quite a few people would have given anything for the opportunity presented to me, and I only wanted a temporary job. Of course it was nepotism. But nepotism at least has the advantage that if you come into the film industry via family, as so many of us did, you already know what is expected of you in terms of discipline and punctuality.

I quickly fell in love with my work in a team of young enthusiastic editors, recutting foreign films (German, French, 'Bollywood') and dubbing them into English. The first such picture to pass through my Moviola was Tati's soon-to-be-classic *Les Vacances de Monsieur Hulot* (1953). Less well-starred was an obscure Indian picture titled *Arzoo* (*Desire*). At a fateful point in this assignment the producer, one Mr Chaudhury, came steaming into the editing suite, grabbed the print and took off with it, to the astonishment of both me and my fellow editors. We speculated that this unshowable film was destined to be the subject of a mysterious accident – thereby qualifying for a compensatory insurance claim. Mr Chaudhury further succeeded in leaving the country without paying us.

Still, by and large, I was having the time of my life, increasingly immersed in the movie world and no longer intending to head off to university. My experiences had brought home to me what a socially sheltered life I had led from my schooling up to the end of my National Service. Most of my fellow technicians were Jewish and had left school at fifteen or sixteen, but they were much more worldly wise and, in some areas, more experienced than me. I soon realised that I should flatten out my public school accent: it would not have boded well for the most junior member of the cutting-room staff to seem to be putting on airs.

I moved on to the hit American TV series *Robin Hood,* which starred Richard Greene and was made at Walton-on-Thames Studios. The series was produced by Hannah Weinstein, efficient in her job and a good businesswoman. Politically left of centre, she provided shelter and work for like-minded writers who had been locked out of Hollywood by the 'blacklist' that arose from the work of the notorious House Un-American Activities Committee (HUAC). Many of the first thirty-nine episodes of *Robin Hood* were written by Ring Lardner Jr and Ian McLellan, who used different pseudonyms for each script so that the US advertisers wouldn't boycott the show because of its association with so-called political undesirables – Joe Losey and Carl Foreman were there, too. *Robin Hood* ran for three years, and its theme of thieving from the rich and giving to the poor was heaven sent for writers of a progressive bent: every episode duly contained some element of high-minded redistribution of wealth. (I wound up trying my hand at writing one of these half-hour episodes myself, and was paid a useful £100 for my effort.)

Otherwise my editing partner Harry Booth and I found that we were working incredibly fast and finishing a day's work in a couple of hours. With time on our hands we decided to become part-time producers: we were emboldened to start at the top, and felt that we had as much experience of the job as half the so-called producers hustling round Wardour Street.

In common with a large chunk of the British population, Harry and I were then fascinated by the radio comedy *The Goon Show,* which had made stars of Peter Sellers, Spike Milligan and Harry Secombe. We wanted to transform the show into a TV series, and hired *Goon* writer Larry Stephens to write a script while we set out to raise the necessary finance (which we budgeted at £4,500). None of us had actually prepared a budget before but the task was made easier by an enormously detailed template document that was standard in the days before computer software. Across forty huge pages were itemised every conceivable aspect of a production, and it was a matter of simply filling in the blanks – not a difficult job on a small picture which we knew we would have to shoot in a week, at a rate of about seven minutes a day. A neighbour of Harry's, John Penington, had worked as a producer in the theatre and we brought him in as our partner so that he could do the legwork while we were spending the morning over at Walton doing our daily stint on *Robin Hood*.

We raised the finance from three sources. Archway Film Distributors put in £1,500 to obtain distribution rights. They were a modest young company specialising in short films – a handy back-up in the likely event that we failed to sell a TV series, and so could recut the pilot as a short for release theatrically. Peter Weingreen, an American assistant director on *Robin Hood*, liked the idea of a share of the profits and also put up £1,500. Joe Sterling invested the remaining £1,500 and for that price he also achieved his wish to become the director. My first producer's fee was £125 – perhaps the equivalent of £1,000 today, or roughly a fortnight's wages from *Robin Hood*. Peter Sellers, our star, was paid for this, his first film, a princely £900 – a sum negotiated by his clever agent Beryl Vertue, who operated from a tiny office above a greengrocer's shop in Shepherd's Bush and later became a successful producer.

The Case of the Mukkinese Battlehorn, as the film was called, tells the story of an antique musical instrument which is stolen from a London museum. Detective Inspector Peter Sellers of Scotland Yard is assigned to retrieve the artefact and solve the crime. We shot in five days at a small studio in Merton Park, near Walton. Hannah Weinstein knew what we were up to and was amused at the idea of her cutting-room staff producing a TV pilot in their spare time – amused, that is, as long as we kept up to date with our *Robin Hood* chores.

Sellers was clearly ambitious and well disciplined. In other words, he gave no hint of the neuroses that would later ravage his life. But Spike Milligan was clearly deranged, or so he seemed to us – hyperactive, with none of the professional calm exhibited by Sellers. On the first day of shooting Milligan rushed up to me and said, 'Why don't you nail a white sheet up on the studio wall?' I looked at him oddly – puzzled. 'Sometimes I suddenly get a great idea,' he explained. 'And when that happens all you have to do is wheel the camera over to the wall and photograph me.' I explained the rather more complex logistics of film shooting to him, and he clearly thought I was a bit thick.

The third Goon, Harry Secombe, had proved too rich for our modest budget, since he had by this time developed a fantastic solo singing career. Thus Dick Emery, an occasional understudy for Milligan on radio, was drafted in to replace Secombe. Thankfully, Sellers and Emery had perfect timing. In one scene, Emery plays a security guard injured during the robbery. Detective Inspector Sellers enquires of him, 'Describe to me in your own words exactly what happened.' Emery has taken off his cap to reveal a head swathed in bandages. 'Well, I was doing my rounds and this geezer hit me on me 'ead. WALLOP! WALLOP! WALLOP! On me 'ead. Down I goes. I gets up again. WALLOP! WALLOP WALLOP! on me 'ead again and down I goes.' Sellers asks, 'Did you notice any- thing unusual about this man?' The guard thinks carefully before replying. 'Yes, sir. There was something odd. He kept on walloping me on me 'ead.'

The final cut of *Mukkinese Battlehorn* ran to twenty-six minutes, the ideal length for US television. Thus we gathered all our American TV film friends into a small theatre to enjoy what we thought was a hilarious little film. Their subsequently stony response was not what we had hoped for. Clearly the humour was strictly British. Mercifully we had our Plan B. Back in 1950s Britain a typical trip to the movies would entail sitting through one ninety-minute feature presentation, one sixty-minute B-movie or two thirty-minute 'shorts', on top of a newsreel and advertisements. So we recut our film to thirty-three minutes and it played on the cinema circuits.

Mukkinese Battlehorn is over fifty years old now but it remains the most profitable film I have ever made – relative to cost – having recouped its original budget ten times over. *Pirates of the Caribbean* it was most certainly not, but no studio could sniff at such a favourable rate of return. And in 2007 I had the pleasure of donating a copy of the picture to the British Film Institute's National Film Archive, so converting an amusing jape into *bona fide* cinema history.

After our first little flutter in the world of producing, Harry and I continued our respectable jobs on *Robin Hood*. A couple of years later Hannah Weinstein transferred us to Twickenham Studios to work on her first colour TV series, *The Buccaneers*, an ambitious pirate yarn with Robert Shaw as a swashbuckling hero. But soon we felt the urge to produce another picture, and our confidence was sufficient for us to embark on a feature-length production. In 1957 I co-wrote *At the Stroke of Nine*, a so-called 'quota quickie' that cost £20,000. Come 1958 our main TV serial assignment was the producer Jules Buck's *OSS*, an ambitious World War II behind-enemy-lines spy thriller. In due course we would squeeze in another B-feature, *Crosstrap* (1961), which starred Canadian actor Robert Beatty and was shot in the studio in which we were editing *OSS*. This time out, I felt that with our growing experience, Harry and I should be entitled to a slightly larger fee than we had been receiving – perhaps £600 apiece per picture. Thus I bowled into the office of financier/distributor Steven Pallos in the hope of negotiating a better deal. 'My boy,' hissed Pallos, 'you are too young to earn more than £300!' Such was the received wisdom of the day; nowadays his equivalent would probably tell me I'm too old.

Jules Buck had also produced such impressive film-noir features as *Brute Force* and *The Naked City*, and he became both friend and mentor to me. As production wound down on *OSS* Buck took me out to lunch. He told me it was time to upgrade. After all, there was only so long I could carry on in the cutting rooms. Buck said, 'It's time for you to find out about the business side of the movies – get out of your sweater and jeans and into a suit.' Buck set up a meeting with Cecil Tennant at MCA Universal, the biggest TV producer and talent agency in the world.

Although I had no film distribution experience, Cecil gave me £40 a week to manage their UK TV film sales operation. He could also see that my experience of shooting low-budget movies might be of use to the company. If MCA decided to shoot some TV shows in Britain, I suppose it was good for them to have someone like me around. I was given top-class shows to sell – the likes of *Dragnet* and *Wagon Train* – both to the BBC and to local independent broadcasters scattered across the UK. I had a wonderful time travelling all over Britain and learning about the business side of the industry.

In 1962 MCA acquired Universal Studios and under anti-trust laws had to give up its agency business. But in 1958 it was still able to produce television films, which it did under the name Revue. I worked for Revue but shared offices with the talent agency at 139 Piccadilly. A constant stream of stars passed through the place, as did the great Lew Wasserman, who was then head of MCA Universal and would remain so until the mid-1990s, becoming, as one filmmaker aptly put it, 'the closest thing Hollywood has to a pope'. Wasserman would visit the UK twice a year and on such trips I was allocated two hours of his time. I learned more about the film industry from Lew in those few hours than I had in the preceding five years. (Years later I ran into him in the famous black tower office block on the Universal lot in LA while I was setting up *The Deer Hunter*. He looked at me, paused, and said, 'Didn't you used to work for me?' I nodded. 'I wondered what became of you . . .' he said.)

After three good years at MCA I wanted to get back into film production. The distribution experience had been valuable, and I had been judged a success. Now with a string of contacts, I set up a partnership with a US television producer, Bruce Yorke, who had managed the mid-Atlantic Bermuda Playhouse owned by Huntingdon Hartford, the eccentric A & P grocery-store magnate. While working for Hartford, Bruce had produced two series for US television. Now we began trying to set up a variety of features. Bruce had enough money to cover the overheads and we operated from his house in Montpelier Street. Our next-door neighbour was Ken Adam, who was and still is one of the world's greatest production designers, responsible for the most spectacular James Bond sets as well as the stunning designs of Kubrick's *Dr Strangelove* and *Barry Lyndon*.

The early 1960s brought the advent of a curious phenomenon called the nudist film, devoted to avid sun-worshippers and packed with people frolicking around swimming pools or volleyball courts. Never was there a glimpse of male or female genitalia, but of course there were breasts everywhere, albeit discreetly masked by a flower pot, ping-pong bat or some other inoffensive object interposed between the camera and the owner's modesty. Small theatres in the West End of London played these pictures and attracted enough of an audience to make them worthwhile. Nat Miller, a small-time British distributor, approached Yorke and me with a proposal to make one of these 'nudies'. I never imagined I would make such a movie, but for a production fee of £1,000 how could I possibly refuse? In the event, we had a lot of fun making the picture, though I was credited as M. D. Lee lest any of my friends called into one of those West End theatres . . . My very efficient girlfriend Susan Mitchell wrote the script and my mother, between more respectable jobs, became the continuity girl.

Thus *Sandy the Reluctant Nudist* went into production. We assembled a group of nice young actors and actresses who didn't mind stripping off and gambolling around in the Buckinghamshire woodlands. We obtained permission to shoot background atmosphere for one day at a real nudist camp. Spielplatz had been established in the 1930s at the height of the naturism craze. Many of the campers were keen to be photographed, although some of them had unusual physical characteristics. One twelve-year-old boy was endowed with an absurdly large penis and he had to be forcibly removed from the set – he had obviously been told that it pays to advertise, but we had the wrath of the censor to think about.

After one sweltering morning shooting under the hot summer sun, our six-man crew retreated to the on-site canteen. The only

A US advert for *Sandy the Reluctant Nature Girl* (note the alteration to our original UK release title). Prospective viewers were being deceived, insofar as none of the 'luscious lovelies' depicted in the artwork actually appear in the film.

choices were salad or salad, and we were served by an elderly, life-long nudist, who was of course dressed accordingly. On bringing our salads she stretched across the table to place a plate in front of our cameraman Terry Maher and inadvertently (and without real-ising) pressed her crotch into my meal. Once she had gone, Terry's eyes were transfixed upon the food on my plate. I followed his gaze and noticed – atop my lettuce and tomatoes, glistening in vinai-grette dressing – a single grey pubic hair. On that note, we resolved to head to the nearest pub for a liquid lunch instead.

A string of B-movies followed for me, some European co-produc-tions, none very notable. In my mind, I was fighting to make it into the big time. Then I read a script titled *The White Rabbit* – a drama-tisation of the World War II story of Wing Commander F. E. Yeo-Thomas, who famously gave assistance to the French Resistance and later escaped Buchenwald concentration camp. The tale was so rich that it struck me as our big chance. Bruce and I obtained a temporary approval from the writer: we certainly couldn't afford to buy the property before we had finance. A string of meetings ensued with agents, stars and directors as we compiled a package to pique the interest of a distributor who would finance the movie. We talked to Dirk Bogarde, John Mills and James Mason, and to directors such as Guy Green, Robert Siodmak and Roy Baker.

Then we struck gold. Kenneth More, then one of the biggest stars in Britain, read the script, loved it and was available. I went to British Lion Films to meet John Boulting, one of the twins who ran the company. He read the script and quickly called another meeting. They were looking for an A-picture so we were really excited. He asked, 'Have you signed an agreement with Kenneth More?' I said no, but told him that if he called More's agent, he would confirm the actor's interest in the picture. Which he did. Boulting then said, 'Show me the contract you have with the writer.' Again I said we hadn't got the cash to buy it, but if he called the author he would confirm that I had an informal permission to purchase the script. Boulting said, 'I'll be in touch.'

He wasn't. Nor would he return phone calls. I became suspicious and within days found out some disastrous news. Boulting had gone behind our backs, bought the script and was negotiating with Kenneth More. I bumped into Boulting at the White Elephant restaurant where I publicly gave him a good dressing-down. He simply laughed and said, 'You should learn to be more careful.' In the event it wasn't until 1967 that a five-hour mini-series was made with More in the lead role. Boulting blew our chance of making a movie, and without any ultimate benefit to himself. The movie world's reputation for back-stabbing and double-dealing has some basis because movie people are instinctively competitive. But over ten formative years in the film industry I had been given so much help and kindness from various mentors that Boulting's treachery was a shock. I marked it down to bitter experience, and moved on.

2

Getting *The Knack*

Woodfall was the British production company of its day. While British cinema had become naturally associated with stiff studio-bound romantic movies or the pleasing whimsy of Ealing comedies, Woodfall arose as a sort of natural extension of the boldness of London's Royal Court Theatre (as exemplified by John Osborne's *Look Back in Anger*) as well as the uncompromising 'Free Cinema' documentary movement of Karel Reisz, Lindsay Anderson and Tony Richardson. Woodfall took pride in its association with the 'Angry Young Men' writers noted for their unflinching realism, and in the fact that they shot everything outside of the studio to maximise said realism.

The company was formed by Osborne and Richardson, spurred by their artistic and financial success in live theatre, and in partnership with Canadian producer Harry Saltzman. But Saltzman's acerbic attitude led to his early departure from the partnership. Harry was a hard bastard, extremely brusque. If he saw no advantage in having a conversation with you then he likely wouldn't reply to 'Good morning'. His lovely French wife made up for a lot of her husband's roughness, but there was a vulgarity to Harry that didn't sit well with Osborne or Richardson. Those two were both of striking height and each, in his own way, very English. Harry was short, round, Canadian, and had once been a circus barker. Loaded with aggression, he loved to cause an argument. From Woodfall he disappeared into the wild blue yonder before returning a few years later – in the company of James Bond. Harry had managed to secure the rights to Ian Fleming's novels, but he was broke. It is rumoured that Cubby Broccoli gave him £1,000 to get to New York to set up the franchise at UA. In return Cubby got fifty per cent of the Bond movies, a most favourable exchange as it turned out.

Woodfall's ties to the Royal Court would furnish it with material for several of its early productions. The first of these was *Look Back in Anger*, released in 1958 and something of a landmark for British cinema. Reisz's *Saturday Night and Sunday Morning* followed in 1960, probably the first really serious post-war British film on a working-class theme. The Royal Court's much-vaunted 'kitchen-sink drama' was now committed to film.

Around this time, I got to know Peter Yates, who had just finished his debut feature assignment directing *Summer Holiday*, starring Cliff Richard. We used to hang out together, and so went to see N. F. Simpson's play *One-Way Pendulum* at the Royal Court. It was the story of an eccentric family, the Groomkirbys, all of them given to barmy behaviour, in the manner of the then-fashionable 'Theatre of the Absurd'. But we were impressed by what we saw, and Peter was yearning to try his hand at subject matter a little more serious than Cliff Richard and pals singing their way round Europe in a red double-decker bus. He suggested we try to set *Pendulum* up at Woodfall. After all, they were the production company to be seen with, and this was undeniably 'their sort of thing'. Moreover, they happened to be flush.

Unable to find British money to finance Tony Richardson's film of Fielding's *Tom Jones*, Woodfall had turned for the first time to an American major, United Artists, who were impressed by their string of artistically successful films. *Tom Jones*, shot on a modest budget of $1.25 million, hit the big time and scooped four Academy Awards, returning to UA about ten times its cost. Richardson offered Albert Finney and Susannah York each a share of profits rather than a fee. Finney agreed and has made about $1 million from the picture to date. York was strongly advised by her agent, the extraordinary Al Parker, that she would be better off taking the $10,000 fee. (Even after his death Al continued to advise his clients, through the medium of his wife Maggie . . .)

In short, money was rolling in and Woodfall could now make any picture it wanted. The company set up an eight-picture deal with UA, and it was during this optimistic era that Peter Yates took *One-Way Pendulum* to John Osborne, who loved it. So did Tony Richardson and Oscar Lewenstein, who became the new partner in the company after Harry Saltzman sold his interest. Oscar was great for Woodfall; he provided their offices in Curzon Street and had strong links to the Royal Court, which meant he could get his hands on material or talent before anybody else. Oscar was also a keen supporter of the Socialist Party, which practically had a branch office in the Royal Court. The early sixties saw the first widespread emergence of working-class achievers in the arts and fashion. Some of them made a great deal of money very quickly, and Oscar's finances were many times multiplied by his five per cent share of *Tom Jones*'s profit. To his house in Hampstead he added a smart chauffeur-driven car and an expensive villa, one of only half a dozen actually on the beach in Brighton. One day I asked Oscar how he could rationalise the apparent conflict between his oft-expressed egalitarian principles and his new and sumptuous lifestyle. He responded without a flicker. 'You must understand that one of the most urgent aims of the Party is to ensure that every working person in Britain will as soon as possible be blessed with a house in Hampstead, a chauffeur-driven car and a villa on the beach in Brighton.' Oscar was nobody's fool.

So Woodfall's first studio picture, *One-Way Pendulum*, began shooting at Twickenham Studios in March 1964. Our cast included some popular faces of early 1960s cinema, including Julia Foster, George Cole, Mona Washbourne and the incomparable Eric Sykes (who as recently as 2001 was giving as good as he got alongside Nicole Kidman in *The Others*). But when *One-Way Pendulum* opened in January 1965, it was a resounding failure: only five people turned up for the first screening. It had cost a mere £40,000 to make, but Peter and I were disappointed none the less. The play had been a hit, but maybe the cinema-going public of 1965 felt it had no business creeping off the stage and into their local Odeon.

I felt at least that I had done an efficient job of producing the picture. Woodfall seemed to agree and asked me to join the company to assist Lewenstein (who described *One-Way Pendulum* as 'the sort of flop we could afford to have') and also bring in movies I wanted to produce. This was a fantastic break for me. For one thing I learned the beauty of working on location, by comparison with which studio-bound production was a cardboard-cutout way of doing things. But above all, for the first time I was dealing with one of the elite band of US majors who really run the movie business. We were entirely financed by United Artists and I would watch skilful operators such as Tony Richardson treading carefully between their own sensibilities and ambitions and what an American company wanted and would be prepared to finance.

The next film I began work on was *The Knack . . . and How to Get It,* a fast-paced adaptation by Charles Wood of Ann Jellicoe's play directed by the American Richard Lester, who had made a great splash for himself by his clever handling of the Beatles in *A Hard Day's Night.* Michael Crawford, then an affable comic performer (later to be known worldwide as Andrew Lloyd Webber's Phantom of the Opera) played naïve schoolteacher Colin, who becomes fascinated by his lodger Tolen's 'knack' for picking up girls. Joining Crawford were Ray Brooks as Tolen and Rita Tushingham as Nancy, the girl over whom the two men would duel. Set against the backdrop of swinging London, it captured the city at the height of its hip Carnaby Street period. The timing was perfect. *The Knack* reached the screen in 1965 just as England was revving up for an unprecedented celebration of youthful hedonism. Released in June, it was followed a couple of weeks later by Lester's second Beatles film, *Help!,* which also proclaimed a spirit of youthful *joie de vivre.* Kitchen-sink realism was placed on the back burner for a while.

For one scene we needed a crowd of nubile young girls and, sad to say, the extras sent to us by the crowd union lacked the necessary bloom of youth. Thus we had a problem. Where in London do you go to find quickly a dozen sexy young virgins? An idea struck me. One of the few parental chores I undertook, when I wasn't filming, was to take my two young daughters to the Lycée Française in South Kensington. I must confess it had not escaped my notice that the sixth-form girls were generally gorgeous, and so we recruited the prettiest of them. This was to be Jacqueline Bisset's first job in film – Jane Birkin's and Charlotte Rampling's too. French cinema has special cause to be grateful to London's Lycée Française, as do the horde of male movie lovers for whom Bisset, Birkin and Rampling soon became pin-ups.

The Knack was a huge thrill for me: the first real commercial A-film that I worked on with the guarantee of a worldwide release. It could well have been a chaotic production because we were shooting on between three and five locations a day and bad weather would have been a catastrophe. Fortunately, Dick Lester proved a very efficient director, adaptable enough to work his way round any everyday location problem. If the police moved us on because we were obstructing a street, or if shopkeepers demanded excessive fees (with threats to interfere with the filming if we didn't pay up), then we always had a stand-by location to zip into.

The most contained location was a small terraced house which we bought for the interiors of Tolen's lair, so providing excellent back-up cover if rain forced the unit off the street. But Woodfall's almost obsessive insistence on using real locations was inconvenient, if correct: the cramped rooms made camera movements and lighting very tough, quite apart from the fact that the amount of light cinematographer David Watkin pumped into each room made it terribly hot. But on screen that little house looked marvellous, which was all that mattered.

Dick Lester shot and cut the picture in a style akin to *A Hard Day's Night*. Although the fast-paced action of the cast running all over Notting Hill, propped up by John Barry's score, was engaging, to me it still felt a bit mechanical. There wasn't much warmth in Lester's early movies; he seemed to cringe at the idea of emotion and romance. He wanted action, which isn't necessarily a bad thing. *A Hard Day's Night* and *Help!* had a shared puppet-show feel to them – people jumping up and down all over the place. This was how Crawford, Tushingham and Brooks carried on in *The Knack*, and it, like the two Beatles films, did well at the box office. The picture cost $364,000 to make and United Artists took in $2.5 million in the US theatrical market.

Further validation arrived when *The Knack* was chosen as the official British entry to the 1965 Cannes Film Festival. I didn't think it was good enough to win the Palme d'Or and yet it did – and allegedly by an odd quirk. Three movies were put forward by the jury, half of whom voted for the first of the three and the other half for the second. They couldn't arrive at an agreement so they simply chose the third picture . . . which was *The Knack*. No *cinéaste* could hope to plan a route to Cannes glory by such roundabout means, and there are surely more emphatic ways to win such high honours. But you didn't hear anybody connected with *The Knack* complaining – or, indeed, saying anything other than 'Merci beaucoup'.

Not long after, a script landed on my Woodfall desk entitled 'Rhinoceros': a version of the absurdist play by Eugène Ionesco to be directed by Alexander Mackendrick, famous for the Ealing comedies *The Man in the White Suit* and *The Ladykillers*. The script dictated that we create a herd of rhinos. Of course, today with CGI (computer-generated imagery), this would be a cinch, but we had to be slightly more resourceful in the mid-sixties. I decided I needed to acquire a well-tempered white rhino from which two dozen rubber moulds could be made. I looked around and ended up in Germany at the Hanover Zoo, where I purchased a fine example for £5,000. His name was Gus and he came back to

London with me. Gus lived happily in a field near Elstree Studios – appropriate for a soon-to-be movie star. He was a big bugger, but patient enough to let us use him to tailor the rubber moulds. The project eventually collapsed under the weight of its own absurdity and Gus was returned to a zoo, where I'm sure he had a much happier life outside the film business.

But as time went by, Woodfall became more and more self-indulgent, ignoring changing tastes and public opinion. Tony Richardson had been off in France carrying on a passionate affair with Jeanne Moreau and with her was making two films *Mademoiselle* (1966) and *The Sailor From Gibraltar* (1967), both of which barely saw the light of day but, sure enough, were borne along by the proceeds of *Tom Jones*. It was then that some bright spark came up with the idea of making a trilogy of half-hour films by three prominent directors: Karel Reisz, Peter Brook and Lindsay Anderson. The combination of the two Free Cinema stalwarts and Brook, the theatrical genius who had successfully filmed William Golding's *Lord of the Flies*, seemed to promise a *portmanteau* film of depth and integrity, if not necessarily a box-office bonanza.

Oscar Lewenstein sent me to Manchester to supervise Lindsay's contribution – *The White Bus*. This short film was somewhat surreal, mostly about a young woman riding around Salford in a white open-topped bus to a chorus of social comment from a host of pompous passers-by, including one played by Arthur Lowe of *Dad's Army* fame. Oddly enough, this device felt brazenly 'borrowed' from Dick Lester's more sophisticated chorus in *The Knack*.

I was still young, still learning, and from *The White Bus* I took away one valuable lesson. I had believed that the producer's job was to whip the production along and finish on time and on budget, taking no nonsense from directors, stars or anyone else along the way. One day Lindsay said to me, 'I have got to go to London for a couple of days.' I was aghast. 'You can't stop shooting, it will cost a fortune,' I told him. Lindsay just smiled. His director of photography, Miroslav Ondricek, was Czech and didn't speak a word of

English. Lindsay was a huge admirer of the Czech films of Milos Forman (*A Blonde in Love, The Fireman's Ball*) and had insisted upon hiring Forman's trusted cinematographer – Ondricek, who hadn't previously travelled west of the Iron Curtain – so as to give the picture a richer, more artistic feel. Now Lindsay told me, 'Don't worry, Miroslav knows what to do.' Straight away I got on the phone to inform Oscar about this absurd situation but he calmly said, 'Let him go.' And with that Lindsay took off to London.

While he was gone, we photographed scenes of the heroine strolling through parks and along streets. All the material shot by Miroslav fitted seamlessly into the finished movie. I had not understood that some creative partnerships are based on a complete understanding of the whole concept and that words aren't always essential in order for artists to work together. Lindsay and Miroslav had achieved that level of communication. Miroslav went on to shoot *If . . .* and *O Lucky Man* for Lindsay and to follow Milos Forman to Hollywood, where he became a top cameraman, his notable credits including *Silkwood* (1983) and Forman's *Amadeus* (1984).

As for Lindsay Anderson, I have to report that in my work with him I found him mean and grudging. His idea of humour was a sneer. He didn't think much of me at all: I suspect that in our relations he found me superficial, perhaps rightly so – I was only interested in ramrodding the show through, I wasn't there to stand agape in admiration at the gorgeousness and intelligence of the work, neither of which were much in evidence as far as I could see. But respect for Lindsay's talent was more common among the film unit than respect for Lindsay Anderson the man. I don't mean to imply that he was hated by anybody, but nor do I think he was widely liked. Lindsay was a snob, although he would have fought to say he wasn't. But I always had the feeling he was a self-invented creature. His father was a brigadier, he was educated at Cheltenham College and Oxford – but all such details he was vehemently pushing behind him in order to pose as the man of the people he wished to be.

Karel Reisz soon announced that his contribution to the trilogy, *Morgan: A Suitable Case for Treatment*, was so good that it should be extended and shot as a feature – which it was. It starred David Warner and Vanessa Redgrave, who picked up the Best Actress award at Cannes. To replace Reisz's entry, Tony Richardson made a short with Vanessa, his wife at the time. The two of them shared an amazing house in St Peter's Square, Chiswick, which uniquely had a glass box thirty feet high built on the back overlooking the garden. This was Tony's aviary. When I visited there, toucans were popular, half a dozen of them roosting in their glass home. On another occasion Tony waived a £10,000 directing fee in exchange for a huge exotic blue parrot, which was presumably nicer than paying taxes.

The final leg of our now-listing trilogy was Peter Brook's *The Ride of the Valkyrie*. It starred the great Zero Mostel, soon to ensure his comic immortality in the original filming of Mel Brooks' *The Producers*. Mostel played an opera singer who is let down by every mode of transport imaginable as – dressed in full Wagnerian costume of bearskin, helmet and spear – he tries to get from Heathrow airport to the Covent Garden Opera House in the centre of London. The rushes worked, but when they were cut together we had an exceedingly boring forty minutes of film. After the dust settled, I asked United Artists if they would like me to cut the film to its natural length irrespective of commercial practicality. I did, and it became a nice little sixteen-minute short. The trilogy, finally entitled *Red, White and Zero*, was briefly screened years later in New York but the profit-and-loss account would show that Woodfall had wasted yet more of its *Tom Jones* riches.

I was now keen to set up a relatively large commercial movie and the ideal project seemed to be an adaptation of Peta Fordham's book *The Robbers' Tale*, the story of the great mail-train robbery which took place in England in 1964. Peter Yates was also keen on the project, but Woodfall turned it down: they weren't interested in action-adventure, perhaps deeming it beneath them. Since the commercial success of _Tom Jones_, Britain's most innovative production house had become introspective and artistically out of touch with mainstream cinema. After Tony Richardson's years of self-indulgence in France he had begun to face the fact that Woodfall had lost its way. His solution was to announce as his next picture a major production of _The Charge of the Light Brigade_ (1968). I was so keen to make _Robbery_ that I decided to leave the company. Thus resolved, I went into Tony's office, which was astonishingly decorated with three _Tom Jones_ Oscars acting as door stops. I delivered my resignation but promised to stay at Woodfall through the pre-production of _Charge_, the largest film the company was ever to make.

During pre-production, a curious lawsuit arose. The best book on the Charge of the Light Brigade, its causes and aftermath, was _The Reason Why_ by the historian Cecil Woodham Smith. She had sold the film rights to Laurence Harvey, a star of 1950s British cinema who relocated successfully to Hollywood. Once John Osborne wrote his script adaptation of _Charge_, Harvey somehow got hold of a copy and had his lawyers bring a lawsuit against Woodfall for plagiarism. Tony Richardson and John Osborne vigorously denied that they had ever read _The Reason Why_, overlooking the fact that we had several copies in the office and it was pretty much 'the bible'. Judgement went in favour of Harvey because of one line of dialogue which appeared in the script as well as the book. Since the book was a reconstruction of an event which had taken place 150 years earlier and there was no record of the words actually spoken on the battlefield, the line had clearly been written by Cecil Woodham Smith. Harvey was awarded £100,000 in damages and, curiously, it was agreed that he would also play a part in the film, for which he would be paid and credited. The part – appropriately, since he came from Lithuania – was to be of a Russian officer.

Tony Richardson was not a man to let bygones be bygones and

was furious at having lost the money and seen his reputation tarnished. When Harvey turned up in Turkey to shoot his scenes for the picture he found that he was to be on horseback in a hard-fought battle with British troops. This required him to fall off his horse, which Tony made him do about twelve times. Harvey gallantly did as he was asked, quite possibly without suspecting that Tony was punishing him. The final kicker came when Tony didn't include the scene in the finished picture: although the lawyers had insisted he shoot it, they had omitted to contract that it had to remain in the film.

On *Charge*'s first day of principal photography I was free to leave Woodfall. I had enjoyed my time there but three years was enough. In that time I had graduated from being a B-picture producer to something more serious. I had worked closely with some very clever people, and had enough on-the-ground experience to feel confident that I could handle my next project as an independent producer.

3

Hollywood UK

I spent most of 1966 lunching at the White Elephant and at Arethusa, twin universes of the London film world, in the company of (inter alia) the likes of Tom Courtenay, Omar Sharif, David Hemmings, Terence Stamp and Audrey Hepburn. We talked about a lot of film projects, but none of them materialised. This was no great hardship – in the film business, we love meetings. Probably only one in every one hundred professionally written scripts actually gets made. In the interim, lunches are some recompense for the frittered energy (and money) of development.

But one of these meetings did bear fruit – a sit-down with actor Stanley Baker who, by the mid-1960s, was not only starring in movies but also producing a few of them, the most famous of which was Cy Endfield's *Zulu*. Stanley came from a Welsh working-class family but, like his friend Richard Burton, had the good fortune to run into a local teacher, one Glyn Morse, who saw in him sufficient qualities as to suggest the life of an actor instead of the drudgery of employment at the nearest colliery. In an era when leading men were romantically handsome, Stanley had his own slightly rougher set of good looks, austere and at times almost menacing. Inevitably, in most of his early films he was the villain, and a very thorough job he made of it too.

Peter Yates and I were developing *The Robbers' Tale* book into a script for the film *Robbery* and we approached Stanley to play the key heavy. This was to be the beginning of a curious partnership that would last well into the 1970s. Stanley, as it happened, was full of ideas for projects he wanted to realise, and was seriously in search of someone to work with. We got on well. He had just finished setting up a London production company, Oakhurst, and he asked me to come in on the venture.

From the start of our partnership, Stanley and I decided not to follow what is still in Britain the common independent practice of shopping a project around different prospective funding sources in order to piece together a budget. No British company was financing a programme of major international pictures, but this seemed to us much the most attractive model, the one on which Hollywood operated. For a producer, Hollywood is a fertile financial source. Independents who favour multiple backers sometimes go down that route so as to retain creative control, knowing that if they were fully financed by a studio then they would become, to some extent, servants of that studio, and of Hollywood's famously dishonest profit-sharing practices. But, on the other hand, the Hollywood majors are the worldwide film business and their marketing skills are famously effective – not only because their home market is half the world (and financially eight times the size of any other single film market) but because they have been doing it for nearly a hundred years and have (mostly) got it right.

Joseph E. Levine had created Embassy Pictures from a very narrow base, importing a *Godzilla* picture from Japan and then half a dozen Italian projects which he dubbed and retitled. His first legitimate production success was *Zulu* and from this he developed a great respect for Stanley Baker, as well as a willingness to finance Stanley's pictures. On the surface Joe was conspicuously vulgar. For example, the collection of Impressionist paintings on his yacht was distinguished for containing the worst example of each of the most famous artists' works. But if he couldn't recognise good Monets, he certainly knew a good money-making venture when he saw it. And in 1968, he agreed to finance *Robbery*.

Originally I wanted to cast Vanessa Redgrave opposite Stanley in the movie. One evening I received a very angry call from Vanessa's husband, my old Woodfall boss Tony Richardson. He said, 'How could you possibly involve my wife with a thug like Stanley Baker?' Stanley may have played thugs, but he certainly wasn't one in real life. Nevertheless, that was the end of any hopes for Vanessa's participation in *Robbery*.

Still, the picture got up on its feet and running. Yates was serving up fast-paced action, and Baker and I were keeping the movie on schedule. That was until I took an absurd phone call from Joe Levine. He said, 'Michael, I think the movie is looking too *British*.' Within a week, on Levine's orders, a new ending had been written, set in New York, explaining that that the whole heist had been masterminded by an American (he to be played by the outstanding stage actor and future Oscar winner Jason Robards). When we cut these scenes into the picture, they were so discordant and unbelievable that no one argued when we decided to dump them. In actual fact it didn't cost Levine a single dollar more to shoot this material. The movie was funded in dollars, and while we were filming the exchange rate changed dramatically in our favour, with the effect that the entire New York shoot was funded by favourable currency conversion. If nothing else, I had a wonderful time filming the US scenes on Levine's luxurious 150-foot yacht moored in New York harbour. I also experienced for the first time the incredibly lavish generosity of a Jewish wedding thrown by wealthy New Yorkers. For Gentiles in the American film industry there is always some degree of separation. The combination of creativity, business acumen, ambition and willingness to take risks which characterises a successful film producer is particularly noticeable in the Jewish community. It is no coincidence that, over the decades, only one major Hollywood studio has been occasionally managed by non-Jews – Fox, whose bosses have included Zanuck, father and son, and latterly Rupert Murdoch.

Robbery went into post-production and on release it did good business. Thereafter Stanley and I had several promising projects kicking around, but nothing that was truly amazing. I was sitting in the office one day and I took a telephone call from Paramount executive Michael Flint. He said, 'We've got this project, Michael Caine's attached to it, are you interested?' On 23 August 1967 I wrote to Flint confirming my agreement that I would produce, on behalf of Paramount Pictures, *The Italian Job*.

Paramount was keeping itself very busy in Britain during the late 1960s. The studio had come under the control of Charlie Bludhorn, CEO of Gulf & Western, a conglomerate of the old-fashioned type. (One division manufactured motor-car parts which had nothing to do with other divisions.) When Paramount was at a low ebb Bludhorn pounced and acquired the famous, debt-riddled old 'mountain' studio for peanuts. Entranced by this glamorous new activity, Bludhorn thoroughly enjoyed mingling with pretty girls and being respectfully addressed by living legends of the movie world.

Because he regarded himself essentially as a businessman, Bludhorn applied 'business methods' to his new toy. Research told him that over the previous three decades the films that had *cost* the most money went on to *make* the most money. Thus, in his first year as Paramount boss he embarked upon on six movies that were, for their time, colossally budgeted: each was to cost $20 million, and some went far in excess of that. *Paint Your Wagon* was green-lighted because it was the first musical Charlie saw on Broadway after his emigration to the United States. He cast Lee Marvin, whose growled rendition of 'Wand'rin' Star' probably made more money in record sales than the misbegotten picture.

Another of Charlie's 'big six' was the ambitiously titled *On a Clear Day You Can See Forever* (1970). Vincente Minnelli, Hollywood veteran and father of Liza, directed this fable about a psychiatric hypnotist who falls in love with a patient's alter ego. Then Martin Ritt directed Sean Connery in *The Molly Maguires*, the story of Pennsylvania coal miners who resort to murder and sabotage to achieve their union's goals. This grim story is reported to

have grossed less than $2 million worldwide. *Darling Lili* (1970) was
a World War I spy-comedy-musical. A major inquiry would have to
be convened in order to decide what possessed anyone to think
such a collision of elements could work. Blake Edwards directed
his wife Julie Andrews, and lurid tales of on-set extravagance made
the rounds of the industry. (It was said that Edwards, dissatisfied
with the look of the clouds in the sky above their Irish location,
shipped the crew to South Africa where the formations were more
to his taste.)

After a few more such 'blockbusters' had eaten into Gulf &
Western's resources, Charlie came up with a new business plan.
Further 'research' delivered a new mathematical certainty. The
average worldwide gross for any given picture was $5–7 million.
Thus, the theory went, if one produced a lot of pictures that each
cost $3 million or less, then clearly the studio would make a large
cumulative profit. This theory is, of course, true when applied to
automobile fenders: if you produce them efficiently below the sale
price, the balance is profit. Unfortunately, motion pictures cannot
be turned out like fenders. But it took Charlie a while to figure this
one out. Lots of Paramount pictures were made in the UK only
never to see the light of day in any other territory. I too would
make my fair share of duds for Paramount.

Finally, Charlie stopped playing at being Irving Thalberg (the
legendary hands-on head of MGM production) and decided to
step down and hand the reins to someone else. The shock came in
his choice of a new Head of World Production. Robert Evans had
once partnered his brother in a New York trouser-making business
(Evan-Picone). He then proceeded to a career as a movie actor that
proved patchy in spite of his dashing Mediterranean good looks,
and so he stepped sideways into the business of trying to produce.
Still, an article in the *New York Times* by Peter Bart (now the editor
of the showbusiness bible *Variety*) dared to propose that Evans
might be the new Thalberg. In short order he was anointed at
Paramount. Whether it was what he read in the *Times* that made

Charlie choose Bob I do not know, but however his instinct got him there, he made the perfect choice. Bob Evans was the best studio chief I worked with. His early pictures would include Roman Polanski's film of Ira Levin's *Rosemary's Baby* (1968); *Goodbye, Columbus* (1969), based on the novel by Philip Roth; *Love Story* (1970), which broke young hearts the world over and made a star of Ali MacGraw, whom Bob promptly married; and *The Godfather* (1972), of which little more need be said.

In 1966 Bob had appointed George 'Bud' Ornstein to head up Paramount's rejuvenated London office. Bud was a very sympathetic person with a solid film background. More to the point, at last it was possible for a British producer to set up a picture with an American major without travelling six thousand miles to knock on Hollywood doors.

During the winter of 1967/68, while I was busy setting up *The Italian Job* – casting, script-tuning, location scouting and buying the mass of cars from Lamborghinis to Minis which I planned to smash to pieces – I was also preparing and shooting a small picture called *Sleep Is Lovely*. I set this up on a tiny budget of $75,000 at Paramount to be directed by a dangerous young would-be Jean-Luc Godard called David Hart. The picture starred Peter McEnery and Maud Adams, a successful model and later a Bond girl.

I was very impressed with David Hart. He was the son of Louis 'Boy' Hart, a violin-playing Hungarian immigrant who by then was chairman of Henry Ansbacher and Company, a merchant bank in the City of London. David's mother was a very potty Irishwoman called Theresa, and they lived in grand style in Essex. David had been kicked out of Eton for some reason about which I never enquired, and made himself an active participant in the mid-sixties 'Chelsea set'. At twenty-two years of age he owned an aeroplane (a Mooney) and at least one Ferrari. He also went bust a couple of times only for his father to bail him out. Third time round 'Boy' didn't come to the rescue, but David was smart enough to make a lot of money in property when he had to. David was one of the cleverest men I had met and when he decided he would like to be a film director it seemed a good idea for me to help him.

He followed what he believed to be Godard's filmmaking method, relying upon improvisation with the actors' help and without a formal script. He even hired Godard's cameraman, Raoul Coutard, who had photographed the classic *A Bout de Souffle* (1960) and *Alphaville* (1965). But, sadly, *Sleep Is Lovely* was not so delectable. In fact it was seriously dreary and David wisely abandoned his plans to be Godard Mark II – though he didn't abandon the creative life. He later wrote a novel, so he got that out of his system, and finally achieved a kind of infamy when he became Prime Minister Thatcher's adviser on all sorts of dangerous and secret matters, acting as her 'enforcer' during the miners' strike of 1984–5. *Private Eye* hated him for his mysterious influence: perhaps he was twinned in their imaginations with the murderous Lord Lucan, whom he somewhat resembled and whose body had never been found.

Parallel to my setting up *The Italian Job*, my other half in Oakhurst, Stanley Baker, was busily making arrangements for another Paramount production, *Where's Jack?*, to be directed by James Clavell. How this picture was set up remains one of my happiest memories, as well as proof positive that elements of the movie business are certifiably crazy.

The script was barely complete when Baker's agent, Marty Baum, called me and instructed us both to be in Charlie Bludhorn's office in New York at three o'clock the following afternoon. He bet Baker and me $100 that *Where's Jack?* would be set up on the spot, for he had an audacious sales pitch to put to the Paramount chief. We duly presented ourselves in New York the next day at the headquarters of Gulf & Western. Marty Baum had set up a blackboard and as a group we waited, baffled, while he chalked upon it the words:

SCRIPT
DIRECTOR
PRODUCER
STAR

Marty turned to Bludhorn and said, '*Where's Jack?* has been written by the Newhouse Brothers, who wrote *Point Blank* – which has made a profit of twenty million dollars.' He chalked up this fine figure next to the word SCRIPT, then continued. 'The director has just done *To Sir with Love*, which cost one million dollars and has already made back ten.' Marty, naturally, wrote this figure next to the word DIRECTOR. He then addressed the matter of the PRODUCER, Mr Stanley Baker, whose recent production *Zulu* he claimed to have made a profit of $16 million.

'Based on their record,' said Marty, roaring toward the finishing line, 'the combined profit of this group is *over forty-five million dollars*. So if you divide by four you are looking at a ten-million-dollar profit on a film that is only going to cost you three.'

Having avidly watched as the numbers went up on the board, Charlie Bludhorn was, by this point, practically panting. He leaned over the table and shouted, 'What about the star? Who is he?'

Stanley and I were flummoxed, but Marty calmly met Bludhorn's eye.

'I didn't want to oversell you, Charlie,' he said. 'But it's Tommy Steele. *Half a Sixpence* is coming out soon, everyone says it's really great and you wouldn't have made it if you didn't *know* it would make a fortune. Tommy Steele is the bonus.'

Bludhorn loved Marty's pitch and we had a deal. We all wanted to get out of his office as quickly as we could before something went wrong – and it did. From the next office emerged Martin Davis, a former publicist who had become Charlie's deputy at Gulf & Western. Davis greeted us warmly and asked, 'What's up?'

We were spared the embarrassment of answering because

Charlie leapt in and repeated Marty's spiel, word for word, chuck-ling away at the business-like logic of all those good numbers. Davis was a smart cookie (and a few years later he was to take over the entire Gulf & Western empire when Charlie died of a heart attack). Unfortunately he was not lost for words on this occasion.

'But Charlie,' he began, 'we agreed we wouldn't ever commit to another movie without reading the script.'

Our hearts sank. An uncomfortable pause cast the room into silence, and we started to come to terms with the fact that we might have just lost the deal. The pause was broken when Charlie angrily spat out, 'Goddamn it, Martin, I've read it *mentally*. This picture will be a smash hit. Now get out of here.'

4

Gearing up for *The Italian Job*

I am the first to admit that, while I was in the midst of bringing the city of Turin to a standstill for the purposes of *The Italian Job*, I didn't dare to imagine that the finished picture would become a cherished cult classic to so many moviegoers. At the time, as I recall, I was more concerned to avoid being lynched by a horde of enraged Italian motorists. But in the long run the effort proved worthwhile.

The Italian Job was made at a time when Paramount was indulging in an orgy of production, and it would plummet from sight after the studio's dire advertising campaign and America's rejection of its humour, which only the British seemed to understand. But in the forty years since its making, *The Italian Job* has become the cinematic equivalent of England's legendary 1966 World Cup victory, an evergreen topper of polls in lads' mags, the all time fantasy flagship of *Austin Powers*-style Britpop pride. If its reputation was first built on the back of multiple bleary-eyed TV viewings on Boxing Day afternoon, *The Italian Job* has become a cherished part of British culture, embedding itself quite firmly in the psyche and the vocabulary.

The script began as a modest concept for a TV drama concerning a robbery set in and around a traffic jam in London's hectic Oxford Street thoroughfare. The idea was conceived by screenwriter Ian Kennedy Martin but never came to fruition, and so Ian's brother Troy, the well-regarded writer of the BBC's *Z-Cars* series, bought the concept from him with the vision of creating a feature film set in Italy. Troy has always claimed that from the word go he envisaged nobody but Michael Caine in the lead role of Charlie Croker, and he wrote the character accordingly.

Troy's completed spec script was then hawked around the Hollywood majors, and was eventually picked up by Paramount. Michael Flint, a top Paramount executive in London, had just seen a working print of *Robbery* and he asked me to look at an early draft of *The Italian Job* in the hope that I might be interested in shepherding a Paramount production. After reading the material I immediately accepted, on the condition that several changes were made.

The great difference between persuading a studio to finance your project and being invited by them to produce a picture based on material they own is that in the latter case you are regarded as being 'on the same side'. They have invited you on to the show because they want you to be there, and there is no question of an adversarial relationship. You are part of their team, not the leader of a gang of outsiders who might have deliberately under-budgeted or been in some other way economical with the truth in order to get a project off the ground. With my status secure in this way, and the production at a nascent stage, I could express any doubts or criticisms of *The Italian Job* without fear of reprisal.

One of my concerns was the style of Troy's script as it stood. The first draft had a political emphasis, and was somewhat 'complicated'. I thought that the picture should be a light-hearted caper and nothing more. A movie is a motion picture, so it has to have motion, it has to be visual and it doesn't often allow room for political discussion. Troy was and is a serious writer, but he is also possessed of a good sense of humour. *The Italian Job* was his work and I had to find a way to turn it into what I wanted for Paramount.

I don't think you can ever run into a truly insurmountable problem with a writer. It's true that writers have a rotten life: they work their guts out for month after month, and very rarely do their films get made. When something does finally lurch into production, the writer then finds himself entirely at the mercy of the director, who has had guaranteed to him the right to change anything he cares to, and interpret anything in the manner he sees fit, no matter how the writer has created it. The scriptwriter's creativity is constantly being challenged, and constantly being diminished. But a truly intelligent writer soon catches on to the fact that it is better to agree to changes while the pen is in his hand, so to speak, rather than handing it to the director and walking away from the project altogether. Screenwriters have since showed some muscle by pushing through a deal with the Motion Picture Association of America whereby they receive their screen credit second only to the director, and one notch ahead of the producer. One could argue that producers and writers have much in common when it comes to being unsung. But, all things considered, I don't begrudge them their promotion.

While Troy Kennedy Martin reluctantly began to tailor the script, I went looking for a director. My initial instinct was to hire Peter Yates, who had masterfully shot some rip-roaring car chases around London for the opening of *Robbery*. Yates was the perfect director to cope with a movie of this size: he was marvellous at shooting all mechanical objects, not least cars. Were further proof required, one would only have to glance at his debut Hollywood picture, *Bullitt*, starring Steve McQueen, which he shot in 1968. It's tempting to imagine what *The Italian Job* could have been if Yates had occupied the helm. But Paramount had other ideas.

Charlie Bludhorn was adamant that Peter Collinson should direct the film. I was baffled by this choice, but soon suspected that Bludhorn's affection for Collinson was founded upon a certain 'little black book' of Peter's that he liberally shared with Bludhorn while the chief was in London. Collinson had previously worked for Paramount directing *Up the Junction*, a movie version of a BBC play done rather more effectively by the young Ken Loach, and Collinson had never directed anything on a grander scale. I feared that Peter might not have the experience to undertake a three-million-dollar production, but the studio's decision was final: it was their movie and Collinson was signed up. Peter was a very good example of someone 'making it' in the sixties: one of a new group who appealed to the Americans because he wasn't stuffy or pompous. Peter had charm and a wicked smile. He was most definitely part of that time and he dressed like it too – a mod, with a flowery shirt and flared trousers.

Worried by Paramount's choice, I convinced the studio to let me make a low-budget picture with Collinson before production started on *The Italian Job*, so as to watch and assess the way he worked. Robert Evans green-lighted an anti-war picture called *The Long Day's Dying*, based on a novel by Alan White, a project that had been the brainchild of Peter Yates and myself. I had commissioned my old friend Charles Wood (*The Knack*) to improve our co-authored screenplay. By the late sixties Wood had become a very accomplished writer and he was angry to discover that Collinson had arranged for sections of his dialogue to be rewritten. A dispute arose, and the original dialogue was written back into the shooting script.

But this wasn't the only dispute concerning the screenplay. Its history was that Peter Yates and I had scripted Alan White's book, and Charles Wood had rewritten the dialogue and certain other scenes: thus we proposed that the screen credits should reflect this distribution of labour, crediting the screenplay to Charles and the adaptation to Peter Yates and me. The Writers' Guild was asked to sign off on these same credits – which they duly did. But what Yates and I hadn't realised (but Harry Fine, who worked for Peter Collinson, had figured out with some clarity) was that if the Guild hasn't arbitrated within two weeks of receiving the submission, then the production company can pretty well do as they like in terms of credits. Fine waited until three weeks had passed and then he and Collinson decided to strike Yates's credit and my own. The Guild apologised for the delay which had cost us in this manner, and couldn't seem to imagine why Collinson had used this sneaky method to deprive Peter and me. But I had a notion. I believe he was jealous of Peter Yates, a more accomplished director at that stage, and he had probably heard that I had tried to persuade Paramount to hire Yates for *The Italian Job*. The saddest part of this affair was that even before we started shooting *The Italian Job* I realised I couldn't always trust my director.

I wanted to get Collinson dealing with character rather than cliché. *The Long Day's Dying* told the sombre tale of three British paratroopers whose internal monologues describe the squalor of war – the terror and sheer brutality of it. Our stars were David Hemmings, Tony Beckley and Tom Bell. Trapped in German territory, the three principal characters await the arrival of their commanding officer to rescue them. John (Hemmings) detests war, Cliff (Beckley) revels in it with a perverse enthusiasm and Tom (Bell) is simply weary of the whole business.

Peter Collinson efficiently delivered *The Long Day's Dying* on time and on budget, shooting the picture with a distinctive documentary feel which realistically presented the deaths of both British and German soldiers. The picture cost nothing, between £150,000 and £200,000, and was shot in three or four weeks. I daresay everybody on the crew, from the production designer to the editor, was of the view that it was a rehearsal for the bigger *Italian Job*, which was to be made immediately afterwards. But *The Long Day's Dying* was original because, as relatively few other pictures had done, it showcased the horror of war, eschewing any attempt to glorify battle or trade in xenophobic delight at the besting of an enemy. No restraint was shown in confronting the audience with graphic images. There was a particular power in a screaming soldier hobbling round in a mud-filled trench, holding the side of his face together having had it blown to pieces by a hand grenade. It seemed to me that the very odour of fighting men in close proximity, the smell of nervous sweat and bad breath, was conveyed.

Thus, satisfied with our efforts, we lobbied hard and somehow managed to get the picture selected as the official British entry to the Cannes Festival in 1968: a pleasantly surprising achievement for such a modestly budgeted film. The distinction was sufficient without our hoping too hard for a prize, since in any case I knew Cannes juries to be notoriously unpredictable – not least after my experience of *The Knack*'s triumph in 1965. To top it all, the festival was handily scheduled to take place between 10 and 24 May, just weeks before we started shooting *The Italian Job* on the other side of the Alps. In short, the timing seemed perfect. If we had not been so naturally immersed in our movie and its prospects, would we have guessed that May 1968 was about to enter the annals of great symbolic dates in world history? Hindsight is a gift, but this was set to be a Cannes where movie projections were shoved firmly to the sidelines.

Since March, France had been in a state of social turmoil; workers and students were occupying factories and university faculties, and the entire country was grinding to a standstill. Revolution was palpably in the air. As the Cannes Festival opened on the night of 10 May, students and police were exchanging savage blows on the streets of Paris, with hundreds injured and much damage done to property.

Cannes had its usual business set out before it. The jury included Roman Polanski, Louis Malle, Antonioni's favourite actress Monica Vitti and Bond director Terence Young. We were competing against such luminaries of cinema as Alain Resnais (*Je t'aime, je t'aime*), Milos Forman (*The Fireman's Ball*) and Richard Lester (*Petulia*). But the word I was hearing from the jury room was that *The Long Day's Dying* was a possible prize-winner. Its anti-war theme was certainly in tune with the spirit of the age, in France and elsewhere. The United States was fighting its increasingly unpopular war in Vietnam, a conflict that had been ratcheted up by the Tet offensive that January, and a groundswell of opposition to 'US imperialism' was building across the globe.

But that spirit of the times was not entirely pacifist. Paris was burning and alive with insurrection. The big unions had joined with the students in mass demonstration. Public transport and the postal system were shut down. In Cannes the French Critics Association had already demanded that the Festival be suspended, and it was the firebrands François Truffaut and Jean-Luc Godard who prevailed upon critics and filmmakers to close the 1968 gathering altogether. Once Louis Malle had convinced his fellow jurymen to resign, the Festival authorities had no option but to tell everyone to pack up and go home. None would have prizes in 1968.

I daresay one could argue that a cohort of anti-war activists helped to prevent the thoroughly anti-war *Long Day's Dying* from reaching the far wider audience it would have enjoyed had it won a major *prix* at Cannes. *Peut-être, peut-être* . . . It was a picture specifically crafted for that moment in history, and it worked very well in that context. But from the vantage of today, I have to confess it was no classic.

On 24 June, with that abortive Cannes episode well and truly behind me, I drove over the Alps and into Italy to begin work on *The Italian Job*. Only days into the production Paramount made a shock announcement in the trade papers. Its recent orgy of overproduction in Europe hadn't been as successful as Bludhorn had hoped. On 13 July Paramount informed the industry that the company would be returning international control to Hollywood. To us filmmakers it was obvious what was happening. Paramount's West Coast side of the company was asserting dominance, and the British side was being firmly demoted. What had looked like a promising advantage for a growing British film industry now looked bleak. By the time *The Italian Job* was complete, I would no longer be reporting to Bud Ornstein in London but to Robert Evans in Hollywood.

Even though *The Long Day's Dying* had added to Peter

Collinson's experience, I still wasn't entirely confident about the technical talent he had at his disposal. It was vital that the camera department bring depth and proficiency to the project. I was impressed by the work cinematographer Douglas Slocombe and his crew had done on *Robbery* and they seemed an ideal choice for this movie. But the erratic manner of Collinson married to the traditional style of Slocombe was to pose its own problems. Peter wasn't at his most comfortable with people who had been educated to any great degree, and Doug Slocombe was the sort of man he would have seen as very 'old school', despite the fact that this same traditional apprenticeship had put Doug firmly in the habit of serving his director and endeavouring to give him entirely what he wanted. Doug was beautifully mannered, an ideal English gentleman, and one could tell as much from the way he talked. Peter Collinson spoke in a markedly different way – he was from the other side of the tracks, and I think he felt a bit annoyed by how genuinely superior Doug was as a person. But then a lot of things annoyed Peter. He had endured an awful childhood, and been raised in an orphanage – that's got to affect anyone to an extent.

If our director still gave us some pause for thought, we had no such worries to reckon with in respect of our chosen star – or so I thought. From an early stage Troy Kennedy Martin had managed to persuade Michael Caine to commit to his script, and it was Caine who made the project really sing to Paramount. Charlie Bludhorn wouldn't have needed figures on a chalkboard to gauge the appeal of the star of *Zulu*, *Alfie*, *The Ipcress File* and others, already an iconic figure of the British cinema and an obvious candidate for our Jack the Lad lead role of Charlie Croker. But once the studio committed itself to the project, some bright spark volunteered that Robert Redford might be better casting. Troy had to fight hard for Caine, taking pains to stress that the character of Croker had been tailored to Caine's specific persona. Paramount finally yielded, and I doubt they ever had cause to regret it.

But as I began packaging *The Italian Job*, it was in my mind that

I needed another big name above the title, however bright was Michael's star. He had punched his weight in the two Harry Palmer pictures and starred in *Gambit* (1966) for director Ronald Neame in Hollywood, but because of the essentially light-hearted nature of this very British production I was afraid it might be seen as *Alfie 2*. Caine's interpretation of Alfie was strongly imprinted on British film audiences at that time, and I wanted a completely different signal sent out about *The Italian Job*.

This was what led me to lure from retirement the legendary English playwright/actor Noël Coward to play the aristocratic crime lord Mr Bridger. He wasn't looking for work, and I never quite knew why Noël did it. In 1968 he had worked on Joseph Losey's *Boom!* as a favour to Richard Burton and Elizabeth Taylor, but nothing since then. Thus we rather dragged him out of his armchair, so to speak, for the sake of two very hectic weeks of shooting into which we crammed all of his scenes.

With Coward nearing seventy and increasingly frail, his long-time partner Graham Payne accompanied him on the shoot and ended up with a part as Bridger's sidekick, Keats. But it was something of a dream come true for Peter Collinson to have Coward in the cast of his picture, for the great man had been a governor of the orphanage where Peter had spent much of his childhood. Peter always claimed that Noël was in fact his godfather. It seemed rather implausible that Coward would assume such a position of responsibility for young boys in a properly regulated orphanage – particularly as he made no secret of his homosexuality – but Peter insisted on addressing Noël as 'Master', and a few eyebrows were raised when he further demanded that the crew also use this title on set rather than addressing him as 'Mr Coward'.

One of the many reasons *The Italian Job* has become so iconic for British audiences is its diverse range of cameo performances by well-loved entertainers, from the likes of Benny Hill, John Le Mesurier, Fred Emney and Irene Handl. I wanted to pack the film full of people who were loved on British television. These characters weren't evident in Troy's early draft and were added later to inject more humour into the film. They add so much colour, so much richness; they bring their own characters with them. Benny Hill and Irene Handl, with just a flicker of the eye, can tell a whole story.

In person Benny Hill was a mystery to us all: impeccably courteous, completely professional – and yet we never really knew what he was thinking. When not needed on set, he would disappear. Where he went, none of us ever knew. He either had some secret hobby which occupied all his spare time, or else he slept fourteen hours a night.

It would have been crazy to cast non-Italian actors for two principal Italian roles – particularly since so many great people were available. Rossano Brazzi had had a very big Hollywood career starting with *Three Coins in the Fountain* (1954) followed by *The Barefoot Contessa* (1954) with Ava Gardner and Humphrey Bogart, and *South Pacific* (1958). His English was excellent and he generously agreed to play the brief part of Beckerman who had invented the robbery and who dies on screen practically before the titles are over.

The second Italian starring role went to Raf Vallone. We cast him as the Mafia boss, perfectly in our estimation, because he simply looked and sounded like pure Cosa Nostra. His first major picture had been *Bitter Rice*, which scandalised the world in 1949 not so much for its neo-realist social concerns as for the daringly displayed thighs of its female lead Silvana Mangano. In 1961 Raf made *Two Women* with Sophia Loren and *El Cid* with Charlton Heston. But a serious problem for Raf was his spoken English: a halting delivery tended to obscure his considerable acting talent. He never struggled for work, and as late as 1990 he had a small but memorable role in *The Godfather, Part III* as the Italian cardinal who takes Michael Corleone's terrible confession of the murder of his own brother. But I found Raf to be an impatient man: impatient with himself because of his language difficulties, and with anybody else who didn't extend to him the respect he considered due to a major movie star. In those days, actors didn't seem to last as long as they do now, when Michael Caine and Sean Connery, for example, have only improved with age, doing more varied and interesting work. I know Raf felt bitter that his lustre had faded, and he was no longer playing the virile leading man he still felt himself to be.

The remaining principal, playing Charlie Croker's girlfriend, was Maggie Blye, a pretty young American actress whom we introduced to the mix specifically in the hope of adding some appeal to the US audience. Maggie came to Italy accompanied by her boyfriend Brian Kelly, who became a good friend of mine, later visiting me in Venezuela on *Murphy's War* and then bringing to me a piece of first-draft material from which would emerge *Blade Runner*.

While the rest of the subsidiary parts were being cast under the supervision of casting director Paul Lee Lander, location scouting began in Italy. A city was needed in which to film the huge traffic-jam sequences and the fast-paced car chase, both vital elements of the story. Although Troy Kennedy Martin's original draft had been set in Turin, I first sent production designer Disley Jones on a reconnaissance mission to Milan. But it soon became apparent that Milan wasn't going to be an amenable city in which to work. Rome didn't seem very accommodating either, while Naples was totally controlled by the Mafia – not the ideal situation when you are trying to make a movie with Mafiosi characters as villains.

I happened to relate my difficulties in this line to my close friend David Ormsby-Gore, Lord Harlech, whom I had befriended when Stanley Baker and I, in a nice bit of side-business, had put together a consortium chaired by Harlech to bid successfully for the independent commercial TV franchise that served Wales and the West of England. Harlech was still only fifty but had already enjoyed a highly distinguished political career. He had been British ambassador to the United States during the presidency of his friend Jack

Kennedy and, before that, minister of state for foreign affairs in the government of his uncle, Harold Macmillan. In 1965 Harlech was also made president of the British Board of Film Censors, and would attract a great deal of publicity when he was obliged to make a decision as to the suitability of *Last Tango in Paris* (1973) and, particularly, the scene where Marlon Brando gets to work on Maria Schneider with a pat of soft butter.

Harlech proposed that I think again in respect of the script's nominal location, Turin. This was because Harlech happened to know Gianni Agnelli, the celebrated proprietor of Fiat – and Fiat practically owned Turin. It was clear that Signor Agnelli could make any number of things happen were he so inclined, and Harlech offered to arrange a meeting between us, a notion I accepted with alacrity.

Gianni Agnelli was one of the most charismatic men I have ever met. His manners were of the utmost elegance, everything about him was beautifully produced. He certainly knew how the world works, and how to work the world. I don't doubt that it was out of his affection for David Harlech that Agnelli instructed his staff to give us whatever we needed – most particularly a firm word to the Italian police so that they would not interfere with our shooting on the streets of Turin. Agnelli had given us the keys to the city – everything we needed to allow location work to run like clockwork.

I sent production designer Disley Jones off to Turin and in due course he returned with positive feedback. I now had my city. Turin was basically an untouched town. Cities that have heavy experience of film crews at work on its streets don't always welcome you back, because filmmakers are a pain in the neck. We take up space, we cause trouble, we stop traffic – we are an all-round nuisance. So if you can find a virgin city, unspoiled by cameras and cranes and shouting first ADs, full of innocent people who think it would be nice to have a film shot in their town – then you have died and gone to heaven. Moreover, it's much easier to shoot a picture under a dictatorship than a democracy. You have control: one nod from the boss and nobody dares say a hard word to you.

Today, as a result of the sideline business known as 'product placement', we are all too well accustomed to movies that act as shop windows for all manner of consumer items, from cars and gadgets to coffees and colas. *The Italian Job* was a project tailor-made to make a movie star of the small but loveable Mini motor car, and in 1969 I fully presumed that its manufacturer the British Motor Corporation (BMC) would be thrilled that a Paramount picture, to be shown around the globe, was ready to offer such a wealth of free advertising: the dollar value of same would have been a phenomenal sum. By the same token I had presumed that the English car giant would want to assist our production in every way possible. Astonishingly, they couldn't have cared less.

Eventually BMC sold us six Mini Coopers at trade price and the rest – about thirty vehicles – we had to buy at retail. Even for such components as bonnet straps, fog lights and all those extras which adorn the Coopers in the film, the production had to cough up full price. My dealings with BMC were thus very limited and generally regrettable. *The Italian Job* would be the longest commercial for a car ever made, and many of those who worked on the picture felt that BMC's attitude was a sad reflection of the British car industry's waning marketing skills. Today, of course, the Rolls-Royce and the Mini are made by BMW, Aston Martin and Jaguar by Ford Motors, and the Bentley marque is now owned by Volkswagen. Even sadder, all these classics are better built under foreign ownership.

On a happier note, Fiat's attitude to our production couldn't have been more different. Effectively they told us, 'Listen, we can be very helpful here if you switch the Minis to become Fiats.' They were prepared to offer me as many Fiats as I needed to crash and smash, as well as trained stunt drivers to pilot the vehicles, a $50,000 cash bonus, and the current top-of-the-range Ferrari as a personal gift. This proposal was too good to be true. But, after not much reflection, I had to decline.

The whole point of the movie – very clear in my mind by this time – was the theme of 'us against them'. Though in real life General de Gaulle continued to veto Britain's desired entry to the European Common Market, *The Italian Job* was a picture in which a bunch of British rogues and rascals were seen to do a job far better, and with a better set of tools, than their Continental counterparts. It was to be, if you like, the first 'Euro-sceptic' movie: the Brits showing the Italians a thing or two, our lads against their lads, us being terrific and them being silly. And yet, even after I was forced to refuse their generous offer, Fiat still provided us with the three Ferrari Dinos for Raf Vallone and the Mafia to drive in the movie, together with dozens of Fiats for the traffic-jam sequences. In short, and even though *The Italian Job* is always seen as a film that waves the Union Jack, it was a production on which I had greater cause to say, '*Grazie, Italia.*'

5

White-knuckle Ride: Making *The Italian Job*

The Italian Job has become the ultimate cinematic indulgence for car junkies across the globe. The evocative title sequence with its distinctive orange lettering, overlaid with the haunting voice of Matt Monro, featured Rossano Brazzi throwing the world's first 'supercar' – a Lamborghini Miura – around snow-capped mountains in the Italian Alps. The Lamborghini was and still is a car for multi-millionaires, and we couldn't possibly afford to destroy one. Instead, we rented a Miura for two days to shoot the driving sequences, and switched to a car of the same colour – with all of its vital parts removed but still looking good from one side – which we could smash up with impunity. After all, movies are shadows on a wall, and illusion is a critical part of the process. If you look closely at the film as the car makes its final descent into the ravine, you will notice that the 'Miura' doesn't even have an engine.

The Lamborghini was not the only 'supercar' to feature in the movie. I also had to lay my hands on an Aston Martin DB4 and a couple of E-Type Jags. Blenheim Motors of St John's Wood, London, had been our car suppliers on *Robbery* and Phil Salamone and his son David were happy to do the same job again. They trawled the used-car world to find rubbishy (i.e. cheap) cars that looked good on the outside, sometimes only from one side if they had been more thoroughly written off. The £900 Aston Martin DB4 convertible was a good example. It was drivable – but only just. Salamone and Son were very resourceful in finding the vehicles required by the script. The Dormobile van was owned by

David and his father, and had been used to transport David's go-kart when he was a kid.

For the sequence at the beginning of the film in which Croker is picked up from outside Wormwood Scrubs, we needed a Daimler Consort. Luckily for us, a particular Daimler made regular visits to the Salamones' garage for servicing. Very slyly we borrowed it while the owner wasn't looking . . . In fact the owner of this magnificent machine was Pakistan's ambassador to Great Britain. We found this immensely funny and ended up writing it into the scene.

Filming began in Turin in the summer of 1968. As is the lot of the producer, I was constantly paying close attention to our cash flow and any available opportunity to save money was seized upon immediately. The additional cost of our purchase of the Minis and their various accoutrements put pressure on our props budget, so we found ourselves having to skimp in other sections. One potentially dangerous economy was that we bought only one bus for the now-famous cliff-hanger ending. Normally we would have bought a spare so that an accident wouldn't stop us from getting such a vital sequence in the can. As it happened, we were lucky that day, and the bus survived. Moreover, this hardy vehicle was also deployed to transport all our camera and lighting equipment from England down to Italy.

Meanwhile, Peter Collinson had asked Disley Jones to cast two dozen tough-looking Mafia foot soldiers, extras for the confrontation scene between Raf Vallone and Michael Caine. It wasn't the easiest of assignments; moreover, Disley himself was a grade-one eccentric who would maintain his extravagant individuality right up until his untimely death in 2005. Being Disley, never one to under-do anything, he trawled through the gay clubs of Turin and offered the customers a chance to be in a movie. When, on the day, Peter saw Disley's 'heavies' posing languidly in their Armani-styled suits he was far from pleased and had no alternative but to move them as far away from the camera as possible and tell them to stand up straight.

In order for the big car-chase sequence to be as spectacular as humanly possible I required the services of a group of the most talented stunt drivers. This is a specific area of skill that cannot be faked or fudged. So I contacted Frenchman Rémy Julienne, who had not long been working in films but was already – perhaps still is – the most accomplished stunt driver in Europe. (He would go on to coordinate half a dozen Bond films and was still at work, aged seventy-five, on *The Da Vinci Code* in 2006.) During our initial meeting with him Peter Collinson and I were delighted to discover that Julienne was prepared to take the chase sequence even further than we had been envisaging, as he began suggesting a range of different hair-raising stunts that could be written into the script.

With Peter busy shooting the dialogue scenes, it soon became obvious to me that the picture needed a second unit. That said, I didn't go about sharing my realisation too widely, the main reason being that the decision to engage a second unit can be a source of great resentment to a director, whose natural instinct is to want to shoot everything – it is, after all, 'his' movie. But it had become perfectly clear to me that we weren't going to get away with that. I wasn't about to enter such a quarrel with Peter upfront, so I waited until we were a few weeks into shooting, slowing down as was to be expected and not quite keeping to schedule. In that state, Peter reluctantly accepted that we couldn't get back on track without a secondary camera crew picking up those minor scenes that didn't feature principal actors. I had known Philip Wrestler for several years – in fact, almost my first job was as his assistant in the cutting rooms. He was a very accomplished film editor, technically very sound, and he understood the process of directing. I telephoned Wrestler and within twenty-four hours he had flown from London to Turin and begun work on the picture, shooting the black-and-white exposition scenes of the job's set-up.

Screenwriters can be very modest and economical in their conception of scenes on the page, mindful perhaps of how an overblown budget may prove a sizeable obstacle to a script ever getting made. When Troy Kennedy Martin wrote *The Italian Job*, he envisaged that the traffic-jam sequences would be faked by the usual cutting-room trickery of close-ups, inserts and cutaways. In short, he never dreamed that we would undertake to create real traffic jams and so bring the city of Turin to a complete standstill. But such was the good Agnelli-sponsored state of our relations with the city authorities that we simply asked the police to ignore what was going on – to look the other way for up to several hours. I instructed Phil Wrestler to set up cameras where nobody could spot them from ground-level – in other words, on top of the tallest building in Turin. Our canteen van blocked off one exit to the square, our camera van blocked off another, and the wardrobe van occupied the last remaining exit. Everyone was going home for lunch, and yet they simply couldn't move. The noise was unbelievable. If these honestly frustrated citizens of Turin had seen the cameras and realised the scenario of which they were an unwilling part, then I suspect we would have been lynched. As it transpired, I think they just assumed it was some dreadful and entirely accidental mess.

My crew was, like most British units, hard-working and happy. Michael Caine seemed pleased with progress, and doubly content to be visited by his girlfriend, a stunning Nicaraguan by the name of Bianca De Macias. He might not have been quite so pleased had he been around to hear a confession that Bianca offered to other ears on the set. One day she said quite plainly, 'I like Michael but I'm going to get Mick Jagger. That's my plan.' And that, in fact, is what she proceeded to do.

However, early in principal photography there was a serious accident, one that threw a pall over the movie. A stuntman was asked to drive Peter Collinson's own white Rolls-Royce rapidly round a circular gravelled driveway outside the Villa Sassi – a location which was acting as Michael Caine's hideout before his team pull off the gold bullion heist. But our stuntman wasn't driving as fast as Peter wanted him to, explaining that there was a danger of the car skidding on the gravel. Peter became impatient. Ordering the stuntman out of the Rolls, he put his personal driver into the car. This driver was very used to driving the Rolls but, as the stuntman had forecast, the car couldn't handle this particular surface at the speed Peter wanted. The car went out of control and crushed our clapper loader, David Wynn-Jones, against a wall, seriously injuring him. David wasn't expected to live. In the event, after a year in hospital and sixteen internal operations, he made a full recovery.

When this awful incident occurred, I halted production for two days. The stoppage was essential. Two days of shutdown on a studio picture ran to many thousands of dollars, but such a stupid and avoidable accident was a serious blow to crew morale, and to Peter's standing as the director. A lot of confidence rebuilding had to be done, and tempers needed to cool down. So we took those forty-eight hours and then, with Wynn-Jones still fighting for his life in an Italian hospital, I instructed Collinson to recommence work on the picture.

One of the most dangerous stunts to film was the leap the Minis make between the roofs of two Fiat factory buildings. It was Rémy Julienne who insisted that the stunt was feasible, but I wasn't taking any chances. I wanted to see a test done first on the ground. Julienne and his boys practised many times on the flat. We watched keenly, and I was persuaded that they could do the job – but it is a different matter when those engines are revving at eighty feet above ground. Not only was I concerned for the safety of the drivers, I also had my own fate to worry about. I was told that, as the person in charge of the enterprise, I would be the one held liable if there was an accident. I would immediately be nabbed and thrown into a Turin jail if something went wrong. Thus we arranged that there would be a getaway car by the side door of the factory where we were shooting, and a plane fuelled and ready at the airport. If the worst happened, I could argue my case from outside the country rather than from inside an Italian prison cell.

When it came to get the scene before cameras, the emotion on set was so intense that one of the extra Italian cameramen broke down in tears, unable to witness the action. The crew really didn't want to watch the stunt. Imagine if one of the drivers' feet had slipped off the accelerator at the crucial moment just before he took off? He would have just splattered against the opposite wall. It makes for sobering reflection. As it happened, the three Minis achieved the twenty-four-metre jump at 110 kph (or just under 70 mph). On landing, one Mini broke its suspension, another its engine. With the death-defying sequence in the can, Collinson emerged on the rooftop with his jacket full of bottles of champagne.

And yet, incredibly, the rushes were disappointing. The eye-level angle at which the cameras had been stationed just hadn't managed to capture the true audacity of the stunt we'd all seen with our naked eyes. It was my feeling that a greater tension could have been created by taking a bird's-eye point-of-view, one that would not only have produced more excitement through a sense of giddy height but would also have emphasised the great distance that these cars were travelling through the air. But the eye-level vantage foreshortened that sense. It was a strange failure. Collinson had become pretty good technically, but he blew this one. We couldn't repeat such a risky and expensive stunt.

I suppose I am partly to blame, because I could have said something to my director before we shot the sequence, but it's very difficult for a producer to interfere with a director's set-ups during shooting. He has to have a hundred per cent concentration, and is working with so many people around him that his authority and decisions shouldn't be questioned, particularly by the producer, one of whose jobs is to support the director. In this case, though, we were left with a daredevil stunt that had proved more thrilling to watch in real life than on film: so much for the magic of the camera.

One unscripted sequence that Collinson spent several days filming showed the three Minis waltzing around an exhibition hall to the strains of Strauss's 'The Blue Danube'. We had time in reserve to shoot this somewhat luxurious sequence which nevertheless held out the prospect of some quirky visual interest. Indeed it was very pretty and elegant in its own right. Sadly, in the event, its pace seriously dragged down the action when the getaway was at its most furious. Peter reluctantly had to agree that it would hurt the picture. (Later, when I showed a working print to Robert Evans at Paramount with the 'Blue Danube' sequence intact, he went so far as to order its removal on the grounds that it was 'nothing more than directorial masturbation', which I thought was a bit harsh.)

Another action sequence which caused concern was that of the Minis ascending at high speed into the coach after successfully escaping traffic-jammed Turin. This was shot on a brand-new stretch of as-yet unopened motorway outside the city. Its potential danger was that the tyres on the coach could burst from the sudden weight of the cars entering the vehicle while it was travelling at such high speed. It was also very hard for L'Equipe Rémy Julienne to plan, because they could not calculate accurately the braking distance for each car as it entered the cabin. A steel plate was placed behind the coach driver, Fred Toms, so that if the Minis couldn't stop in time they wouldn't kill him. The first Mini came in and kissed the barrier, the second came in and clipped the back of the first. The third Mini came in and hit the other two, pressing Fred forward by about four inches. By the time Julienne's team had finished, Fred's belly was resting on the steering wheel.

The figure seen in the movie waving the Minis into the coach was in fact Peter Collinson who, in my absence, grabbed an opportunity to appear in the picture. I was furious when I heard about it that same afternoon. Not only could Peter's presence have distracted the drivers, but also he completely breached our insurance conditions with this hazardous behaviour. This was the second time Peter had thoughtlessly risked life and limb. On the back of Wynn-Jones's accident I reminded Peter that one more escapade of this sort could result in our insurance being cancelled, and probably in his replacement as director.

The car chase was later completed back in Britain, where a Coventry sewer pipe doubled for underground Turin. Phil Wrestler shot the Minis zooming down a brand-new section of sewer before it was connected to the existing system. That was another stunt which could have gone better. Rémy came to me with the idea of spinning one of the Minis inside the pipe so that it would perform a complete loop. He tried several times, destroying one of our cars in the process. But he just couldn't generate enough speed on that slippery surface, so the G-force was insufficient. In rehearsal the stunt was achieved admirably but unfortunately no film was in the camera. With the Minis eating a serious chunk of the budget I wasn't prepared for Julienne to work his way through half a dozen Minis for a five-second shot.

I might say that ever since *The Italian Job* went into release, Mini enthusiasts around the world have been claiming that they own or have owned a Mini that was used in the movie. Contrary to those rumours, I can assert that there was not one roadworthy Mini left by the time we wrapped – if there had been, I would have nabbed it for myself.

A further headache for me occurred when the Aston Martin was destroyed accidentally, and a replacement had to be found overnight. How the hell were we going to find in Turin a reasonably priced Aston Martin that matched the one we had already shot for the movie? We didn't have a chance. But the resourceful David Salamone came up with another of his bright solutions, sourcing a Lancia Flaminia convertible and rebuilding it overnight to look like an Aston. A close examination of the sequence when the Mafia destroy the three sports cars will reveal that as the Aston disappears over the cliff it is in fact an Aston one minute and a Lancia the next.

Even in the midst of our various car wars, there was a nagging script problem that preyed on me at all times. The fact was that we had begun shooting without an agreed and satisfying resolution to our story on paper. So, while we were busily shooting all the car stuff in Turin, Troy Kennedy Martin was still devising a number of different endings for his script. But none of them was suitable. It was not that I didn't like any of them on their own terms – I just couldn't see the one that would wrap up our picture in the required fashion. Most of the concepts Troy devised required a number of the principals to meet in some dialogue scene intended to provide a twist for the end. But these scenes all fell under the banner of what Ridley Scott would later condemn on *Blade Runner* as the work of 'Irving the Explainer'. In other words, the filmmakers end up depending on dialogue to wriggle out of a conundrum which ought to be settled visually, and the audience can plainly see the cop-out. I knew we had to do better.

Towards the end of the Italian location work, I flew out to Hollywood to update Bob Evans on the film's progress, and to sort out conclusively what would be the final few minutes of the film. During the course of my long-haul flight to LA I was quite selfishly thinking of the pleasures I would get from shooting a sequel if this picture were to be successful. And as I sat on the plane I devised an ending for *The Italian Job* which would become one of the most famous in movie history . . . if also one of the most frustrating.

'Hang on a minute, lads, I've got a great idea.' So declares Michael Caine at the cliff-hanger conclusion of *The Italian Job*. But what was this great idea? The movie's cultists will debate endlessly about how a sequel would have started. In devising that ending I was as keen as anyone on the notion of a sequel and had we been sanctioned to make one I had a clear vision of how it would begin.

The sequel would have opened with the original footage of the bus racing downhill, through to Michael's famous last line. After a pause, aircraft-engine noise would have caused a reaction from the gang in the bus, and slowly the front of the coach would have lifted into the air. Cut outside – and two helicopters linked by a cable underneath the front of the bus are slowly pulling the coach back onto the road. The gold and the gang tumble out, and find themselves surrounded by the thirty armed Mafia men led by Raf Vallone. With his shark smile, Vallone tells Caine, 'Be sure that I will let Mr Bridger know you are on your way home – empty-handed.' The Mafia push the coach into the ravine below, load the gold into their Dino Ferraris and are away. What happens after this I was going to leave to Troy Kennedy Martin.

I checked into Bob's office at Paramount on Melrose Avenue. His assistant was now the astute ex-journalist Peter Bart, who had come to the studio from the *New York Times*, where his original profile of Bob as a producer had actually helped Bob into the Paramount job. Peter had become a good friend to me, and he immediately spotted my strategy to ensure a sequel if the picture was a hit. It amused him, but he didn't think it a bad idea. Bob, who also spotted my ulterior motive, was happy none the less to approve it on both creative and commercial grounds.

From Hollywood I headed to Ireland, where the next leg of the picture was getting under way and where Noël Coward was set to join the production. I showed Peter Collinson the new ending which Paramount had approved. 'I'm not shooting this shit,' Peter snapped. He may have been flexing some of the muscle he had built from successfully vetoing my and Peter Yates's writing credits on *The Long Day's Dying*. Here, though, he wasn't in a position to exert the same kind of authority. 'Okay, Peter,' I responded, 'you don't have to shoot it. We'll do it second unit.'

Peter never grasped one essential fact about *The Italian Job*. He went along with a traditional and usually justified view that the interaction between the characters is supremely the most important part of the creative process. Generally that is true, but here he couldn't see that the characters of the three Minis, mere automobiles though they were, were as emotive to the audience as any of the actors. Even the bus had its own character. He should never have let the second unit shoot the end of his picture – but I'm very glad he did.

With Peter in Ireland, Phil Wrestler remained in Italy and headed up into the Alps with the coach to shoot the new ending of the Harrington Legionnaire teetering over the precipice. I did later return to Italy to see how Phil was getting on, when what was supposed to take a couple of days turned into several weeks owing to extreme weather conditions.

There were other problems, too. One Sunday, beautifully sunny and perfect for shooting, I had the police close one of the mountain roads so that we could shoot the coach hurtling out of control downhill. We didn't actually know that at the top of the hill there was a famous picnic spot and a large restaurant which was doing blockbuster business every weekend. By midday, forty cars were being held up by the police and others were joining the traffic jam every few minutes. After about an hour, when the picnickers realised that something as trivial as filmmaking was standing between them and lunch, they became enraged. Led by a local politician they crashed through the police barrier and sped up the hill – by this time, a convoy of probably 150 cars. I'm glad my limited knowledge of Italian did not permit me to understand precisely which insults they hurled at us. That was certainly the end of shooting for that day.

Later, when filming recommenced, my worst fear of losing the bus nearly became a reality. It was a very dangerous stunt. The bus had to be exactly positioned when it skidded over the side of the hill, and needed to be restrained by cables so that it didn't tumble to its doom in the valley below. As the helicopter swooped down for a rehearsal, its downdraught began to upset the balance. This terrified me. The lads ran in, grabbed the landward bumper – which at this point was about six feet in the air – and hauled it back into position. Fortunately, like any experienced producer on location, I had a bottle of brandy in my car. This was dispensed to the second-unit heroes who had saved the day – and who probably needed it more than me.

Phil Wrestler later recalled to me that when he was in Rome to post-sync some of Raf Vallone's lines, Raf had expressed considerable displeasure that the new cliff-hanger ending had replaced a scene in a Swiss bank of his character Altabani triumphantly confronting and demolishing Charlie Croker. This ending would have destroyed the heart of *The Italian Job* which was, of course, Michael Caine and our British boys making the Italians look daft. But you can see how that ending would have pleased Vallone – probably making the picture successful in Italy, but certainly wiping it out in Britain.

Back in Dublin, the main unit was busy capturing Noël Coward's scenes. We had the maestro's services for only ten days, though we had hired him on a flat fee of £25,000, which wasn't bad at that time. Coward was, of course, a legendary figure to have on board but he had started to lose his self-assurance, which was sad because this had been a man of what some might call excessive confidence. I was never really very happy with Coward's scene as he gives his cronies a final briefing in the graveyard before they embark for Turin. It isn't vigorous or tough enough. The way it's played, he isn't the boss he's supposed to be. But it was the best Coward could do at the time, no doubt.

One typically Irish moment occurred when it started raining. The art department had rented six sombre black horses to haul in the fake coffin containing Great Aunt Nellie. These fine beasts were willing to prance and perform their hearse-pulling duties as necessary, but the downpour was their undoing. Within minutes of the rain starting, our six matched black stallions were in a state which must have embarrassed them – shedding their glorious ebony colour and revealing themselves as unmatched greys, duns and chestnuts as the water-based paint dribbled onto the ground. In short, we had been scotched by the Irish. But it was nothing that a respray couldn't fix once the rain stopped.

The location used for Bridger's patriotic prison cell was the disused Kilmainham Gaol at Inchicore just outside Dublin, the infamous site where the leaders of the Easter Rising of 1916 were executed. The Irish Free State had closed the prison in 1924, and I had used it previously for *Robbery*. (It has starred in other famous pictures since, including Jim Sheridan's *In the Name of the Father* and Neil Jordan's *Michael Collins*.)

With all location work in the can, the unit moved back to Britain to complete the film at Twickenham and Isleworth studios. Twickenham had been reopened in the mid-1950s to make half-hour TV films for the US market, and I had worked there on *Buccaneers* and *Fabian of the Yard* so I was very familiar with this boutique studio only a thirty-minute drive from London. It was interesting to come back as a grown-up producer to somewhere I had worked as a cutting-room lad.

These smaller London studios were very useful for limited sets. Isleworth, with only one stage, was perfect for Irene Handl's living-room scene and at Twickenham we could fit in only two different sets. We cut costs even further by shooting Michael Caine's conference with his band of crooks on the eleventh floor of 93 Albert Embankment, premises owned by Stanley Baker and me.

Another crucial scene that remained to be shot was 'to blow the bloody doors off'. Peter shot the sequence on Sydenham Common in South London. We purchased an old Post Office van and sprayed it grey. I later heard when the unit returned to the studio that the rushes would be far more exciting than planned. Pat Moore, the special effects supervisor, created an explosion that was slightly larger than the crew was anticipating. When the van exploded it was so big that it broke windows on the other side of the common.

Peter was shouting, 'Wrap! Wrap! Wrap!' and people were flying in all directions, jumping into cars and getting out as quickly as they could because the police were on their way.

Principal photography was finished by early 1969. It was Peter's idea to approach Quincy Jones to write the score, having greatly admired his trumpet music. When Quincy came to London to begin work on the movie his personal fortunes were at a low ebb: he was short of money, his wife Ulla was pregnant and we felt he really needed to be befriended. We all concentrated on creating a warm family atmosphere to make him feel as comfortable as possible. He and I became great friends.

Jones's music has become just as iconic as the film itself. In recent years 'The Self-Preservation Society' has been used in a major television commercial and has been a mainstay in the repertoire of England football fans since the Euro 2004 tournament. I feel that without Quincy's contribution, *The Italian Job* wouldn't have worked nearly as well. When the picture was cut together, before the music was put on, I was very worried about it, very depressed, because it was extremely choppy at the end. The last twenty-five minutes had been shot by different people – Collinson and Wrestler – at different paces, and it didn't hang together the way it should. Quincy's music stitched the whole mishmash together to provide a seamless climax to the movie. This understanding of film and music is a rare talent, and Quincy had it.

He came to dinner one night with Michael Caine, Peter Collinson, Troy Kennedy Martin and me, and at an advanced point in the evening Michael started singing cockney East End tunes including 'My Old Man's a Dustman' to a fascinated Quincy. This was the stimulus needed to get both Don Black and Quincy to produce 'The Self-Preservation Society'.

The movie was eventually released in the summer of 1969. Although popular in Britain, its uniquely British style and humour failed to excite the American public. There are profitable hit movies and unprofitable hit movies. The difference lies primarily in the speed of a film's income. Hollywood studio contracts provide for the cumulative addition of interest at a high percentage on the film's production, advertising and distribution costs. Thus, if a picture costs $3 million plus $1 million for prints and advertising, the studio's accounts department is adding interest on the first dollar spent even before the film starts shooting, so that by the time it is released and before a penny is earned at the box office, 'the juice' has been running for over a year on $4 million. This interest is generally nearer to credit-card rates than those of the banks, and in 1973 it was nearly twenty-three per cent. It is sadly reminiscent of the 'vig' paid by people borrowing from Mafia loan sharks, but producers put up with this and other inequities just to get their films made.

Pictures which are instant hits – and, nowadays, this means taking box-office receipts of $50 million-plus during the first weeks of US release – have a chance of paying out net profits provided the box-office volume holds up. A case in point is *Coming to America* (1988), starring Eddie Murphy, which cost about $28 million to make. Yet the studio argued that it needed to earn over $140 million at the box office to break even. Writers Andre Bernheim and Art Buchwald sued Paramount for their piece of the profits but the studio argued in court that, sticking to their contracted formula, the picture was not profitable for the producer and writer. Paramount eventually settled the lawsuit after a great deal of bitterness had been generated. (The picture has been reported as having finally grossed $288 million worldwide.)

Of course, studios who invest in productions are entitled to recoup those costs. They also recover a distribution fee of thirty-five per cent of the amount received by them from the theatres plus the cost of advertising and a further ten per cent surcharge on that cost. They also recover the cost of the thousands of prints as well as the expense of shipping them to the theatres around the world. And – would you believe it? – they charge the cost of prints purchased from laboratories at the retail invoice price, not at the actual price after the lab has paid them a substantial discount for volume. Film distributors over the years have become cannier at chiselling than car dealers and are just as legal.

Now, with that diatribe out of the way, I have to say that I've always been somewhat sympathetic to the studios' need for 'creative book-keeping'. For the amount they spend and risk, their financial return isn't that high. I have made my share of failures so I suppose I can't blame the studios for milking the profitable pictures to pay for the turkeys. However, I do have to say that, looking at Paramount's 'cumulative distribution statement' for *The Italian Job* (which cost a little over $3 million), it seems to me a masterpiece of creativity to conclude that the film's recent reported deficit is nearly three times that amount at $8 million. The film has in recent years been reissued theatrically, been a tremendous success with hundreds of thousands of DVDs sold

Paramount Pictures

5555 Melrose Avenue, Hollywood, CA 90038-3197

Release Date:

CUMULATIVE DISTRIBUTION STATEMENT

08/28/69

With
REGENT ESTABLISHMENT
(f/s/o Michael Deeley)
Agreement Dated: As of April 23, 1968
"THE ITALIAN JOB" 06928
Period Ending: 9/25/99

Net Participation		
Gross Receipts		$ 9,472,070
Less: Distribution Fees		3,403,443
Gross After Distribution Fees		$ 6,068,627
Less: Accounts Receivable (Net of Distribution Fees)		11,894
Balance		$ 6,056,733
Less: Distribution Expenses		1,956,110
Balance		$ 4,100,623
Less: Interest on Production Cost From Date of Delivery (Estimated)	$ 9,440,000	
Production Cost (Note 1)	3,533,698	12,973,698
Balance		$ (8,873,075)
Less: Deferment - Paramount Pictures (UK) LTD 3,000 Pounds		0
Net Profits		$ (8,873,075)
Regent Establishment - Share @ 7.5%		$
Less: Previously Paid		
Balance Due		$

Note 1: Includes interest to date of delivery $176,605

Paramount's 'cumulative distribution statement' for *The Italian Job*, as of 25 September 1999. As you will see, somehow we still appear to be nearly $9 million in the red . . .

and in 2003 was 'remade' at a cost exceeding $50 million. Whenever did Hollywood remake an unprofitable picture?

Many theories have been put forward as to why the film didn't gel in America, the most popular being that the publicity campaign in the States came shortly after the shooting of anti-Vietnam war student protestors at Kent State University when public opposition to firearms was at a peak. The poster design that Paramount produced showed Michael Caine with a massive sub-machine gun in one hand and a cup of tea – to signify trendy London – in the other. A tattooed, naked girl knelt in front of him. I find nothing wrong in principle with naked girls, but this one was hardly relevant to the film.

Today the influence that *The Italian Job*'s winning cocktail of larger-than-life characters and street-smart London dialogue has had on films like Guy Ritchie's *Lock, Stock and Two Smoking Barrels* is obvious. As Michael Caine enjoyed an iconic rebirth so did the film – it spoke to the phenomenon (or oxymoron) we call 'lad culture'.

I have come to the conclusion that the reason the film did not click in the USA is because it had nothing to do with America – nothing at all. It is a playful look at the differences between the British and their European neighbours. It would have worked equally well had we shot in Paris instead of Turin because it was the same old 'us against them', love/hate relationship that flourishes to this day between mainland Europe and Britain. Looked at this way, it makes perfect sense that *The Italian Job* received a Golden Globe nomination in the category of Best English-Language Foreign Film.

Peter Collinson and I didn't work together again, but he subsequently relocated to America. When next we met, he and his wife Hazel had a very pretty house in Brentwood and they seemed happy. Peter wasn't getting the quality of script he wanted, but he was working regularly. Alas, he was to die of cancer in 1980, at the age of forty-four. I wish he had lived long enough to see his best film become a classic.

Hollywood Foreign Press Association

Certificate
of
Nomination For Award

Be it known that

The Italian Job

was nominated for a Golden Globe Award of Merit
for Outstanding Achievement

Best English Language
Foreign Film

This judgement being rendered with reference to Motion Pictures
which have qualified for consideration by the Hollywood Foreign
Press Association during the year ending **1969**

PRESIDENT

SECRETARY

The certificate that marked *The Italian Job*'s nomination for a Golden Globe as Best English Language Foreign Film of 1969. If the movie seemed 'foreign' even to the Hollywood Foreign Press Association, then I suppose we were in the right category.

6

The Greatest Film I Never Made, and the Hellish One that I Did

A lesson one learns quickly as a producer is that it's just not enough to have made a good movie. You still have to expend a lot of time and energy and money telling everybody that you made a good movie, and be sure that they heard you – hence the indispensable functions of the press and publicity machines. I learned to engage with these forces as fully as I was able, though in the course of trying to promote *The Italian Job* I was taught another key lesson, which is that the discretionary term 'off the record' doesn't mean the same thing to all journalists.

As the release date drew near, the veteran British film PR specialist Theo Cowan invited me to lunch with Lee Beaupre, a key journalist on the leading Hollywood trade paper *Variety*. After a well-lubricated lunch at A L'Ecu de France, with all business talk concerning *The Italian Job* completed, we began gossiping off the record about the film business over coffee and brandy. Lee asked me what I thought of Charlie Bludhorn's theories about how to make Paramount profitable – particularly referring to this new burst of production in Britain. I said that although we had all benefited from the excess, it was not nearly discriminating enough to be successful. I threw out the scenario that if Charlie met a taxi driver he liked, he would probably offer him a picture to direct. A few days later *Variety* accurately printed what I had said. Mr Beaupre died soon after, but not without having made a great deal of trouble for me.

Charlie Bludhorn was sufficiently displeased to make one of

those 'You'll never work for Paramount again' speeches. As it turned out, Charlie – who was waking up to the folly of his studio leadership – either decided the comment was fair, or else he just forgot about it. In any event, I was soon contracted to make another picture at the studio, and nothing more was said.

While post-production was being completed on *The Italian Job*, Oakhurst was also finishing *Where's Jack?* for Paramount, with Stanley Baker producing and starring. Our audacious pitch to Charlie Bludhorn had promised a great deal, not least the marquee value of Tommy Steele. But looking at the picture as we delivered it, I felt there was something missing. It looked beautiful, but possibly the script hadn't fully exploited the potential of the subject matter. Maybe the director, James Clavell, was not the right man for the job. Certainly he gave up directing soon after *Where's Jack?* flopped and concentrated on becoming the hugely prosperous author of *Shogun* and other such literary blockbusters.

Not a success for us, then. But Robert Evans, knowing that Peter Yates and I were friends, suggested that we make a movie for Paramount. He handed me *Murphy's War*, a novel by Max Catto that Paramount had acquired, an all-out action piece set during the last weeks of World War II. It was the story of the sole survivor of a British ship torpedoed in the South Atlantic: Murphy, a seaplane pilot, wages a one-man war against the German submarine responsible for the death of his fellow crew members. Evans had already commissioned Stirling Silliphant, Oscar-winning adapter of *In the Heat of the Night*, to develop Catto's novel into a screenplay and was keen to attach a producer and director too. This was merely one of the many projects that Stirling had accepted in the wake of the Oscar bumping up his asking price, so we weren't expecting to see anything too quickly. Whether Stirling was too busy to pay attention to *Murphy's War* or whether it was basically just an old-fashioned pot-boiler of a story, the fact was that the early drafts were seriously dreary – hardly the stimulus to drive one back into the fray of a big production.

★ ★ ★

Come the spring of 1969, I felt I needed time off. I was waiting for a workable script of *Murphy's War* and the idea of several months on the Californian coast sounded tempting. So we rented a former Mrs Paul Getty's cottage on Carbon Beach, Malibu. I asked Paramount to lend me an office and a secretary for half a day per week so that I could keep in touch with Oakhurst and personal business in London. Amazingly, they installed me in the enormous office of Paramount's ninety-year-old founder Adolph Zukor. The first day I arrived at the studio there lay on the vast mahogany desk an envelope addressed to Michael Deeley. I opened it and took out a $2,000 cheque marked 'Expenses'. I drove back to Malibu and popped it in the Bank of America.

The next week the same thing occurred, then again, and again. Clearly the accounts department had presumed, since I was at the studio, that I should be paid the expenses for which I was con-tracted when outside London. After the sixth week, the suspense of it all began to affect my holiday. From Monday to Wednesday I worried about whether the cheque would be there on Thursday. And from Thursday to Monday I worried that it might have been cancelled. I suppose this is not a level of stress which would bother most people, and probably didn't bother me either in the end, because I was sure that at some point in the future the studio's cre-ative accounting would find a way to recover this generous mis-take.

But this Malibu sojourn was proving a very happy time – until early August 1969, when appalling events took place. These were at the instigation of Charles Manson, a sociopath, would-be rock star and 'guru', who had spent his youth in and out of reform schools and prisons before founding a cult-like hippie 'Family' of female followers in San Francisco. Obsessed with apocalyptic violence, and upset that he couldn't get a record deal, on the night of 8 August Manson ordered some of his drones to a house on Cielo Drive in Benedict Canyon, which he thought to be the home of a music-business executive who had snubbed him. Manson's instructions were to commit bloody murder. But the place was being rented by Roman Polanski, who was away in Europe, and his young pregnant wife, Sharon Tate. That night she was entertaining three of their friends, including the well-known Hollywood hairstylist Jay Sebring. All four were viciously murdered in cold blood.

The following night the Family killed again, in Los Feliz, the victims a supermarket executive and his wife. But Hollywood was rocked above all by the Tate/Sebring murders, for it seemed that everybody knew at least one of the victims. The seemingly random nature of this bloody and murderous attack sent a ripple of fear through the film community. Everyone felt it could have been them – and maybe, next time, it would be.

One night, only a few days later, I was at home alone when I was certain that I heard something – some*one* – moving on the roof of my house. I grabbed the pump-action shotgun I had recently bought, along with a powerful flashlight, and ventured outside. Instead of a band of psychopath cut-throats, I was met by the sight of a respectably dressed young man who appeared completely dis-orientated, and obviously under the influence of some drug that he believed had bestowed on him the power to fly. The police came and took him away. If only all of the chemical/visionary 'experiments' of the late 1960s had been so harmless in their folly.

Though pre-production on *Murphy's War* trundled along apace, I sensed Paramount's attitude toward the film starting to cool. One afternoon Robert Evans called me into head office on Melrose to discuss the project. 'I know you and Peter are on pay-or-play contracts,' he told me. (In other words, we would be paid our fees even if the film was cancelled.) 'But I don't like the way this picture is coming along. We'd like to switch you to another project.' Bob then presented me with the galleys of a fat soon-to-be-published novel. I took it away to read. 'If you like it,' Bob advised, 'I want you and Peter on it.' I left Bob's office and proceeded to devour the novel over the course of a weekend. It was by an Italian–American writer of whom I had never heard, but it was plainly fantastic. I was so excited that I wanted Peter to read it immediately. I jumped into my car and drove the manuscript over to his house. Then I waited, breath bated. Peter isn't a fast reader but eventually he did plod through the book. He called me back after a few days and said, 'Yeah . . . it's okay, but I don't want to swap it for *Murphy's War*.' I had the distinct impression that Yates didn't want to do another crime story so soon after his smash with *Bullitt*. I was extremely disappointed. I tried to make him change his mind but he wasn't having any of it. I returned to the Paramount lot to speak with Evans. 'Sorry, Bob, its bad news. Peter doesn't want to do it.' Bob looked astonished, though he accepted Yates's decision.

In fact, that decision turned out to be one of the luckiest in the history of Paramount Pictures. Instead of having Peter and me, Paramount struck gold – a smash-hit masterpiece and a multi-Oscar winner – when they decided, against the odds, that the hitherto little-known Francis Ford Coppola should make Mario Puzo's *The Godfather*.

Of course, I wasn't the only one to 'pass' on this material, though I was perhaps the most reluctant. In his memoir Bob Evans recalls that 'Richard Brooks, Costa-Gavras, Elia Kazan, Arthur Penn turned it down. "Romanticising the Mafia is immoral" was their single voice.' Personally, I hadn't identified that moral problem; I simply couldn't persuade my director to commit. Back in London I would make a similar blunder when an agent sent me Frederick Forsyth's novel *The Day of the Jackal* and I simply couldn't see how it would work on screen. After all, everyone in the audience would be aware that de Gaulle was still alive, so where was the suspense? I had completely misinterpreted what the book was all about. It was not about whether de Gaulle would be assassinated or not. It was about *how* the assassin would be prevented from killing him. I blew that one.

The strangeness of this period in Hollywood is further summoned for me by the memory of another slightly chilling event that occurred at the time. I belonged to an informal group who would play tennis together regularly, one of these being a Beverly Hills police officer named Jim. One day I called Jim to excuse myself from a match we had scheduled: I said I was running into difficulties on the picture I was preparing for Paramount. Everyone in Hollywood loves movie gossip and Jim duly asked me what my problem was. I told him that the head of the studio was having second thoughts about the project and it might get cancelled. Jim leapt in. 'You can't let them do this to you,' he said. I replied that if they wanted to I couldn't stop them. 'But *I* can,' said Jim. If I gave him the number of the executive's automobile he could stroll by and 'find' some illegal substance in the trunk. In Jim's eyes this seemed very much one of those 'What are friends for?' conversations – but it scared the hell out of me. I said I would 'get back to him', and called the next day to assure him the problem was amicably settled – which in fact it wasn't. But that was the end of my enthusiasm for the Hollywood tennis circuit.

Come October, it was time to get back to England, and I drove the Corvette that Paramount's accounting department had kindly provided for me across country and over to London via Portugal. In due course Bob Evans finally came back to me. Paramount was unwilling to fully finance *Murphy's War*. We haggled our way to a compromise deal. Paramount put up half the money in return for domestic rights. By mid-November I had found Dimitri de Grunwald, a veteran producer in England who had set up a finance/production company called London Screenplays. With Dimitri on board, the picture finally had a licence to roll.

But even with a reduced stake, Paramount still wanted a bankable star to look after the box office, so we engaged the services of Peter O'Toole, already a three-time Oscar nominee, who came to us with the added and less happy reputation of being one of the movie world's *bona fide* hell-raisers. There was no denying that Peter's life story was littered with accounts of famously drunken brawls: it was as if he revelled in playing up to some mindless Irish stereotype. But the rumours had it that on certain occasions he was too bashed-up or hung-over to do a day's work. *Murphy's War* was liable to be a demanding and stressful location film, so in the eyes of some we were taking a risk here, even with a star of Peter's magnitude. But, much as this may disappoint those who prefer the legend, I have to say Peter was impeccable for us – much to my own great relief. He certainly wasn't drinking, was always on time and always cheerful. I should say that I slyly cast O'Toole's then wife, Siân Phillips, in the film as an English doctor working among the indigenous people living by the Orinoco River – the calculation being that it would be much harder for Peter to raise hell with Siân at close quarters, keeping an eye on him.

Murphy's War ended up being shot almost entirely on location in Venezuela, but I had first investigated the possibility of making the movie in Jamaica. Alas, we showed up there at the precise moment that the inhabitants woke up to the fact that independence from British colonial rule had not given them the wondrous prosperity they felt they had been promised. The Jamaican government certainly wanted a big motion picture there as a boon to the tourist trade, and they generously gave me a helicopter to scout the entire island out of reach of the angry population. But quite clearly it would be impossible to shoot a picture in that atmosphere. Instead Peter Yates and I went to Venezuela and found some breathtaking locations along the Orinoco, miles away from any of the logistical support necessary for film crews but undeniably perfect to look at. This decision made on aesthetic grounds had the unfortunate consequence that, in practical terms, the *Murphy's War* shoot was probably the toughest I have ever experienced in my producing career.

Because the production was so far away from hotels and amenities, we devised a strategy whereby we would hire a cruise ship – a floating hotel big enough to house the entire unit and all our equipment. Our production manager went to Athens and chartered the

1 Lobby-card artwork for *One Way Pendulum* (1964).
2 *The Knack* (1965): Oscar Lewenstein, Richard Lester and Michael Deeley.
3 MD with Lindsay Anderson, on location for *The White Bus* (1967).

4 *The Italian Job* (1969): MD with, (seated left to right) Tony Beckley, Noel
    Coward and Michael Caine.
5 MD receives a fine piece of Italian knitwear from soon-to-be wife Ruth.

6 *The Italian Job*'s stunt of Minis jumping factory roofs.
7 Michael Caine and MD on the streets of Turin for *The Italian Job*.

8 MD in the midst of the hellish production of *Murphy's War* (1971).

9 Nic Roeg directs David Bowie on *The Man Who Fell to Earth* (1975).

10 The Cannes Film Festival, 1975. MD with EMI Entertainment chairman Bernard Delfont.

11 *The Driver* (1978): MD with producer Larry Gordon.

12 MD, Bob Sherman and Sam Peckinpah on location for *Convoy* (1978).
13 Michael Cimino and Robert De Niro on location for *The Deer Hunter* (1978).

14 'Oscar Night' 1979: MD with John Wayne. (© Academy of Motion Picture Arts and Sciences.)

SS *Odysseus*, an outwardly pristine vessel painted white and air-conditioned throughout. The *Odysseus* was made available for our collection in Trinidad, and we loaded up and set out on our journey. But we hadn't gone too far before a couple of carpenters made an alarming discovery in the hold: a pile of mouldy life-jackets marked *Belfast Queen*. It turned out that before the *Odysseus* had received its recent (and largely cosmetic) makeover, it had put in years of service as a ferryboat on the run across the Irish Sea – hardly a record that boded well for an extended stay in the tropics.

Then, as the ship entered the mouth of the Orinoco, the captain brought me disastrous news. The sandbar across the mouth of the river where we were to shoot had slowly silted up over the course of the last fifteen years. The boat's draught was more than a foot too deep to gain access, even at high tide. We were stuck. We could have abandoned the ship, flown back to London and sued the Greek hire firm, who already had our charter fees in hand. But *Murphy's War* would have been sunk right there, and the production costs and expenses and other financial commitments would never have been recovered. The only alternative was to improvise a costly solution and tough out the production. We managed to lay hands on a pair of thirty-two-seater flat-bottomed river boats, and pressed on into the Orinoco. In hindsight, since the making of the picture was to prove more thrilling than the results on screen, I wonder if we shouldn't have abandoned our efforts when we had the chance.

The fabled 'Murphy's Law' has it that if anything can go wrong, it will go wrong. *Murphy's War* soon began to live up (or down) to such pessimistic imaginings. This was Venezuela, and we could have predicted that our location would be beset as it was by hazardous yellow snakes and piranha fish. I had anticipated that commuting to and from the location could cost us valuable time, and indeed it did. Other misfortunes were more freakish, such as the hugely regrettable fact that our chief daredevil stunt pilot Frank Tallman had lately suffered an accident whereupon he had the further indignity of having the wrong leg amputated.

In any event, our schedule was soon in trouble, the atmosphere of the shoot grew tense, and so did relations between Peter Yates and myself. I found Peter just as efficient as he had been for me on *One-Way Pendulum* and *Robbery*, but in the interim he had of course decamped to Hollywood and made himself a heavy hitter with the success of *Bullitt*. He had also learned a thing or two about how to throw his weight about. The only way for our production to communicate with the outside world from the Orinoco location was the radio room on the *Odysseus*: all cost statements, purchase orders and progress reports went through there. It will not surprise anyone who has ever worked with me to hear that I had sight of all outgoing transmissions. As our woes deepened, Peter began communicating with his agent Dick Shepherd, to have it made plain in Hollywood that any delays on the picture were not his fault – which meant they could be safely presumed to be mine. I never told Peter I knew about these self-exculpating cables, but sadly they spelled the end of a long friendship and a good professional collaboration.

When a production is in trouble, more than ever the answer to the question of what a producer actually does is 'Everything necessary.' We needed shots of a German submarine surfacing out of the river, and for that purpose the Venezuelan government had agreed to lend us a 1942 submarine given to them by the US Navy after the war. But when it came time to get the vital shot, the submarine captain refused to submerge his vessel. My interpreter relayed to me the bad news that I by now might have guessed: that this submarine was prone to leak below a depth of twenty metres. I pointed out to the captain that without the shot of the U-boat surfacing, we would have to abandon the film and go home, and everybody would have to be told precisely why. A deal was hashed out. I agreed that the submarine didn't have to be completely out of sight before resurfacing. The captain added one condition of his own: the producer had to be aboard during the manoeuvre. We got our shot.

Next in the succession of headaches, we made a flight of some 450 miles from Caracas to look at an abandoned coal mine as a possible location, when our first-rate pilot Luis tripped over a railway line, fell and broke his leg. There was nothing for it but for him to fly the twin-engine Beech Baron to Barcelona, the nearest airport – two hundred miles away. Barcelona, it transpired, was fogged in, entirely inaccessible, and Luis was by now barely conscious from the pain. Finally we reached the Caracas airport, Maiquetia, only to be told by the army that we were denied permission to land in heavy fog even with a seriously injured pilot. Luis summoned all his remaining energies, aimed the plane at the cliff on which the airport sat, and at the very last moment he gained enough altitude to slip through the thirty-foot envelope between the runway and the fog. The army were ridiculously furious, and would have arrested Luis had he not needed to go straight to hospital. In the event, they fined him heavily and suspended his pilot's licence for six months. We managed to replace poor Luis with another pilot who, I later learned, would not be in danger of having his licence revoked, for the simple reason that he had already lost it.

For me, this had long since come to feel like a very unlucky picture. But then I had one big stroke of fortune. I had to arrange to go back to London after the production lost time, so as to reassure our financiers that we were *somehow* going to get back on schedule. But come the day of my travel the road to Caracas airport was beset by high winds, and I had not left any margin for delay. A traffic accident on the road meant I reached the airport half an hour late. I repaired to the bar which overlooked the main runway, and while I gulped a restorative brandy I watched the plane I had been due to board revving its engines and accelerating down the runway. It took off smoothly and climbed until it was quite small in the sky, before suddenly exploding into a ball of fire.

As *Murphy's War* began to wind down, the relationship between Peter Yates and me was worsening yet further as a consequence of our disparate views on some of the big creative decisions about the direction of the movie. Our lead character Murphy had been conceived as a wry, sweet-tempered sort, and I had stressed to Yates that this movie was in the action-adventure mould. He had other ideas, and wanted to turn it into a serious anti-war statement, even shooting a climax which would result in the death of Peter O'Toole. I fought with him, and I lost the bout – O'Toole's character duly died in the end. Such battles are rarely won by producers because the studios are anxious to protect their relationships with directors, and in this case Paramount went with Peter Yates's vision. Given that Bob Evans had hardly wanted to make this picture in the first place, it's possible that by this advanced stage he didn't give a damn. No doubt he was more preoccupied by the process of getting a workable draft of *The Godfather* from Mario Puzo and Francis Coppola, as well as a cast that could make the film work. As it turned out, *Murphy's War* limped into cinemas in January 1971, following a royal premiere. From the vantage of today the film looks dated: nothing more than a string of clichéd scenes, centring on a clichéd character. The aerial photography still looks good, at least. But at the time my chief emotion was, 'Finally, it's over . . .' Indeed, for a while I felt that I would never personally want to produce another movie ever again. I suspect I would have been in a much different frame of mind had Yates and I spent 1970 making *The Godfather* instead – but then again, who knows?

7

Mr Wilson, and His Plans for British Film

The early 1970s were an action-packed time for Stanley Baker's and my Oakhurst Productions; though I must confess that they yielded no actual film production.

It was simply the case that by now I was very much a part of the London film scene, an independent producer who had delivered a string of movies for Paramount Pictures. We were having the time of our lives, spending long lunches at the White Elephant, *the* restaurant for striking deals, run by Stella Richman, a greengrocer's wife who also happened to be the head of TV drama at Associated Rediffusion. That place became our club: we drank generously at lunchtime and somehow managed to do some work in the afternoon. And then every evening there was a private screening of some big new movie to attend.

One evening at the Warwick Theatre we were all set to be treated to a new Joe Losey picture, and Michael Caine and I were in the audience. *Secret Ceremony* starred Elizabeth Taylor, Robert Mitchum and Mia Farrow. Losey's pictures could be pretty turgid but with that cast we figured we were in for a treat. In the event, the film ground on as if without end. Though there was evident restlessness in the theatre, nobody walked out – but then they never do at private screenings, such is the etiquette, and the fear that the artists on screen are also in the audience, primed and ready to be offended by such a slight. Still, after the credits rolled on *Secret Ceremony*, the lights came up to a deadly silence. For a moment nobody said a word or indeed moved a muscle. And then Michael

Caine's voice rang out from the back of the theatre, enthusiastic, even joyful. 'Well, Joe,' he cried, 'you've done it again.' The theatre erupted with helpless, grateful laughter.

Back in August 1967, when I had joined in Oakhurst Productions with Stanley Baker, we had leased 3,500 square feet on the eleventh floor of Alembic House, a fourteen-storey block overlooking the Thames, across the river from the Houses of Parliament. Richard Harris was on the tenth floor, James Bond composer John Barry on the twelfth. (The penthouse is these days occupied by Jeffrey Archer, when he isn't residing at Her Majesty's Pleasure.) Our office became a play-pen for the London film community, actors and actresses, producers and directors. A stream of visitors would pass through, happy to enjoy the fabulous view of the mother of parliaments as well as some fairly lavish hospitality, and we were glad to entertain them. It was with rather more trepidation that we occasionally received Albert Dimes, a Soho gangster who became infamous after tales circulated of a knife fight with a rival (one Jack Spot) said to have lasted three-quarters of an hour. But then working in the film business has always offered the opportunity of making friends on both sides of the law-and-order fence, and this was especially true in England after the 1960s.

I probably met more senior policemen than serious crooks – especially during the making of *Robbery* – though I do remember one brush with people reputed to be rather more serious than Albert Dimes. It was rumoured that a certain criminal organisation in New York, one that had enjoyed much success in laundering money through car parks, had then decided to launch another 'laundry' venture by acquiring a major Hollywood studio that had become rather run down during the late 1960s. It was believed that organised crime saw the overseas distribution of films as an excellent way to legitimise large sums of cash. And yet, perhaps a little indiscreetly, they loved to use their Las Vegas connections to entertain film people. I myself was wafted over to Vegas on a grand private jet to see Elvis Presley's famous come-back performance in 1969. Now it's possible that all of this was no more than movie-business gossip, and the Mafia never had a hand in any major studio. But there is a modicum of evidence.

It seemed then a heady time to be in the business, and yet I was supposed to be making movies for a living, and nothing was on the horizon. Then Richard Burton's and Elizabeth Taylor's agent John Heyman came and asked me to help him make a movie based on the marvellous Flashman books by George Macdonald Fraser. I persuaded Ismail Merchant (later to team with James Ivory in making *A Room with a View* among others) to become my Indian co-producer and I spent an amazing few days with him in New Delhi. I quickly realised that apart from his charm and doggedness he had extraordinary energy. Through Stanley Baker I had become great friends with Prime Minister Harold Wilson, and Harold kindly gave me a letter to Indira Gandhi, then prime minister of India, in case I needed help at the highest level. But after seeing Ismail Merchant operate, I suspected that he could get more done than even the head of state. The Flashman project came to nothing, and as my break from film producing lengthened I began to involve myself in Labour Party politics with Harold Wilson and his most trusted aide Marcia Williams, now Lady Falkender.

I have fond memories of Harold Wilson, who led Labour to four general election victories and yet, in my opinion, has never been fairly treated by history. His dealings with the trade unions were, by political necessity, perhaps less than entirely frank, but he pulled them off for the country's good. Back in 1952, as the youngest ever president of the Board of Trade, he had used his ministerial clout to push through a scheme devised by Sir Wilfred Eady to provide financial support for the British film industry. The Eady scheme was simple: every British cinema ticket sold carried a levy of a penny or two, and this money was paid into a fund managed by the National Film Finance Corporation (NFFC). The sums collected could then be apportioned to the makers of qualifying British films – usually up to thirty per cent of the film's budget. If and when the resultant film turned a profit, the NFFC were last in line to recoup their investment. The trick behind the Eady scheme was that, of course, the largest contributors to the fund were the Americans, whose films dominated our screens.

In 1973 I travelled by train to Blackpool for the Labour Party Conference, sharing a compartment with Harold. While I chatted with Wilson, my wife was in the next carriage with Mrs Wilson, and spent most of the journey being regaled by her companion's readings of her own poetry. But for four good hours Harold and I talked about films with great enthusiasm, as well as of the many problems that were facing the British film industry. Harold promised that if Labour got back into power at the next general election he would do something to help us. Through this private talk I gained huge respect for Harold's intellect and essentially good character.

In February 1974 the Conservative prime minister Edward Heath finally went to the country, asking the question 'Who governs?' This was in the wake of the OPEC crisis, a miners' strike and the three-day week. For Labour Oakhurst produced and donated a series of TV commercials, and Wilson won a narrow victory. True to his word, Harold found time to plan an inquiry into the problems of and remedies for the British film industry, increasingly dominated by Hollywood production. He invited half a dozen people to Chequers, the prime minister's country retreat, these including Richard Attenborough, Bernard Delfont, a couple of financial people from the City of London and me. As a result, Harold formed the Prime Minister's Working Party on the Future of the British Film Industry. (More than thirty years on this body still exists as the British Screen Advisory Council, although it now has a much wider remit than simply films.)

The Chequers meeting was very productive from a professional point of view, but for me it was also very interesting socially.

Chequers is like a beautiful aristocratic country house with first-class staff. If today you were to visit a British embassy in a reasonably important foreign country, you might yet be astonished at the number of footmen standing behind the chairs at dinner. This level of service and opulence still goes on. Certainly it did in 1974, even under a Labour government. Yet I also visited Number 10 Downing Street, and I was surprised at how modest were the Wilsons' living quarters upstairs. The flat was pleasantly middle-class with chintz-covered sofas, knick-knacks and a comfy family atmosphere, much in contrast to the grandeur of the public rooms downstairs. From the outside, Downing Street looks quite modest and somewhat unprepossessing, but it stretches back a long way to accommodate the civil servants beavering away inside.

Until the IRA tried to lob a mortar bomb into the back of Number 10 during John Major's tenure, it was my impression that security provisions around the prime minister were moderate and scarcely visible. The bobby standing by the front door seemed hardly likely to intimidate a potential assassin. The rigmarole was quite different, though, when Harold and Mary Wilson came to dinner at our house. Three very tough security men checked the house and the garden, as well as David Frost's house on one side and Lord Vestey's on the other. No parking was permitted outside, and uniformed and plain-clothes policemen patrolled Egerton Crescent. The Wilsons left very late, which gave the secret-service men who were grouped in the kitchen plenty of time to enjoy our wine cellar.

Stanley Baker and I decided it would be beneficial to widen our range of entertainment activities. We had a foothold in the movie business and our interest in Harlech Television was paying dividends. Now it came to our notice that a lot of money was being made in live music festivals. The Isle of Wight festival had been cancelled after its stunning 1970 swansong, when the 600,000 who came witnessed instantly legendary performances by Jimi Hendrix and the Who, but Glastonbury and Reading had since picked up the baton. We felt that with enough money and good management such events could become respectable as well as profitable. So we set up a series of companies under the name Great Western: 'Great Western Music', 'Great Western Investments', 'Great Western Festivals' – all had a similar logo to that of the defunct Great Western Railway.

Stanley and I had a new accomplice for these plans of ours. Back in 1969 I had met Barry Spikings, a journalist working on *Farmers Weekly*, a journal owned by the publishing corporation IPC. Barry had since advanced to the point of working on a strategy for the establishment of an IPC film production division, for the purpose of which he travelled to Los Angeles and head-hunted widely for a chief executive. But in the end it was me he proposed for the job. The notion of trying to crank up an entirely new business with £10 million of capital was an exciting prospect, and Barry and I spent a lot of time working out how we could leverage these start-up funds into a truly substantial film programme, drawing up the rudiments of a pre-selling strategy.

The project seemed to be gaining board approval at IPC until it was suddenly scotched by Cecil King, a veteran newspaper man who chaired the company. Unbeknownst to us and, I suspect, to most of the board, secret negotiations had begun for IPC to be taken over by the giant paper company Reed International. Thwarted at this turn, Spikings decided to throw in his lot with Great Western, and Stanley and I gave him five per cent of the company, though Stanley had his doubts – suspicious, perhaps, of the high-voltage charm-assaults that were Barry's strong suit.

Fortified thus, we quickly began setting up our first pop festival. By now Lord Harlech had become a good friend, and just as his children were regular festival attendees he himself was also a great pop fan. We planned our first big event as a three-day concert over the May bank holiday weekend, and found a seemingly perfect site in Bishopsbourne, Kent, owned by a retired colonel. We set up a meeting in the village hall to tell the local folk what our intentions were, but we ought to have prepared ourselves for a little native hostility – the *bourgeoisie*, when excited, can be very strident. A faction opposed to our plans had printed up some pungent leaflets depicting a chamber-pot pouring its vile contents – labelled 'VD', 'excreta', 'crime', 'rape' et cetera – upon the sleepy village of Bishopsbourne. At the meeting I was duly cornered by someone with whom I had served in the army, demanding to know how a former officer could be associated with such depraved activities.

In the months to follow we were chased out of Battle in Sussex, Castle Combe in Somerset, White City in London, Towcester and Lingfield race courses, and Wadhurst Park. If it wasn't the locals it was the police or county authorities. Finally, we found a site in the middle of nowhere – Bardney in Lincolnshire. We prepared facilities for the 150–200,000 people we were expecting, and special buses were laid on. But come that weekend, from Friday through to Monday, we had nothing but driving rain and howling winds. Only the most hardy enthusiasts made the trip though, amazingly, there were 45,000 of them. Sadly this was no more than half the number we needed to break even. But the late John Peel was our DJ, and John Cleese and the Monty Python team performed a wonderful comedy routine. The music, lest we forget, came from the likes of Joe Cocker, Rod Stewart & the Faces, Don McLean, Genesis and the Beach Boys (who doubtless felt themselves to be very far from home in drenched and windswept Bardney).

Great Western Festivals did manage to mount a further big pop concert in Scotland, and then a more genteel series in 1973 tying in to the government's celebrations upon finally entering the European Economic Community (an occasion over which Charlie Croker might have wept). But that proved the height of our ambitions in this area: Michael Eavis of Glastonbury would henceforth have the field largely to himself.

In February 1972 Great Western Investments had pulled off an extraordinary deal to buy the whole of Alembic House, in which we had previously leased our office. The building's owner Felix Fenston had died, whereupon I discovered that there was some dispute over what shares his partners were due from the disposal of the property. It looked as though probate of his will might be delayed for as much as six years. I paid a visit to Mrs Fenston and put to her a proposition. The building had cost £456,000 a few years previously. On behalf of Great Western Investments I offered her £457,000, the idea being that if she accepted there would be a profit of only £1,000 and she might as well share that equally with the claimants. It took her only twenty-four hours to agree. Stanley and I went to Barclays Bank and, on our personal guarantees, were loaned the purchase price.

This purchase wasn't a complete bargain. There were rumours of some inherent structural engineering problems in the building – and indeed it did sway in heavy winds. The limited permitted business uses also yielded very low rentals, though within a year the property market had improved, and the value of Alembic House rose. That I couldn't bank on at the time, and so I was worried about maintaining my share of the mortgage – about £40,000 per annum. Oakhurst still wasn't shooting any films or earning any fees. After the misery of *Murphy's War* this suited me personally to some degree, but was a serious problem on the financial front. Stanley was in a slightly less precarious position, since he was still working regularly as an actor.

One barrier to our making a profitable sale of Alembic House was that the government had imposed a punitive tax of ninety-eight per cent on profits from the sale of commercial real estate. But there was a solution. Alembic House was the only real asset in Great Western Investments. Even though Stanley and I were the loan guarantors, we could exchange our shares in GWI for shares in another company. We looked around and finally lighted upon Lion International, a public company which owned British Lion Films, Shepperton Studios, Pearl and Dean cinema advertisers, and Mills and Allen outdoor advertising. This swap would allow Lion to sell Alembic House for cash, offsetting the profit against existing losses it had incurred in some of its subsidiaries.

British Lion Films was rather a difficult little sector for Lion International. It had been producing movies since 1919, and had to its credit the likes of Carol Reed's *The Third Man*, Powell and Pressburger's *Tales of Hoffmann* and David Lean's *Hobson's Choice* as well as some amusing *St Trinian's* movies and the distribution of the Boulting brothers' comedies (*Lucky Jim, I'm All Right, Jack* and so on). But it was now a somewhat rundown business. Lion International was forced to rely on their people at British Lion Films knowing something about movies, because they themselves didn't. Longstanding managers such as the Boulting brothers were still hanging round, but weren't especially helpful – in truth, they were out of date. I felt British Lion Films could benefit from the blueprinting Barry Spikings and I had worked out when it seemed likely that an IPC film company would be formed. But negotiations with Lion International dragged on and on. John Boulting, one of the managers of British Lion during its declining years, strongly opposed my entry into the company. But he was rebuffed, and that was the last I heard of him for some years. Finally, in January 1973 I was appointed managing director of the British Lion Entertainment Division and joined the board of British Lion Films. Within three months I was MD of the film company. It was past time for me to dirty my hands once again in the actual making of movies.

8

Don't Look Now, or The Prudery of Warren Beatty, and *The Wicker Man*, or The Wrath of Christopher Lee

We arrive at a somewhat pained passage in this story, but one where the truth must be faced. My connection to a macabre low-budget British film called *The Wicker Man*, which I inherited upon the purchase of British Lion Films in 1973, has led down the years to my being dubbed a rogue and a villain in the eyes of a dogged number of *Wicker Man* cultists, outraged by tales told of how their all-time favourite movie was brutally cut down by 'the money-men' and cursorily shunted off to a very limited theatrical release.

In particular, the decisions I made at that time as to how to handle the picture have been endlessly questioned by an irritable Christopher Lee, long peevish about his undying public identification with the Hammer horror films, and firmly of the view that his performance in *The Wicker Man* (in the supporting role of the saturnine Lord Summerisle) has never been correctly appreciated. But grieving *Wicker Man* aficionados should take note – I can fairly say that, were it not for my actions, the picture would never have been released at all; it might even to this day be mouldering in cans in British Lion's cellar on Broadwick Street, Soho.

By 1973 the renaissance enjoyed by the British film industry during the sixties appeared to have expired. Apart from the increasingly tired *Carry On* series little was being churned out other than appalling big-screen versions of TV comedies such as *Dad's Army* and *On the Buses*. Hollywood, too, had fallen out of love with

Swinging London and the policies of the Exchequer, and had cut back on making films in Britain. And yet, the early part of the new decade was notable for such offerings as Sam Peckinpah's *Straw Dogs* (1971), Mike Hodges' *Get Carter* (1971) and Stanley Kubrick's instantly notorious *A Clockwork Orange* (1972), all of which seemed to reflect an increasingly edgy and violent Britain. Darker, more sexually explicit product was also coming out of British Lion Films, and upon my arrival two were in the works.

Lion International had kept the film company on a tight rein, short of cash, and so much depended upon the box-office results from *Don't Look Now* and *The Wicker Man*, both of which were in the post-production stage of music scoring and dubbing. My Canadian predecessor in the company, Peter Snell, had been responsible for green-lighting Nicolas Roeg's *Don't Look Now* starring Julie Christie and Donald Sutherland, based on a story by Daphne du Maurier. When I saw a rough cut I was delighted: the picture had been beautifully shot in Venice during the winter, and told an original and disturbing story of an architect and his wife trying to cope with the unimaginable trauma of the drowning of their young daughter. The girl's death was realised at the start of the film, with great artistry and in a manner most dreadfully affecting to the viewer. There was no doubt that this theme of loss would be a tough sell to the movie's first audiences: potentially so strong as to obscure the underlying love story of a husband and wife trying to remake their marriage and their lives – which is, in fact, the real subject of *Don't Look Now*. To that end Roeg's film featured an astonishingly poetic and elegant lovemaking scene, made all the more moving and unusual in film terms because the intimacy was between a bereaved married couple, rather than the usual cliché of two young lovers falling into bed at first sight. Nic Roeg's films were already famous for their enigmatic, fragmented editing style which seemed to make the past and the present exist in the very same moment. This particular love scene was a model of that Roegian style, for one moment we were watching husband and wife separately but fondly buttoning themselves back into their clothes in the aftermath, and the next they were passionately entwined between the sheets. Roeg's editor Graeme Clifford had cut the sequence quite brilliantly.

I learned that for the purpose of the scene Nic had cleared the set of all but himself, the actors, and the most vital camera personnel. Perhaps then it was not so surprising that rumours were rife among excluded technicians that Julie and Donald had actually had sex together. A similar legend had attached itself to some notorious footage from *Performance* (which Nic co-directed in 1968 with Donald Cammell), this involving Mick Jagger and Anita Pallenberg, then the girlfriend of Keith Richards. It seemed that parts of said footage had played separately at European festivals of erotic film, as well as causing something of a tiff within the ranks of the Rolling Stones.

As for *Don't Look Now*, there was also an interesting off-screen context, for Julie Christie was very much involved in a passionate affair with Warren Beatty. It may be that Beatty did not believe anything untoward occurred in the making of *Don't Look Now*. At the same time it might not have escaped his attention that Donald Sutherland had also been rumoured to have conducted a romance with another of Beatty's former lovers, Jane Fonda, during the shooting of *Klute* (1971) in Canada. Might Beatty, in effect, have been cuckolded twice by Sutherland? Even if there were no truth in the tales surrounding *Don't Look Now*, Beatty's much-envied reputation as the Don Juan of Hollywood might be compromised.

It was eleven o'clock one night when there came a knock on the door of my mews house in Belgravia. At first I feared it might be the police, or security forces yet more intimidating – the Stasi, even. For that same evening I had been forced to rescue my ginger tomcat Patrick from a tree in the back garden of a nearby house that just happened to be the embassy of the German Democratic Republic. I had strayed onto East German soil (indeed enemy territory) as stealthily as I could, scooped up the ungrateful cat and made my escape, but I couldn't discount the possibility that I had been observed: hence my dread of the late-night rap on the door. As it turned out, my fears were misplaced. It was only Warren Beatty.

Beatty had stepped off a plane from Los Angeles and, it appeared, come directly to my door. After some initial pleasantries, he came to the purpose of his visit. He was determined that the love scene between Julie and Donald be excised from *Don't Look Now*. He described it, essentially, as vulgar, and suggested that Julie had been talked into enacting it without fully understanding how explicit would be its effect projected up on a cinema screen. I countered by asserting Nicolas Roeg's absolute integrity, and my own belief that the scene was so beautiful in its context that any 'smutty' undertones were negligible. I also pointed out that Julie Christie had no call to be concerned by loose talk that emanated from anybody who had not been among the few to witness the scene being shot on a closed set. Above all, I put it to Beatty that the underlying drama of the scene – the repairing of a schism between husband and wife wrought by their daughter's tragic death – had a poignancy very rare in movies.

I didn't resort to a further argument that might well have appealed to Beatty as the resourceful producer he had increasingly become since his work on *Bonnie and Clyde* (1967): namely that the scene's undeniable loveliness and the impact its daring would have on audiences were potentially substantial money-makers. Without it, *Don't Look Now* might have looked a lot more like a modestly budgeted Venice-set horror picture. In short, there was no way that I as managing director of British Lion could make the economic sacrifice that Beatty's proposed cut would have entailed.

Of course, had British Lion been a Hollywood studio and *Don't Look Now* just one of a dozen works on their busy production roster – had we, moreover, coveted the notion of Warren Beatty starring in some future British Lion picture – then, certainly, we would have given in to him, as so many others have done over the years. But we were not in that situation: *Don't Look Now* had to be British Lion's financial lifesaver. And though Beatty and I had the same conversation four or five times over the following days – a process of attrition probably familiar to anyone who has worked with the man – we would not be taking scissors to a scene that, today, is considered one of the boldest and most beautiful elements of an acknowledged film classic.

While in the case of *Don't Look Now* I was being begged to cut down, the other picture in the works at British Lion – *The Wicker Man* – I was being implored to leave intact. This pagan thriller, written by Anthony Shaffer and directed by the somewhat inexperienced Robin Hardy, was shooting in remote surroundings (and amid terrible weather conditions) in Scotland. Peter Snell was the producer, and though it was proving hard to exercise total control over the proceedings he was wrapping matters up efficiently. But still there were obvious schedule and budget concerns.

It was presumed by Snell and British Lion that the Rank Organisation would pick up *The Wicker Man* for their cinema circuit: certainly, any British picture denied access to either Rank or EMI cinemas was as good as doomed. I was told that George Pinches, who booked films for Rank, had allowed Snell to believe that he would take *The Wicker Man*. Perhaps something went wrong in the personal relationship between Snell and Pinches. But it's more likely that Pinches simply didn't like the finished movie. He turned it down flat.

I hurriedly got onto Bob Webster at EMI, already fearing he would suspect he was being offered spoiled goods, and EMI also declined *The Wicker Man*. Thus our cash-strapped new company appeared to have on its hands a rather expensive picture with no UK release, and our new bankers were not amused. I felt more than a moment's panic.

I decided we would have to bypass the UK and go straight to the

United States – a reasonably successful release there might at least recoup our costs. But the first US bookers to whom we screened *The Wicker Man* came back with yet another negative response – whether offended by the film's content, unimpressed by the cast, or simply dubious about whether it would play at Peoria, we simply weren't to know.

Finally, I turned to the living legend of low-budget American cinema, Roger Corman, and offered him the picture. He was aware none of the majors would go near it, and so agreed to acquire it on the condition that it be cut down from its current length. Among the bits universally considered tedious by early viewers was a scene where Christopher Lee's Lord Summerisle expounded at great length about an apple crop. This seemed a clear candidate for the chop, though Lee himself came to see it as the unkindest cut, and just one facet of a larger conspiracy against the film and his performance.

Let me say here and now: I thought *The Wicker Man* was interesting, but it was just unfortunately mistimed for the market. Human sacrifice was not your average everyday amusement for British cinema audiences at a time when a comedy about a penis transplant called *Percy* was cleaning up around the circuit. It was simply a shame that there was no greater enthusiasm evinced in the US, or on the film festival circuit, for that matter.

Meanwhile, *Don't Look Now* had been picked up by Paramount's distribution arm in America, the deal covering much of the $1.1 million cost. The picture seemed to be generating advance interest, and we awaited the US premiere in some anticipation. One morning I got into my London office and was appalled to learn that *Don't Look Now* had opened in New York overnight, more or less unannounced, without trailers or publicity. It transpired that Paramount had just suffered an almighty flop with their filming of a much-praised novella called *Jonathan Livingston Seagull*, a 'lyrical' expression of the philosophy, ethics and wisdom of the aforementioned bird. This movie effort to cash in on the book's cult had resoundingly failed – the public, as they say, queued up round the block not to see it. Furious New York theatre operators demanded the picture be pulled forthwith and replaced with anything that wasn't about a seagull. Paramount had made a number of prints of *Don't Look Now* ready for the scheduled release in a couple of months, following the usual pre-release publicity and advertising. But they now decided to press *Don't Look Now* into the sudden void left by that unloved *Seagull*.

Three or four days went by before the first ads for *Don't Look Now* appeared in the New York press. Until then, the public might have assumed that the seagull horror was still flapping through cinemas. But opening days are critical, not only for word-of-mouth to spread but also because other theatres throughout the US book pictures based upon the early box-office figures. Inevitably, those figures for *Don't Look Now* were terrible. Paramount were undeniably within their rights to have acted as they did, but I doubted they would have treated a bigger production company than British Lion with such scant regard.

Don't Look Now's UK release was near at hand, and so I made one final attempt at releasing *The Wicker Man*, which was sitting gloomily in cans down in the British Lion basement. I re-approached Rank and asked whether it would be possible to release the picture as a supporting feature to *Don't Look Now*. Rank accepted, on the proviso that *The Wicker Man* be shortened to the length of a typical 'supporting feature', around the eighty-minute mark. While I was certainly of the view that the loss of a few minutes wouldn't much hurt the picture, there was, in any case, no choice. I was sure that Peter Snell understood that the only way people were going to see this picture on a circuit in Britain was in a truncated form. I had no reservations, and the deal with Rank was struck.

I set cutter Eric Boyd-Perkins the job of abbreviating the movie in the manner required. But Anthony Shaffer and Robin Hardy were greatly displeased. Shaffer would never concede that anything he wrote was less than perfect, and Hardy was unhappy that his film was not the dream length he would have wished for. Both claimed that they were locked out of the editing room while Boyd-Perkins made the necessary changes. What they failed to appreciate is that the point of making movies is to get people to see them, and to pay money at the door for that privilege. As it had turned out, the running time for which Robin Hardy wished was not suitable to our sole commercial option, and at British Lion we made films for a commercial purpose. I wasn't about to allow the company to go out of business in my first year of ownership. Hardy and Christopher Lee were further aggrieved to discover *The Wicker Man* was to be released as a B-feature, and naturally I sensed it was their view that on any double-bill they should play at the top. But there was no question that Roeg's *Don't Look Now* was the A-list production of the two.

In the years since *The Wicker Man*'s awkward release, the film has steadily acquired what is known as a cult following, and as a consequence I have been dubbed the desecrator of its reputation – the man in the suit who took up scissors and ruined a masterpiece at birth. The chief whiner has been Christopher Lee, who has gone so far as to say that I actually sabotaged Robin Hardy's footage. In fact, this paranoia on his part seems to credit me with suicidal tendencies: British Lion was my company, and to that extent *The Wicker Man* had become my concern. I hadn't swapped our rather grand building on the Thames in order to pursue a personal vendetta against Hardy's film. Yet according to Lee's voluminous and repetitive remarks, British Lion had at one point 'stolen' our own negative, and I had had the footage buried under the construction of the new M3 motorway.

In later years I was more than a little surprised to see printed in *Hotdog* magazine a prominent boxed pull-out quote attributed to myself, shouting, 'Christopher Lee is a fucking idiot.' My first reaction was that the word 'fucking' was inappropriate, and the word

'idiot' a bit weak. Then I recalled the years of mean and petty diatribe from this actor over the necessary editing of *The Wicker Man*.
My next thought was to wonder why he was still raving about my
trimming some ponderous verbiage of his on the subject of apples.

But then it all began to seem like déjà vu to me when I got
wind of Lee's complaints after Peter Jackson was compelled to
leave his wizard character Saruman's seven-minute death scene on
the cutting-room floor of *The Lord of the Rings: The Return of the
King* (2003). Despite substantial screen time in the two previous
Rings films, Lee seemed to feel he had been especially ill-served. 'I
was given plenty of reasons why I was cut out,' he told *Total Film*,
'none of which made sense.' Having read Jackson's account of
trying to lock off a 200-minute movie, during which scenes other
than Lee's simply had to go – 'The longer the film was, the less
strong it got' – I had to wonder what Lee struggled to understand,
and why he had taken it so hard. But then I also discovered that
Jackson was further subjected to an internet-driven petition by
Rings/Tolkien cultists, tens of thousands strong, seeking Saruman's
reinstatement. Such is the people-power behind a cult movie, as I
witnessed with the growth of the *Wicker Man* legend. All I can say
in response is that the people who work to produce and release
movies, and the people who consume the end results, do not
always enjoy the luxury of identical concerns. In making a picture,
certain tough choices and compromises are often unavoidable.

9

British Business

The Wicker Man's failure to achieve a first-feature release on the British circuit pointed to the handicap we at British Lion were bearing by not owning our own movie theatres. At the time we had virtually no production funds at all, and yet while I strove to sell *The Wicker Man*, two further movies had been completed: *The Internecine Project*, an action-adventure starring James Coburn, and *Who?*, a much darker movie with Elliott Gould and Trevor Howard. In terms of cinema history, neither picture is important. What is worth mentioning is the way we had financed them, securing half the costs from a US distribution deal with Allied Artists, and the other half through a German tax-shelter deal. Such clever arrangements were the only means to keep British Lion alive.

Don't Look Now, too, had been part-financed by a US tax deal, and when rooting through the old British Lion 'unmade script' cemetery, I found a project that I knew could be financed almost entirely through such a deal.

Barry England's *Conduct Unbecoming* had been a successful London play but its film rights had been expensive and a number of screenwriters (including Terence Rattigan, who was paid £250,000) had failed to crack the adaptation. In fact there was a very simple solution, which was to go back to the stage play and strip out as much extraneous dialogue as possible. Robert Enders delivered a perfect screenplay by these means.

The piece was set in nineteenth-century India and revolves around the trial of a young officer accused of sexually assaulting a fellow officer's wife. I engaged as director Michael Anderson, the showman who made *Around the World in 80 Days* (1956) and whose efficiency was legendary. Together he and I cooked up a scheme to shoot this film on a four-week schedule, and I set the start date at Shepperton Studios for the middle of November 1974, which gave a maximum of five weeks before the Christmas break closed down the studio.

Our cast was prestigious: Michael York, Richard Attenborough, Trevor Howard, Christopher Plummer, Susannah York and Stacy Keach, who played a British army adjutant with a cut-glass accent. And under Anderson's direction the picture ran like clockwork. Our editor was an old cutting-room friend and colleague, John Glen (who went on to direct five James Bond films). Allied Artists distributed the picture in the USA, where the National Film Board of Review voted it third best picture of the year after Kubrick's *Barry Lyndon* and Altman's *Nashville*. I'm not sure how our picture muscled into the top end of such a splendid list, but it was certainly well made, at the right price, and completely fulfilling British Lion's objectives – to make money.

Then Peter Rawley, a British-based producer, came to me with a script entitled *Ransom*, a drama based on the hijacking of a passenger airliner which he had packaged with Sean Connery and Ian McShane. 20th Century Fox picked up US and Canadian rights for an advance of $800,000 and with Connery in the cast we made excellent pre-sales in Cannes of $1 million for the rest of the world, meaning that we more than covered our $1.5 million production cost. *Ransom* emerged as a cheerless-looking picture, but again it turned a profit.

Nevertheless by the winter of 1973/4 we were getting hurt by a continuing and serious decline in the London stock market. We didn't see the crash until it hit us. In any event we were locked into Lion International, unable to trade our shares for two years, a reasonable condition since it prevented us unloading a sum that would have severely depressed the Lion International share price, and ensured that we stayed with British Lion Films so as to increase the value of Lion International as a whole and of our shares in particular.

The component parts of Lion International, at least, were doing well: they had sold Alembic House for a quick profit, the advertising arms were earning steadily. And yet I had to watch in horror as the share price declined to the point where we had lost over £1 million between the four of us.

John Bentley's controlling shareholding had been taken over by more serious-minded people with very little desire to own and continue to finance Britain's number three film company as well as loss-making Shepperton Studios. In the end, we struck a deal under which – to put it more simply than the complex arrangements deserve – we swapped our twelve per cent share of Lion International for British Lion Films without Shepperton Studios, agreements we completed in June 1975. I flew back for three days from Albuquerque (where I was producing *The Man Who Fell to Earth*) to sign the contracts.

The Italian International Bank, under managing director Russell Taylor, now became our bankers. Taylor owned a small percentage of British Lion Films and so did one of his deputies, Colin Madison. Money was still very tight, but at least we were working for ourselves to earn back our fortunes. One casualty was my friendship with Stanley Baker. It had been impossible to persuade our bankers that Stanley was an appropriate manager: they believed, perhaps correctly, that his primary interest would always be his acting career. (This was déjà vu in the sense that when I had become MD of British Lion Films I quickly gathered that Lion International didn't want Stanley anywhere near the place, knowing all too well that he was 'a producer' only in tandem with other producers, and would want to appear in every film we made.)

Spikings and I buckled down to dig British Lion Films out of the financial hole it was in. I never really knew whether Stanley accepted from his point of view the wisdom of what we had done.

He continued working as a leading man in films, but then tragedy befell him. My wife Ruth had always been perceptive in her ability to detect from someone's appearance if they were not in the best of health, and she started to fear for Stanley long before his doctor had spotted anything awry. But in due course Stanley, still only in his mid-forties, was given the dire news that he had contracted lung cancer.

Though British Lion's traditional choice of UK cinema circuit releaser was Rank, suddenly the other member of the 'Big Two', EMI, was taking an interest. EMI's film management was over the hill and although the chairman of its entertainment division, Bernard Delfont, knew little about films, he realised none the less that the time was coming when he would have to replace the ageing team of Nat Cohen and James Carreras, who had retired handsomely from Hammer Pictures and its run of often hastily conceived and luridly packaged horror films. (It was rumoured Carreras worked backwards toward a script from a given title and a pre-designed poster – *Lust for a Vampire*, say. The formula certainly had a ready audience for a good while.)

I daresay an obvious choice to take over EMI Films was the people running British Lion, who had already demonstrated an ability to make films which were sold worldwide and produced using ingenious financial manoeuvres. As for Spikings, Taylor and me, we had got out of one sticky situation but only with a temporary reprieve. It was plain that just a couple of financial mistakes could topple British Lion from its shaky position. There was no room for number three in Britain and we had to set our sights on one of the big boys.

We knew that if we had EMI's money behind us and we stuck to the same formula of making no film without at least half the budget committed by a major US distributor, then we could significantly increase the quantity and quality of our current output. Moreover, we were sure we had enhanced our standing by having lately opened an office in Beverly Hills that was strengthening our connections and profile in Hollywood – certainly surpassing EMI's relationships at the time. We had realised that for British Lion to have any impact in Hollywood would require a local presence; it was not enough to be making endless runs between Heathrow and LAX. Thus we had established ourselves on the top floor of the building occupied by high-class jewellers Van Cleef and Arpels on Rodeo Drive, already poised to become the most fashionable street in Beverly Hills. The offices were built around an open courtyard where we would host lunches, and our invitations to these were rarely declined.* And yet we were revolving a production fund of only £1 million: EMI could make available at least ten times this, and with movie theatres to feed, they clearly could use more A-quality product by way of films made in-house.

Bernard Delfont decided that he wanted the British Lion team on board; but we were not available for hire. The only way he could get us would be if he were to buy our company – British Lion Films Ltd. The company did have other assets, including a library with more than 400 films, holdings that would form a basis to establish its value.

What of the other big player on the British scene? The Rank Organisation had been founded in the 1930s by the wealthy flour miller J. Arthur Rank. He was a religious man who originally wanted his company to turn out films that would propound the Methodist view of life. How this became a commercial filmmaking

*Around this time, our being 'on the spot' led to a deal with Columbia Pictures to distribute Peter Bogdanovich's $8-million *Nickelodeon* outside the US. Columbia was then a bit rickety financially, and often prepared to part with overseas rights for a capital sum plus a fifty per cent share of further income once the buyer recouped his advance. We wanted a big picture to raise British Lion's profile, and Bogdanovich had *What's Up, Doc?* and *Paper Moon* behind him. As usual we didn't have the $2 million Columbia wanted, so we made a deal with EMI: they would pay the front end in return for a half share of our profits. It looked good on paper, though the resultant film was inexplicably dull, and we were only just able to scrape back EMI's money.

activity based at Pinewood Studios, I do not know, but from the 1940s onwards it grew into one of the biggest production houses in Europe. In the immediate post-war period it had set out to establish itself in the USA as a major film distributor to rival MGM, Fox, Columbia and the rest. By that time, however, the American majors had such a firm grip on the US market that no newcomer would ever have a chance of breaking in. Rank was crushed and returned to London with its tail between its legs – much as others would do in due course, including EMI and Lew Grade in 1983.

If the main problem facing EMI Films was ageing management, Rank had very different considerations. With extraordinary foresight they had invested in a fledgling office equipment company called Xerox. Xerox had quickly grown so large that it completely dominated Rank's other businesses. Films, for instance, had become a minor and unreliable part of the empire: Rank now made more money even from its TV-station ownership than from showing movies. In 1974 the Rank circuit consisted of over 200 cinemas that yielded a profit of only £900,000 – and all of that came from its flagship cinema in London's West End.

British Lion's lack of cinema ownership was a serious handicap, and it seemed to me that Rank's increasing disillusionment with films in general and cinemas in particular made them a plum rich for the plucking. With the help of a Rank Films managing director who had just quit after a row with chairman John Davis, we put together a proposal to acquire the cinema chain.

My friend Harold Wilson regarded Rank Cinemas as a national treasure, and was concerned about any talk of the chain falling apart. However unprofitable cinemas had become in a declining British film market, the Wilson government had refused support for any proposals which would permit them to be converted to other uses. Knowing Harold's feelings, I went to Downing Street to ask for his help, without which little British Lion couldn't swallow this big mouthful. Marcia Williams came up with the answer and Harold called in James Goldsmith.

Goldsmith was already famous, and for many reasons. At the age of twenty, already a gambler and a drop-out from Eton, he had eloped with mega-rich Bolivian tin heiress Maria Isabel Patiño. When in 1954 she died not long after giving birth to their daughter, Goldsmith decided to make himself extremely rich – which he did, initially by acquiring undervalued food companies (including the famous Bovril) which he eventually merged into a conglomerate called Cavenham Foods. Soon he was a multi-millionaire, openly maintaining a wife in London and a mistress at his other home in Paris. (The last consuming passion of Goldsmith's life was to found a British political party – the Referendum Party – that would fight elections solely on a platform of opposition to Britain's membership of the European Union.) In 1974 Goldsmith very quickly grasped Harold Wilson's point and agreed to provide £7 million for British Lion to acquire the Rank cinemas, with the chain to be owned in equal partnership by Goldsmith and British Lion. Following recoupment of his investment plus interest, we would each take fifty per cent of the profits. This deal was made in the blink of an eye, thanks to the prime minister's involvement.

Although returning only two per cent on capital, the Rank cinema circuit was on the company's books at a value of £39 million. At the time, £7 million was a fair price but Rank's shareholders couldn't take the write-off, or loss, of £32 million. To avoid this, we agreed not to buy the theatres but to lease them so that their capital value would be unimpaired. The lease would be for ninety-nine years and if at a later date the rules changed and any of the theatres could be developed into commercial non-theatrical use, we would split the profits three to one in Rank's favour.

Our other possible lifesaver, EMI, initiated acquisition talks at the 1975 Cannes Film Festival. Clearly, this was going to be a protracted negotiation with no certain outcome. Bernie Delfont haggled skilfully, well aware of Lion's weak financial position. Also, we had begun to realise that he was a chronic prevaricator. Throughout the months of discussion that followed, Bernie was promising one

structure for a combined EMI/British Lion to Nat Cohen, his current head of films, and a quite different one to us. His style was
defined by great lies, as I was to observe to more ruinous effect in
the years ahead.

The Prime Minister's Working Party on the Future of the British
Film Industry, chaired by Sir John Terry, reported back to the government before the end of 1975. A prime recommendation was
that a British Film Authority be established to bring together and
coordinate various government-funded operations such as the
National Film Finance Corporation (NFFC) and the British Film
Institute (BFI). The BFA was to be established under royal charter
and plans for its foundation crept forward.

It came as a great shock, then, when Harold Wilson resigned in
1976: not just because the BFA plan ground to a halt but also
because nobody really understood why he gave up so abruptly.
MI5, for base political reasons, had attempted to blacken his character by setting up a forged Swiss bank account in the name of Ted
Short, the deputy leader of the Labour Party, but this was clearly an
absurd deception.

Harold's resignation honours list included a knighthood for
Stanley Baker, whom he had always respected. By this time
Stanley's cancer seemed to have been successfully thwarted, but
three weeks later he contracted pneumonia at his home in Spain,
where he died on 28 June before having the chance to travel to
Buckingham Palace. The Queen agreed that although he had not
formally received his knighthood his widow Ellen could use the
title of Lady Baker.

Unfortunately, Harold's successor was James Callaghan, a career
politician of no great charisma who furthermore had absolutely no
interest in cinema. He limped through the balance of Wilson's
term, presided over the disastrous winter of union agitation that
was 1978–9, and was soundly thrashed by Margaret Thatcher at the
subsequent election.

Wilson's retirement years were tough. Harold had only had his prime minister's pension of £12,000 a year and the family flat in Westminster. The moment she was elected, Mrs Thatcher spitefully confiscated his modest Rover car and dismissed his driver. Marcia Falkender called me one day to say that she had seen Harold sitting in a long queue in a doctor's waiting room in Victoria and was seriously upset to see the humiliation the country's former leader was having to suffer. Marcia had decided she must rally Harold's friends to set up a fund to help him and Mary in his retirement. By then, Harold's health was deteriorating as Alzheimer's began to take hold. A few good friends contributed a few good thousands of pounds, but some of the people who had benefited most from Harold's generosity failed to donate a penny. Lords Grade and Delfont – both of them 'ennobled' by Harold Wilson – were not among the givers.

In 1975 British cinema was in a trough – with hindsight we could call this period the lowest ebb. Radical and momentous action was called for at British Lion. One problem was that the Americans had abandoned Britain. Our solution was simple: we would go to America, make our films there, in American settings, but financed by British money and starring British talents. We had made our proposition to Rank and it was up to them to react. The EMI alternative would only happen if and when Delfont made up his mind. As for me, I flew to Albuquerque to get on with my primary job. I had a picture to produce.

10

Soaring High, Almost Crashing: *The Man Who Fell to Earth*

When I had first arrived at British Lion the production process of Nic Roeg's *Don't Look Now* was nearly complete, but I was highly excited at the prospect of working with Roeg. He was a filmmaker who had served apprenticeships at various London studios, working his way up to camera operator by the early 1960s, while garnering a few writing credits here and there. But it was as a cinematographer that Roeg made his mark, shooting among others Roger Corman's *The Masque of the Red Death* (1964), François Truffaut's *Fahrenheit 451* (1965) and Richard Lester's *Petulia* (1968). Those films were so individually distinctive and yet somehow akin to one another – in their use of colour as much as their boldness of theme and structure – that with hindsight one can see the outline of Roeg the future director.

Indeed, with *Performance* (1970, co-directed with Donald Cammell), and *Walkabout* (1971), Roeg shot to the forefront of British cinema, proving himself to be a director with an utterly distinctive style. As I was to discover for myself, in Roeg's hands a script isn't any kind of blueprint, not in the usual architectural sense. He develops his material as he goes along. And he makes his audience work with him, because he wants to make it just a little harder to perceive what he is offering: he wants the viewer to *think*.

After the *Don't Look Now* experience Nic and I became friends and in due course he brought me a script by Paul Mayersberg based on Walter Tevis's novel *The Man Who Fell to Earth*. The script told the story of an alien who arrives from a distant planet blighted by drought, seeking a means of survival for his race. On earth he adopts the demeanour of an Englishman and takes the name Thomas Jerome Newton – appropriately for one who has had such dramatic experiences with gravity. His intention is to amass an unearthly fortune, fund scientific research into a remedy for what ails his own planet and construct a viable interplanetary vessel to enable his return. In short order he constructs one of the largest corporate empires on earth, this fortune arriving via Newton's exploitation of a number of strange patents for consumer technologies, which he presents to an astonished lawyer. (Nic and Paul Mayersberg had come up with numerous pretend-inventions in this line, mainly inspired by the thinking behind Polaroid, and I know that some readers of the script thought these a bit silly. They included a disposable camera that one discarded after shooting off a roll of film and a camera with automatic focus and exposure . . . Far-fetched, clearly.)

But Newton's success soon makes him the target of aggressive corporate takeover, with his rivals prepared to go to homicidal lengths. Newton himself becomes increasingly frustrated, unable to understand human feelings, fears and aggression. He comes to regard this planet as nothing more than a prison of sex, alcohol and violence. It all sounded perfect for Roeg: hadn't *Performance* and *Walkabout* offered extraordinary visions of individuals cut adrift from their usual surroundings, both moral and physical? And those films had further shown that Roeg had no fear of the violent or erotic currents in his material. The further extraordinary good news appended to Mayersberg's script was that Nic already had David Bowie attached to play the lead role of Newton.

I calculated that we could make the film on a reasonable budget, so long as we were careful. Nic duly came by my Beverly Hills office to discuss the project, bringing along a friend of his by the name of Si Litvinoff, who had produced *Walkabout* and taken an executive credit on Stanley Kubrick's *A Clockwork Orange* (having for some years held the option on Anthony Burgess's novel). I told them both that British Lion couldn't be viewed in the same light as one of the Hollywood majors who, basically, handed over money for the production of a film. Because of our size, financial limitations and modest output we had to be seen as a production house that additionally pre-sold its pictures to distributors throughout the world. This came as bad news to Litvinoff, who had it in mind to be appointed producer of Nic's film; but given the ambition of the project, there was no way I would hand over such financial responsibility to another party. In explaining this, I noted that I would fully understand if they wanted to take the picture somewhere as a team. They may very well have attempted as much, but within a couple of weeks Nic came back and said he would like to set up the picture at British Lion. This was Nic's prerogative, though I understand that Litvinoff cursed me at every cocktail party he attended thereafter.

Paramount had distributed *Don't Look Now* and were very keen on Nic Roeg's work. I made a deal with them whereby they would pay British Lion $1.5 million against all US rights, and our bank loaned us money against this contract.

Our leading man had no experience in movie acting other than an unsung cameo in *The Virgin Soldiers* (1969). But two other big factors had to be considered. For one, David Bowie had considerable on-stage experience: he knew how to look good and move well. Nic had already co-directed Mick Jagger in *Performance* and Jagger's presence had lent a lot to that picture. Nic assured me he could make it work with Bowie, and I was nothing but confident in this director's talent. The second – perhaps more banal – factor that made Bowie suitable was that he would be playing a creature from another civilisation. There seemed to be no standard actor's rulebook on how best to inhabit the role of a man who has fallen to earth . . . and so Bowie had a licence to inhabit the skin of the character as he saw fit.

Moreover, Bowie wasn't even especially expensive and did seem committed to the idea of a film career (although I think he later decided it wasn't fully worth the effort). But he came from a different set of disciplines – was, moreover, coming to us not so long after his huge six-month Diamond Dogs tour of North America – and he was used to being treated as a solo star. When you are working on a film you are in an ensemble business: you have to wait for the cameraman to light the set, for the make-up to be carefully applied, et cetera. It's not one man doing his thing, and I think for Bowie that took a lot of getting used to. American rock journalists Steve Stroyer and John Litflander, who would visit our set to get a story for *Creem* magazine ('Spaced out in the desert', December 1975), observed that 'Bowie is a man well insulated from the world by a retinue of employee-disciples.'

With the script nearly finalised, we chose our location. Nic wanted to reproduce something like the planet that Thomas Newton had fled in his search for water. The production had to be located in an arid part of the US, but we also needed urban locations; and then for practical reasons we needed to have an airport close by, to get our overnight rushes sent back to Los Angeles so we could see the dailies within twenty-four hours. Albuquerque, New Mexico, met this bunch of needs and was ideal for other reasons too. It was out of sight of the movie unions and being, at that time, not too prosperous a town we were welcome to come there and spend our money. The only union we had to deal with was the Teamsters, who are everywhere, but even they were reasonable and we were required to hire only three of their drivers. There was a new Hilton hotel, well managed and tolerant, which housed the crew for $15 each a night and gave us parking for our trucks.

New Mexico had a singular atmosphere that I hadn't experienced before. I have heard the theory that all emigrants keep moving westward until they can settle down: they might start in Russia and move to England and then onward; or if they are Irish, perhaps to Canada before trickling down to New England. Some just keep going west. If they find land to cultivate they might stop anywhere in the heartland. For many, California is the final goal. But on the way, a few very decent folk found the peace and sunshine of New Mexico a lot more pleasant than the rampant commercialism of California.

On the border between the Rocky Mountains and the Great Plains is a town called Las Vegas, New Mexico. The place had been set up around 1835 as a 'great new town' and the centre of it had been founded by some very enterprising people. A railroad had also been built to what was expected to become the sheep centre of the South West. Las Vegas was indeed very prosperous for a while – until the sheep grazed the entire land and there was no food left. What remained was a sort of ghost town with pens for thousands of lost sheep. The place had served as a location for many early silent Westerns. And it was there, too, that Peter Fonda and Dennis Hopper met Jack Nicholson in *Easy Rider* (1969). Its spectral quality made it an obvious choice as one of the towns in which *The Man Who Fell to Earth* would be shot.

If I had hired a crew in Hollywood the cost would have been impossibly expensive: with the studios working flat out and a huge number of television films also being shot, rates were sky high. The British unions, meanwhile, were becoming quite liberal in their terms, especially for such an enviable location as the USA. So we decided to take a gamble. Each member of the crew went to the US embassy in Grosvenor Square, London, and lodged an individual application for a tourist visa. We chartered an Aer Lingus plane and loaded as much of the equipment as we could carry with the entire film crew already aboard. The plane touched down to refuel in Shannon in Ireland, and then flew non-stop to Albuquerque. Two days later the unit started shooting. This was the first time – and will probably stand as the last time – that a full-sized British crew shot an entire feature film in America.

My biggest headache over six weeks during July and August 1975 was in keeping the production on schedule. Nic Roeg wanted to capture some quite complex shots which took considerable time to set up. I found that a certain amount of pressing had to be done on this picture to keep it moving along. It is quite difficult to be brisk on the production side when you have a picture which demands a sort of moodiness and a slightly slower pace, but you do have to force the production through, because each day costs you too many dollars.

Nic is an auteur director, clearly the mastermind of what goes into any film that bears his name, and an artist in whose vision one simply has to trust. So I considered it my job to back him in every way I could – provided there weren't to be any crazy excesses. In fact, such problems as arose on *The Man Who Fell to Earth* were between director and crew – a rift I would observe at a later date when working with Ridley Scott. Traditional 'stolid' English film crews don't always find it easy to work with Nic, precisely because of his distinctiveness. The crew on this picture grew frustrated in the belief that he was being too 'artistic'. Nic began his career as a cinematographer, and good cinematographers are innovators as well as perfectionists: if Roeg seems less concerned with the commercial aspect of cinema then the reason may lie therein.

Nic is not much given to booking in rehearsal time with his actors. He wants to make things happen in the moment, discover things that are surprising to him. (For that reason he was very fond of our prop-man, who kept coming up with unusual items that gave Nic ideas for particular shots or scenes.) Nic's passion is for what the camera can steal: moments in time, which can't be prepared for exhaustively, and would never be quite the same again even if reshot a hundred times over.

Nic could be very specific about the set-up of a given scene: he wouldn't want anybody to move anything in a room that he had laid out, he wouldn't want a location cleaned up or prettified in the routine manner. When it came time to roll he could be much less specific – leading to obvious mutterings from the crew along the lines of 'He doesn't know what he wants . . .' But Nic certainly knew what he *didn't* want, and was ready to stretch time so that an inspiring moment could occur.

David Bowie lived in his own world, and I'm not sure how many other inhabitants it had. His wife of the time, Angie, an exotic lady with an unexpectedly innocent name, made frequent visits to the location accompanied by their four-year-old son, who rejoiced in the name of Zowie. It was a nice rhyme, if a daring choice, but not untypical of the times. Nevertheless I wasn't hugely surprised to be told in later years that the boy elected to be known first as 'Joe' and then 'Duncan'.

Bowie, in any case, was my star; and like any other star his every whim, fear, demand or tantrum would have to be dealt with as promptly as possible, and at the smallest possible expense to the production budget. There was a moment when filming might have ground to a halt: this was when the star became convinced that someone or something had poisoned his preferred tipple, a glass of skimmed milk. He claimed to see some strange matter swimming about in the liquid, and was ill for two days afterwards. On another occasion there was a fuss because the star's mobile dressing room had been set up on a site which he felt must be an old Indian burial ground. There were no grave markers, sign-posts, artefacts or any other necrological indications, but we moved the dressing room anyway. In fairness, he might have been right. Some people do have a special instinct for such things and David Bowie was probably sensitive enough to feel strange vibes.

I think that even Nic Roeg – who clearly has a highly sensitive creative register of his own – felt there was a strange aura around Bowie. Our star was happiest when secluded in his big trailer with his books and his milk – he didn't go out drinking with the grips. But whenever it came time to roll, Nic found Bowie available, accessible and ready for anything. Certainly he was asked to perform some extraordinary scenes, many of which benefited from Bowie's particular quality of otherworldliness. One of the film's most stunning moments is when Newton decides to reveal his true physical being to Mary Lou (Candy Clark), the hotel chambermaid who has become his lover and rashly insists that she can take any surprise he throws at her. Thus Newton retires to their bathroom, where he fastidiously removes his synthetic skin and the fake corneas from his eyes. Mary Lou hammers on the door throughout this process, until the newly denuded Newton finally opens up. Candy Clark, however, had not been treated to a sneak preview of how Bowie would look in his unalloyed alien form, and her terrified reaction to the camera was authentic and unfeigned.

Towards the end of production, Roeg needed to capture one of the movie's key shots: the splashdown of Bowie's intergalactic spacecraft into the remote Lake Fenton, a tarn, or mountain lake, formed in a cirque excavated by a glacier, 11,000 feet above sea level. This and other shots required us to travel by car very early in the morning up a mountain to Lake Fenton. Every car had a big oxygen tank in the back to revive the flagging workers. Nic and I travelled together, and had the good fortune to discover a country bar open at six in the morning which made excellent tequila sunrises. These got us up the hill in no time.

The picture finished on time and on budget; the crew and equipment were loaded aboard their Irish charter flight and flown back to London and we left Albuquerque to go back to sleep.

The editing process on any picture is difficult. There can be conflicts between the director and producer, or between either of these parties and the studio, as to how the picture should finally look. Questions of running time arise, as do all sorts of other vexing matters, not always when expected and never to be desired.

For all that *The Man Who Fell to Earth* was a picture in the popular genre of science fiction, boasting a rock 'n' roll superstar in the lead, it was nobody's idea of a blockbuster. Indeed, Nic had kept his story on an achingly human scale – here, in essence, was the drama of someone cast adrift far away from family and crawling into a bottle for solace. For my part, when I saw Nic's rough cut I liked it very much, and I told Nic so. I further assured him that however the film was received, whatever were its commercial fortunes, one thing was for sure – his fellow filmmakers would be ripping off his ideas in no time. I was only half-joking, because if Nic was not the business's most bankable director he was – and is – truly a film-maker's filmmaker, in the sense that he can make a frame like no one else and come up with images that are unique and indelible, with the result that other directors are forever raiding his work as a visual treasure-trove.

The original plan was to have David Bowie provide the music for the film. After a month locked away in a recording studio, he emerged with one modest song quite unconnected to the picture. Nic's editor Graeme Clifford then wanted to use some existing Pink Floyd tracks, but they were unobtainable and would in any case have been too expensive. In the end John Phillips, once of the Mamas and the Papas, put together a combination of some new tracks and some existing cuts.

While the music was being painstakingly added, I took a rough cut to New York to show to the newly appointed chairman of Paramount Pictures, Barry Diller, who had come to 'the mountain' from ABC Television (so replacing Frank Yablans who had earlier supplanted Bob Evans). The viewing by Paramount of the rough cut would trigger their first payment to us under British Lion's contract.

Now, if you have ever paid attention to the shifting power struc-tures of the US entertainment business, Mr Diller's name will be known to you. He would move on from Paramount to Fox, then to QVC, before his present station as chairman of Expedia and IAC/InterActiveCorp, parent of companies including the Home Shopping Network, Ticketmaster and Match.com. According to the *New York Times* Diller was the highest-paid executive of the 2005 fiscal year, with a total compensation package in excess of $295 million.

But back in 1976 it was just the two of us, Diller and me, in a private New York theatre, and for a few minutes after the lights came up at the end of the screening, Diller said nothing. It's hard to imagine Diller being speechless but I was by now pretty certain he was not struck dumb by any great admiration. Finally, he said, 'This is not the movie Paramount bought. The picture we bought is linear, and this isn't.' This was the first time I had heard the word 'linear' applied to a film. I explained that what I had screened for him was only a rough cut, without any polish or music or post-sync or sound effects. But he was unmoved.

To an extent, I could see Diller's point. Every producer would like to feel that what he's doing is delivering the goods to make a certain piece of work in a form as promised. For me, making a film was about providing material that could be shown in a cinema in exchange for money – so paying for the next one, and so on. Nic, on the other hand, wasn't really interested in anything but his creative process. (I was quite often slightly baffled by what he was doing, but confident in his ability to do whatever he wanted to do well.) If no one came to see the picture Nic would be disappointed, no doubt, but it wasn't his prime objective.

When Diller was at ABC Television he had enjoyed groundbreaking success by introducing simple ninety-minute TV 'Movies of the Week', which certainly were linear and nothing much more, at least in cinematic terms. Nic Roeg's pictures were and are multilayered, demanding more effort from their audiences than would any Movie of the Week. The *Time Out Film Guide* would later report of *The Man Who Fell to Earth*, 'Roeg's hugely ambitious and imaginative film transforms a straightforward science fiction story into a rich kaleidoscope of contemporary America.' Diller wouldn't have chosen those words to thumbnail the movie. And he now indicated his disinclination to honour the deal his company had struck prior to his tenure.

This was a potential disaster for British Lion, and something I had to disclose to our bank the moment I got back to London. I met with our former financial adviser, now CEO of the Italian

International Bank, Russell Taylor, or 'C.C.' (for Constantly Carping) as I had started to call him. Russell duly lived up to his nickname and complained bitterly: he always liked to make his criticisms personal, almost as if we wanted Paramount to renege. British Lion were engaged on two alternative merger prospects, running our company prudently and making films, but in all this time we received no wise counsel or calm consideration of any reversals or advances we faced. Meanwhile the IIB had contracted a number of loans to various businesses and, we learned, many of these looked shaky. (A while later, when IIB closed down, I was told that British Lion was the only debtor over £2 million who repaid the bank's loan in full.)

I instituted a lawsuit against Paramount, but this was largely formulaic. It would have taken five years to come to court and we couldn't compete with their financial clout. Paramount always defended court actions, however much they were in the wrong. I knew that within those five years we could be out of business if we didn't find another distributor for the film. Also, it was our obligation to mitigate the damage and Paramount would use this against us if we didn't genuinely try to find another US distributor, which would not be easy. Hollywood is a village and everyone knows what everyone else is doing – or at least some version of the events. No other major US distributor would want to pick up *The Man Who Fell to Earth* because it was now soiled goods, blighted by Paramount's rejection. A lot of film projects are abandoned by one studio and picked up by another at the script or even pre-production stage, but very rarely after they are shot. Hollywood is, secretly, highly superstitious.

We looked around and finally found a partial solution. Don Rugoff ran an efficient New York company called Cinema V which specialised in unusual pictures, often from Europe (much as Miramax and New Line do today). Don picked up the picture and gave us an advance of $850,000, which got us two-thirds of the way out of trouble. Cinema V didn't have Paramount's clout in the theatres, and an average release on their part might amount to 550 theatres as opposed to Paramount's 2,000. But this was not a mass-market picture, apparently, so we were grateful to Don for what he did.

We were now counting heavily on the EMI deal. We were absolutely worn out, continually strapped for cash. After we failed to get the $1.5 million from Paramount, our bankers wouldn't take our word on anything – though Paramount did make a modest financial settlement of our lawsuit. Meanwhile the British Lion overseas sales department under Sidney Safir worked the foreign sales market a bit harder. Once again, we scraped through.

11

The Lion's Last Gasp

In September of 1975 Bernard Delfont threw a birthday party in Cannes that was used to publicise the growing relationship between British Lion and EMI. Knowing how difficult Delfont was to predict, we still pushed ahead with our preferred acquisition dream. On 11 February 1976 James Goldsmith signed off his financial commitment to British Lion's Rank cinema circuit takeover deal, which was now getting very warm. We were ready to put a formal offer to the Rank board – which, essentially, meant chairman Sir John Davis, since the lesser mortals at Rank were already on side.

As for EMI, we had lots of perfectly pleasant lunches with Nat Cohen. In March, I met with the affable John Read, chairman of the EMI group, who confirmed EMI's wish to acquire British Lion and have us take over the management of EMI Films. All it needed was for Delfont to close the deal. But we had no idea what was really going on in Delfont's duplicitous mind.

At the end of this busy period the Rank board finally met to decide on British Lion's offer. We even provided a proposal for us to take over all their film interests, including Pinewood Studios, Rank Film Laboratories and their production and distribution divisions, if they preferred. Our ducks were all in a row. Later I was told that our proposal was discussed in detail and most of the board welcomed in principle the idea of disposing of films so that they could concentrate on Rank Xerox and Rank Leisure. At the end of the discussion, members dutifully turned to the boss, Chairman

Davis. He pondered for a while then declared: 'I do not wish it to be said that under my chairmanship the Rank Organisation disposed of its historic film interests.' That was that. Later, after Davis had retired, Rank got out of the film business completely, scattering to the four winds its vertically integrated empire of studios, production, distribution, laboratories and cinemas. For now, it was one down and one to go. We stepped up the pressure on the EMI deal.

Finally, in May 1976, heads of agreement were signed under which EMI would acquire British Lion, and an announcement was made at Cannes. The next three months were agonising. EMI had a team of bureaucrats whose purpose seemed to be to chip away at every aspect of the deal, however insignificant. These functionaries were skilfully orchestrated by Delfont, who was promising Nat Cohen that he would remain in control even though I was to be appointed managing director. Bernie was in no hurry, knowing that for us time was valuable and every delay might reduce the price of his acquisition.

At this stressful time, British Lion was waiting for three films to go into release – *The Man Who Fell to Earth*, Peter Bogdanovich's *Nickelodeon* and *At the Earth's Core*, a prehistoric adventure story we had sold to Columbia Pictures. There was no current production, because we were doing our best to conceal the fact that the Italian International Bank would not lend us any cash for filmmaking. Russell Taylor was writing lengthy and intemperate letters blaming us for Paramount's reneging on their commitment to *The Man Who Fell to Earth*. But Nat Cohen, too, was stirring up trouble. On 30 June 1976 Cohen was quoted in Hollywood's *Daily Variety* in relation to the merger and our future with EMI, claiming that 'nothing has yet been signed' which blatantly ignored the heads of agreement. It seemed to me the last gasp of a reluctantly retiring management. We decided to be positive by concentrating anew on the future, preparing some projects for later production – whether with EMI, Rank or anyone else.

It was then that an old Hollywood friend, the English-born agent Robert Littman, brought me a remarkable script called *The Man Who Came to Play*, written by the brilliant – if sometimes erratic – team of Quinn Redeker and Lou Garfinkle. These two were fondly described by their agent as the only Jewish-Gentile writing team he'd ever seen, but in truth Lou was more of a mentor in the relationship than a writer himself, Quinn doing the lion's share of the work on the page. *The Man Who Came to Play* had its origins in a childhood memory of Quinn's: as a boy in Seattle around 1953 he had been leafing through *Collier's* magazine when he came across a short piece about a man who played Russian roulette for a living. The article was illustrated by a triptych of photos depicting this heavyset fellow with a towel wrapped round his head as though he were suffering from toothache, holding a Smith and Wesson .38. Over the three frames he levelled the barrel at his head, squeezed the trigger and smiled in satisfaction having emerged unscathed.

This highly alarming eccentricity would linger in Quinn's mind, and around 1974 he was sufficiently inspired to develop it into the hook for a story, with Lou Garfinkle's advice and encouragement. After a year's work and something like twenty-one drafts which had the basic story set everywhere from the Bahamas to South Dakota, Quinn found his preferred location: a POW camp in Vietnam, where two captured American servicemen – one, Merle, a wounded and vulnerable army grunt, the other, Keys, a shrewd ex-flyer – make money by playing rigged games of Russian roulette. In due course they escape the camp and head to Saigon, there to get ensconced in a professional Russian roulette circuit. The slippery Keys fools Merle into thinking he has died, and returns to the US with their stake money. Merle remains in Vietnam and becomes a yet more proficient player of this deadly game. But in due course there is a reunion and a reckoning for Keys, he and Merle finally playing against one another while Saigon falls.

At first Quinn Redeker lodged the script with a producer friend,

Herman Saunders. Eventually Herman gave it to Bobby Littman, whereupon it reached me. I did find some weaknesses in the characters, but I was struck by the underlying drama and the totally original idea of using Russian roulette, which seemed to me a very strong visual and emotional premise for a picture. I was sure that this could be a major movie. I bought the script for $19,000 and a share of potential profits, and started looking around for a writer/director who could make the changes necessary to define the principal characters more strongly.

I knew Bobby Littman had offered the script to other producers; I subsequently learned that one or two were horrified by what they read. (*Rocky* producers Bob Chartoff and Irwin Winkler had a look, but Winkler had a viscerally negative reaction to the Russian roulette scenes.) A view seemed to have been established among the script's early readers that the picture would never be made and, for a while at least, they were right. Following British Lion's usual practice, I took the project to five major studios. All of them turned it down. The consensus was that American audiences would have no stomach or savour for a picture concerning the Vietnam War: it would simply be too depressing a subject for too many Americans still feeling the anguish, anger or shame of that failed conflict – emotions which, I was told, I 'wouldn't understand, as a European'. In fact, they were dead wrong on that score.

I had been a soldier in the Far East, and had experienced the difference between the conflicts in Malaya and Indochina. The British won in Malaya because the insurgency was led from outside (by China) and supported internally by only a minority of the population. In Indochina, our French allies were fighting a vast majority of the population, and they lost as dismally as they later did in their other colony, Algeria. But the USA was somehow blind when it chose to inherit the doomed French role in what had become Vietnam. It was actually 'as a European' that I felt I understood the lessons of the Vietnam War all too well. Nevertheless, *The Man Who Came to Play* was off to a slow start, but I intended to stay the course.

At the same time, I was talking to an American agent turned producer, Robert M. ('Bob') Sherman, about a truck movie, of all things. Unusually, *Convoy* was based upon a song – a surprisingly popular one of the same name by C. W. McCall which hymned a convoy of trucks that flouted the USA's national 55 mph speed limit and so locked horns with an armada of police cars trying to enforce the law. Sherman had acquired the script by B. W. L. Norton and had set about packaging it. I had a couple of meetings with the proposed director, Sam Peckinpah, who at that moment didn't seem to be as crazy as he was reputed to be. Peckinpah was staying in London, in a Chelsea flat just round the corner from where I lived. He was accompanied by Katy Haber, a London girl (from Dollis Hill), whom he had first met while working on *Straw Dogs* (1971) and who had become his assistant and girlfriend. I sensed that Peckinpah's chief feeling about *Convoy* was that he wanted the money – *needed* it, in fact, because he had very expensive habits. Yet he struck me as quite a mellow soul. We would continue to get on fine, until the picture started.

As I tried to keep these new projects on track, one more hitch to the EMI deal occurred. The government, through the National Film Finance Corporation, owned a 'super share' in British Lion Films to ensure that the company preserved Shepperton Studios as a filmmaking centre and did not redevelop the land. Without settling this problem, British Lion Films could not be cleanly sold. Further, the share carried with it an opportunity to take a £350,000 tax write-off benefit, something the EMI bureaucrats were eyeing greedily. It would take a few weeks for this to go through various government departments so I went to Hollywood for a month to crank up interest in our new projects. By now we were certain the merger would go through but Russell Taylor wasn't. He had switched from his initial 'You failed to make a deal at EMI' to 'Why is it taking so long to complete?' In July he wrote accusing us of concealing income from the bank – based on 'information' from a person he declined to name. Ironically, this income purported to come from a Canadian tax-shelter deal of a sort which the Canadian government had long rendered impossible to make. Taylor had even, at one point, secretly negotiated with a well-known London lawyer, asking him if he would take over my job as managing director. This wasn't too smart, because it was our management that EMI was negotiating to buy.

Finally, on 25 August 1976, at EMI's offices very late at night we signed the papers – the last hour of this procedure being occupied by EMI's most vicious number cruncher knocking a miserable £9,000 off the price they were to pay for British Lion Films Ltd. But it was done. Spikings and I received some EMI shares, £81,000 each and, certainly the best part, the repayment of British Lion's £2 million debt to the IIB which we had personally guaranteed. Closing the company's account with the Italian International Bank meant that we wouldn't have to listen to any more of Russell Taylor's ill-informed opinions as to how we should manage the film company; nor read any more of his bitchy letters. Shortly afterwards the IIB was closed down.

After months of marking time both EMI and British Lion had become practically moribund. John Brabourne's *Murder on the Orient Express* (1974) was earning good revenue and EMI had a low-budget Dick Emery comedy in the works, but that was all. We presented to EMI a much more detailed document setting out our modus operandi. The cost of major American pictures could to a great extent be recouped in the US domestic market, particularly now that network television was kicking in big prices. With a domestic market as small as we had in Britain we either had to make very cheap local films which could recoup domestically and in the British Commonwealth or, if we wanted to go international for the bigger revenues, we would have to lay off much of the financial risk and find co-funding partners around the world even though this would reduce potential profit.

At this time, revenue from a major international picture on average derived sixty per cent from the USA and forty per cent from the rest of the world. If I could not get from a US major a guarantee yielding fifty per cent of the budget plus a commitment to provide the full costs of prints and advertising in their territory we would not produce the picture. While we were closing a US financing and distribution deal, we would be in conversation with our best contacts in Japan, Italy, France and Germany to hear their views, from a local standpoint, about the proposed principal cast and to make sure that financial commitments before and during production (so called pre-sales) were in the works. We liked to start shooting with seventy-five per cent of the budget committed and we needed other deals to be closed from time to time or at the Cannes Film Festival. Nowadays, non-US distribution companies can have a pretty good idea of a film's appeal if they've watched its results in America but with pre-sales this opportunity does not exist and names are vital, sometimes of directors as much as stars. With *Convoy*, for example, Kris Kristofferson's name was barely adequate but Sam Peckinpah's name had great weight because of his earlier successes – particularly in the foreign markets with pictures such as *The Wild Bunch* (1969) and *The Getaway* (1972).

By the time we completed each picture we expected to have ninety per cent of each budget covered with the UK market (where we had our own cinema chain) completely free. Australia also was not pre-sold because we had a longstanding distribution agreement for all our product at the very low fee of fifteen per cent. Ours was a damage-control system but it came at a price. In return for the local distributor's risk and financial commitment he would keep thirty to fifty per cent of the surplus once he had recovered his guarantee to EMI plus distribution fees and costs. But this method allowed EMI to produce much bigger pictures at almost no risk, provided we had the discipline to stick to the rules. At British Lion we had to do this when we had no money and no choice and we wanted to do it at EMI, where we planned a slate of films costing many times EMI's contributions to the budgets.

We planned to shoot an inaugural six pictures in the period January 1977 to June 1978, one of which, *Death on the Nile*, was already at EMI and the others came with British Lion. The three American films were to be *Convoy* with United Artists, *The Deer Hunter* with Universal and *The Driver* with 20th Century Fox. The three British films were to be: *Death on the Nile* with Paramount and *Warlords of Atlantis* and *Arabian Adventure* with Columbia.

This programme would be EMI's first substantial involvement in the US market and I wanted to work with as many of the US majors as I could. If with one of the companies we developed a strong rapport it might be that we would enter into an exclusive arrangement for the next batch of pictures. For the US distributor, the advantage of exclusivity would be that they would be guaranteed three or four major pictures each year with half the cost of each picture paid for by somebody else. For EMI we would expect some improvement in the distribution terms as well as a guaranteed US distribution deal, with few limitations, for each picture we chose to make. Clearly the idea of an exclusive relationship could be achieved only if our American pictures were successful. Time would tell, so we kept this plan to ourselves.

The 1970s were proving a creative high point for Hollywood. At the cusp of the previous decade the likes of *Bonnie and Clyde* (1967), *Midnight Cowboy* (1969) and *Easy Rider* (1969) had marked a symbolic transfer from old Hollywood to new. Restrictions on language, adult content, sexuality and violence had loosened up. A new breed of younger filmmaker convinced Hollywood to experiment and take risks. EMI was now set to join in this revolution.

By the mid-1970s Columbia Pictures was strapped for cash and EMI saw an opportunity to add to its growing presence in the music publishing business by buying from them the Screen Gems music library for $15 million. Columbia negotiated a condition whereby EMI also agreed to invest a total of $5 million in any three pictures on Columbia's current production slate. We picked two hits: *Close Encounters of the Third Kind*, in which we invested $2 million, and *The Deep*, also for $2 million. Both of these made us net profits even under Columbia's poisonous net-profit terms. In fact, the revenues from these films to EMI more than paid for our third punt of $1 million into the unsuccessful biography of Muhammad Ali, *The Greatest* (which it certainly wasn't).

In terms of production control, the British films were self-sufficient. Producer John Brabourne (later seriously injured in the vicious IRA murder of his father-in-law Lord Mountbatten) was experienced and highly responsible. He had earlier delivered to EMI his first Agatha Christie all-star picture, *Murder on the Orient Express*, and his crew on *Death on the Nile* would repeat their efficient work. John Dark was repeating the formula which he had started at British Lion with *The Land that Time Forgot* and his two pictures for Columbia would be smoothly delivered.

The American pictures presented a much greater challenge to me. They were vital as ground breakers for EMI Films Inc., which had taken over British Lion's elegant offices in Beverly Hills. But the company did not have the depth of supervision which existed at the major Hollywood studios, and so I faced a daunting task – which could not be handled from 6,000 miles away. EMI asked me to move out of England and reside permanently in Los Angeles.

By then I had worked with most of the Hollywood majors on one project or another. I had produced *The Man Who Fell to Earth* on American soil, and had made a lot of good contacts and some wonderful friends such as Quincy Jones (after our involvement on *The Italian Job*) and *bon viveur* George Axelrod, whose screenplays included *Breakfast at Tiffany's* (1961) and *The Manchurian Candidate* (1962). Any party at George's place was liable to be graced by the presence of such luminaries as Gregory Peck, Kirk Douglas, Lauren Bacall and Roddy McDowall, the former child star from South London who had successfully managed the switch to Hollywood as well as performing the remarkable feat of seeming to be liked by everybody in town. For me, these gatherings at George's were a very useful introduction to the Hollywood A-list.

I had been a member of the Academy of Motion Picture Arts and Sciences since the producer Walter Mirisch (*The Magnificent Seven, West Side Story*), successfully proposed me in the late 1960s. And since 1964 I hadn't made a single picture that didn't have a US distributor and at least part-financier. The Woodfall films were made with United Artists' backing and British Lion dealt with various US majors. In short, I felt myself comfortable with the Hollywood system.

It was a big physical upheaval to move out of London on a more or less permanent basis but it was the only way to assert control of our new adventure; it would also be easier to raise money there. The late 1970s had been a real struggle in London. The city had been virtually deserted by the US majors and no private investment was available to fill the vacuum. In Hollywood, money was there for the grabbing – it was just a case of finding the right scripts.

The US majors and the bigger independent companies have been controlling cinema worldwide for nearly a century. Their enormous libraries and large annual output of movies and television films over the years have provided them with an ongoing cushion of revenue to offset the ups and downs of annual box-office revenues. For a producer with access to good material and the studios there is a striking difference from the European experience. EMI Films Inc. had that clout – I was only asking the studios to invest fifty per cent of the budget against their market of sixty per cent of the world. They had script, cast and director approval, no responsibility for budget overruns and no supervisory tasks at all.

Provided I could find a studio that liked the basic material, the deal was so attractive to them that it could be wrapped up very quickly. The five aforementioned pictures made during my spell were easily set up with five different studios and each one was net-profitable to its studio as well as to us at EMI.

A few people railed against my 'disloyalty' to the British film industry, suggesting that such a policy of international production was unethical when the native British film industry was flat on its back. Chief among these voices was that of the stentorian Ulsterman Alexander Walker, film critic of the London *Evening Standard*. Always at pains to make himself heard, Walker criticised me in the pages of the *Standard*, to my face at meetings of the British Screen Advisory Council, and in a private letter. I responded to him unrepentantly. 'First, it shows the Americans we really mean business when we take the action to them. We are more heavily committed to making movies in America than some of the traditional Hollywood majors like MGM and Warner Brothers are at the moment. Our show of strength will increase the willingness of Americans to come in on films we are about to make in Britain. We inherited no substantial British projects from EMI, so this will take time to develop.'

Walker refused to grasp that my object was to create a truly international film company, and so I could hardly ignore more than half of the world market. Sixty per cent of our films were American films and the rest were British, but the biggest impact came in the international markets outside the US and UK, where distributors without permanent links to one of the US majors would now buy product of the same quality from EMI.

In fact, unbeknownst to Walker, we were already well on track to make a very British picture indeed. The producer John Goldstone, a friend of mine, had been working with the Monty Python team on a project and when their screenplay was finished John sent it to me. I can truthfully say that I have never in my life read a funnier script than Monty Python's *Life of Brian*, in which a nice and unassuming lad from Nazareth was mistaken for the Messiah in Roman-occupied Judaea. As soon as I could, John and I sat down together to agree a deal to make this picture. While the paperwork was crawling through the contracts department, I returned to

Beverly Hills. Soon an extraordinary cable arrived from Bernie Delfont.

It seems that one of my London-based ill-wishers at EMI had slipped a copy of Goldstone's Python script to Delfont; this was either Nat Cohen or his crony Jimmy Carreras, the company's Roman Catholic. In his cable, Delfont castigated me for wanting to make a 'sacrilegious' film with 'outrageous swear words'. He said that the EMI cinema boss, Bob Webster, echoed his displeasure and disregard for the project. I told Delfont that, speaking as a Christian, I could assure him that this film was not sacrilegious. (In due course the Pythons would be forced to argue the same point until blue in the face, much like the famous purchaser of the dead parrot.) But Delfont wouldn't listen to my case. He was not used to being corrected, and his final furious expostulation was, 'I'm not going to be accused of making fun of fucking *Jesus Christ!*' I warned him that we would have to pay off the producer, and his response was, 'Do what you have to do to get out of this.'

In fact, EMI hadn't completed the contract with John Goldstone but I was so cross that I arranged to have John paid £50,000 in compensation. The project was then taken to Handmade Films, the production house of ex-Beatle George Harrison. Monty Python's *Life of Brian* (1979) went on to enjoy huge success in both the UK and America, far outrunning the predictable quibbles it provoked among the easily offended. And it was shown in EMI's cinemas, too – thus giving the lie to Delfont's assertion that Bob Webster 'wouldn't touch it'.

```
28213  EMICIN G

20TH FEB 1978

ATTENTION MICHAEL DEELEY AND BARRY SPIKINGS
EMI FILMS INC
BEVERLY HILLS. CALIF.
696231


HAVE LOOKED RATHER QUICKLY THROUGH THE SCRIPT OF
THE NEW MONTY PYTHON FILM AND AM AMAZED TO FIND THAT
IT IS NOT THE ZANY COMEDY USUALLY ASSOCIATED WITH HIS
FILMS. BUT IS OBSCENE AND SACRILEGIOUS, AND WOULD
CERTAINLY NOT BE IN THE INTEREST OF EMI'S IMAGE TO MAKE
THIS SORT OF FILM.

EVERY FEW WORDS THERE ARE OUTRAGEOUS SWEAR WORDS
WHICH IS NOT IN KEEPING WITH MONTY PYTHON'S IMAGE.

THIS IS VERY DISTRESSING TO ME AND IS A VERY SERIOUS
SITUATION AND I CANNOT, UNTIL WE KNOW EXACTLY WHAT WE
ARE DOING, ALLOW THIS FILM TO BE MADE.

I UNDERSTAND THIS VIEW IS ABSOLUTELY SUPPORTED BY BOB WEBSTER
AND JIMMY CARRERAS AND I HATE TO THINK WHAT JOHN READ'S VIEW
WOULD BE.

PLEASE ADVISE

BERNARD DELFONT


TIMED IN LONDON AT    16.37.


.
EMI FILMS BVHL

28213  EMICIN G"
```

One that got away: Bernard Delfont's irate response by cable to his reading of
the script for Monty Python's *Life of Brian*, a picture that went on to reach a far
more receptive audience than Delfont could conceive of.

12

Peckinpah, *Convoy* and a Blizzard of Cocaine

Back in 1968 my old associate Peter Yates had made more than the average Hollywood hit when he directed Steve McQueen in *Bullitt*. In fact, Peter's film served as a template for a new kind of gear-crashing, tyre-screeching action picture, where a fast car and a cool actor behind the wheel made for a perfect symbiosis. By November 1977 EMI Films Inc. had a picture of this type well on its way into pre-production: *The Driver*, to be produced by the experienced Larry Gordon and directed by its screenwriter, Walter Hill, who had proved himself a top gun among the rising generation of young American auteur directors headed by Lucas, Spielberg, Coppola and Scorsese.

The plot of *The Driver*, like its dialogue and indeed its protagonist, was lean and pared-down to the point of enigma: a master getaway-car driver tries to elude the attentions of an obsessive detective. And the picture was adroitly cast for foreign markets, with Peter Bogdanovich's favourite actor Ryan O'Neal as the terse lead, the reliably shifty Bruce Dern as the cop on his tail and, as the female interest, the beautiful Isabelle Adjani: a national treasure in her native France, though handicapped in Hollywood by her heavily accented English.

Still, I had plenty of confidence in Walter Hill, who had already directed Charles Bronson as a Depression-era street-fighter in the impressive *Hard Times* (1975), and had as a writer exhibited a great facility for crime, action and tough stuff, from *The Mackintosh Man* (1973) and *The Drowning Pool* (1975) to *The Getaway* (1972), a slick action vehicle that Hill had adapted from a much darker novel by Jim Thompson for that most macho of directors, Sam Peckinpah. *The Getaway* had been a huge box-office hit.

Hill's *The Driver* was indeed a success. So, judging by Hollywood's usual formulas and predictions, the combination of vehicular mayhem and Sam Peckinpah at the helm would have seemed to suggest another sure-fire winner. What could possibly go wrong with such a picture? I was to find out at painful length when I got behind the wheel, so to speak, with Sam.

From 1976 onward I was once more being reminded daily of the difficulty of a producer's hunt for good material. A flood of projects was being submitted to my Rodeo Drive office as the Hollywood community woke up to the fact that British Lion (famous for their great lunches) had now been replaced by EMI (famous for being rich). I was well aware that a lot of these 'new' scripts would have been hastily recopied and retitled to conceal the fact that they had already been sent to and rejected by everybody in Hollywood. (I knew as much because I had often tried the same stunt myself.) If the producer hadn't even bothered to change that original ill-fated title then I would have my assistant call a friend at Fox who would send over the reader's report and so save us all a little time. Even so, everything that came to me from a reputable source had to be looked at, and a lot of time was expended on this chore just in case some golden nugget was concealed among the dross. Guaranteed new material from legitimate sources was very carefully read, and usually by me. I was still attached to that supposedly 'difficult' Vietnam script *The Man Who Came to Play*, by Quinn Redeker and Lou Garfinkle. And there was Bob Sherman's trucker movie, based on the 'Convoy' hit song. But there were other demands on my time.

While I was in LA in December, I had one especially thankless task to deal with. Nat Cohen had committed $1 million to a lion tamer turned director, Noel Marshall, to make an adventure picture called *Roar*. Marshall was certainly charming, and was married to actress Tippi Hedren, star of Hitchcock's *The Birds* (1963). She now helped Marshall look after the large bunch of lions he kept penned on a ranch in the San Fernando valley. I had heard that she had once been almost scalped by an angry lioness. After her gruelling experience on *The Birds*, you might have thought she would have kept away from nature. I could never find out what *Roar* was meant to be about. If there was a coherent script Nat Cohen didn't have it in London and I never saw it. I was asked to 'sort it out' when the million dollars was spent and there was less than half an hour of (admittedly good-looking) footage. EMI abandoned the project and Noel Marshall found another financier to complete the film, which was released a few years later in 1981 – probably without EMI's million dollars being recovered.

On my way back to London, I stopped off in Boston for an important meeting intended to raise financial support for the programme we had devised. My appointment was with Richard Smith, an influential director of the Bank of Boston, who had built up his General Cinema Corporation into the biggest movie-theatre chain in the north-eastern US. Smith's thinking was neat. Build a multiplex of at least five theatres in every new shopping mall, often using basement space. The theatres attracted shoppers to the mall and convenient parking was available after stores closed. The space was cheap and, since malls were being built all over the country, the concept proved very profitable.

I probably should have known better than to talk to Dick Smith about our pictures. For years he had been investing in Lew Grade's famously old-fashioned programme of clunkers (*The Voyage of the Damned*, *March or Die*) which flopped consistently in the US. (When General Cinemas finally withdrew their financial support from Grade, that decision indirectly but inexorably led to the collapse of EMI Films a few short years later.) Dick warned me against making *Convoy* on the grounds that it made fun of the police, and 'Americans don't make fun of the police.' Well, I daresay multi-millionaire Boston bankers don't – but since I knew that Dick hadn't been asleep for the previous ten years I could only assume that he had paid no attention to the US counterculture of the 1960s and its highly irreverent view of authority. American kids were now keen to see the police getting a comeuppance, a fact royally confirmed by the success of *Smokey and the Bandit* in the summer of 1977, the plot of which involved Burt Reynolds giving Texan sheriff Jackie Gleason the runaround.

But doubts about *Convoy* were not all that Smith had to relate to me about my line-up. '*And*, Michael, *nobody* would go to see a picture about Vietnam,' he announced, as had so many before, about *The Man Who Came to Play*. 'You don't realise how Americans feel about that war . . .'

As I settled into EMI in LA, I began concentrating my energies on setting up *Convoy*, which now had a completed script and was ready for pre-sales. From the jumping-off point of the hit song, *Convoy* had become the story of a mile-long caravan of independent truckers – modern-day cowboys, owners of their own rigs and fiercely opposed to steep gasoline prices, unrealistic speed limits and corrupt highway cops. A hundred and fifty trucks strong, they speed along the Arizona highway toward the Mexican border, sustained by the trucker's lifeline, Citizens' Band (CB) radio, each trucker with his own call sign, constantly trading information about looming speed traps, weather problems and traffic jams – or just gossiping about women. A trucker whose CB radio handle is 'Rubber Duck' has a special adversary in Sheriff Lyle Wallace, a.k.a. 'Cottonmouth'. The sheriff's aim was to stop the convoy reaching Mexico and freedom, and he didn't care how he did it.

Bob Sherman had Kris Kristofferson interested in playing 'Rubber Duck' but he also proposed Sam Peckinpah as director, and that to me was the selling point. We had all heard rumours about Peckinpah's bad behaviour but Bob believed that Sam had mellowed. He was to regret this judgement hugely. Bob is a gentleman, and though he knew Hollywood could be tough, he simply didn't inhabit the same jungle as Peckinpah. In pursuing his enthusiasm for the celebrated director of *The Wild Bunch*, Bob had grabbed a tiger by the tail.

As far as I was concerned, Peckinpah was a great choice because his body of work was spectacular, and I knew he would be a very big advantage to foreign sales of *Convoy*. That said, it was clear that none of the US majors would hire him any longer. But if somebody else – in this case EMI – was taking responsibility for the delivery of the picture, then the Hollywood studios certainly weren't averse to acquiring the finished product.

The reasons for Peckinpah's fall within the industry had been much rumoured and debated. His addictions to alcohol and cocaine had long since begun to exact a toll on the discipline and quality of his filmmaking. He had fought with MGM over cuts inflicted on *Pat Garrett and Billy the Kid* (1972), and though the picture clearly deserved far better, it was also plain that Peckinpah's alcoholic conduct on the set had been unsupportable. Cocaine use, meanwhile, had been blatant and rife among cast and crew of *The Killer Elite* (1975). Peckinpah's brilliance could still be discerned in the movies, but it was increasingly obscured by sloppiness, incoherence, grandiosity. The notion of his making a proficient, profitable job of directing a picture like *The Getaway* had receded in the space of a mere few years.

His previous picture, *Cross of Iron*, had been shot in Yugoslavia with a German producer whose background was rumoured to be in softcore pornography. It was a determinedly bleak, even nihilistic study of Nazi soldiers hopelessly mired and feuding among themselves on the Russian front. Though it seemed to play very well in Germany and Austria, in the US it was poorly reviewed and barely seen. In all, *Cross of Iron* might have seemed a poor rehearsal for what we had in mind with *Convoy*. Our picture was intended to be bright, full of sunshine and colour, madness and silliness. But I truly believed that if Peckinpah directed it then it would have the undeniable virtue of being original – by definition, a cut above the average truck movie.

Was I, then, breaking my natural habit of caution? I remained in no doubt that the British Lion/EMI risk-reducing formula of pre-sales was the right way to finance a picture. But creativity without risk rarely makes for a satisfying attainment. Peckinpah was clearly a risk – but his creative history, in spite of his past troubles and the fate of his last film, justified hiring him. It would be Bob Sherman's brief to try to stop him from going crazy – a miserable task, as it transpired.

With Peckinpah's name attached and EMI offering to bear half the cost, it wasn't difficult for me to make a deal for *Convoy* with United Artists. That said, Peckinpah's previous hits had been made with the likes of Steve McQueen and Dustin Hoffman. Our *Convoy* lead Kris Kristofferson was not in that league, and the distinction mattered, particularly in Japan where we were dealing with Nippon Herald, represented by an elegant man called Sam Namba. Sherman and I puzzled over how we could add a further star name without breaking our budget. The script had a lead female role in the character of Melissa, a venturesome society photographer, but this part was not terribly important to the story even though Melissa was scheduled to be on screen a lot of the time. Then we struck gold. I had in mind an actress who was beautiful and famous and who had starred in only three pictures, each of which had made a fortune. I met with Namba and pitched as follows.

Recalling the old trick that Marty Baum had used to sell *Where's Jack?* to Charlie Bludhorn at Paramount, I wrote down three titles and asked Namba to put beside them the amount each picture had taken in Japan. This he did, and the cumulative sum was amazing. The three pictures listed were *Love Story*, *Goodbye, Columbus* and *The Getaway* . . . and the female lead, of course, was Ali MacGraw. I argued that Ali was a talisman, a good-luck charm and the proud possessor of a hundred per cent box-office record; any picture she graced would make a ton of money. Namba bought *Convoy*, promoted it beautifully and it was – thank heavens – a huge success in Japan.

In truth I don't think that Ali would ordinarily have consented to play such an uninteresting part, but at that time her marriage to Steve McQueen was in difficulty. If, as she surely suspected, she was soon to be on her own, then she would certainly need the $500,000 I would pay her for *Convoy*. Ali had done *The Getaway* under Peckinpah's direction and she must by then have fully realised that Sam was not given to being kind to women, particularly the leading lady in one of his films. But Ali is as brave as she is beautiful and she took the job.

In fact, *Convoy* would prove to be the last of Ali's screen successes, her movie career winding down in the years to follow. Movie fame is, of course, very often transient. While making *Convoy*, I was shown one interesting indication of the general public's curious affections. Playing a TV interviewer in the film was Brian Davies, a fine actor whose wife Erika Slezak attended RADA in London but found her fame after accepting a job for one year in the long-running ABC-TV soap opera *One Life to Live*. That was in 1971, and she became a series regular. By chance one day Ali, Erika and I were travelling from Albuquerque to New York, and at both airports Erika was mobbed while Ali, at the height of her fame, was ignored. Such is the curious power of daytime TV.

Convoy was fully cast once we hired our villainous sheriff, Academy Award winner Ernest Borgnine, one of Hollywood's great men. Now a suitable location had to be found. A truck movie clearly needed a lot of road space, preferably uncluttered and controllable for the purpose of big and difficult stunts and set pieces that were unlikely to be pulled off in single takes, however much we wished it so. On *The Man Who Fell to Earth* I had found New Mexico to be a wonderful location, in terms of practicality and economics as well as natural beauty. The highway system there goes on for ever, and it is not a crowded state. Therefore I went with what I knew, and so we once again based our show in Albuquerque. Some advantages were immediately clear: the room rate at the Hilton had gone up by only a dollar a day in the two years since last we were there. That said, for all its good qualities as a shooting base, Albuquerque probably had no great claims to be a major centre of culture or gastronomy; but this was another problem to land at Bob Sherman's door rather than mine.

Convoy undoubtedly had to have size, and the trucks had to look impressive – they were, after all, the greater part of the picture. We budgeted for hire of 110 trucks in all, knowing that there would inevitably be breakdowns and so the number would fluctuate. In addition, we needed doubles for the four 'starring' trucks to be driven by Kristofferson ('Rubber Duck'), Burt Young ('Pig Pen'), Madge Sinclair ('Widow Woman') and Franklyn Ajaye ('Spider Mike'). We planned to rent each truck, with a driver, for $100 a day, and there was no intention of crashing and wrecking these vehicles with the gleeful abandon we had enjoyed on *The Italian Job*. In the event, Kris's leading jet-black Mack truck and its double each cost us $40,000, new. After such outlays we needed to be yet more cost-conscious: Bob Sherman's transport captain and production office scoured the New Mexico area, posting notices in the local papers and printed posters at the most popular truck-stops.

Finally, in the late April of 1977, I was able to send Bob Sherman to New Mexico to start producing the picture. With other projects whirling around the Beverly Hills office, I temporarily set *Convoy* to the back of my mind and awaited the early progress reports. Privately, I was waiting for the bomb to drop.

At moments of stress around a movie I often liked to remember Peter Yates's account of his experience as an assistant director on *The Roman Spring of Mrs Stone*, a Warner Brothers picture made in 1961 starring Vivien Leigh and Warren Beatty. Peter had told me, 'It's wonderful, the smoothest picture I've ever worked on – everyone's friends with each other and everything's perfect.' Well, that smooth and so-perfect production delivered a rather boring picture. By contrast, conflict and stress during a film shoot can express itself on the screen in the form of a perceptible tension. These are not hard-and-fast rules, but the happiest shoots are not necessarily the most artistically striving, while fraught sets can be the seedbed of extraordinary work. A producer doesn't create conflict deliberately, but he certainly must avoid blandness. Sam Peckinpah plainly didn't do 'bland', and the pictures we now consider his masterpieces were not warm-and-fuzzy experiences in their making. You know with a man like Peckinpah that it's going to be difficult: you just won't know quite how difficult.

One thing is for sure – the moment shooting starts on a movie, power shifts from the producer to the director. The producer's pre-production function is to shepherd together the crew, the stars, the director and the money. Once film is running through cameras, the producer's job is to move whatever mountains must be moved so that the director can make his days. Bob Sherman was very experienced in the business side of film. He had been an agent, and a good one, known for his easy relationships throughout the industry. His experience as a producer was limited, though he had solid credits – Jerry Schatzberg's *Scarecrow* (1973), Arthur Penn's *Night Moves* (1975) and *The Missouri Breaks* (1976). Better yet, he had good production people around him. But once the power on *Convoy* shifted into Peckinpah's hands, Bob was in for a testing time.

The progress reports were always going to be crucial. When a picture is being shot on location, the studio receives these daily reports indicating which scenes are now in the can and how much money has been spent on same. These are duly compared to the schedule and budget that was agreed before the picture rolled. It is, of course, immediately apparent when there is slippage, whether of time or money or both; and both factors soon cropped up on *Convoy*.

The first week on a picture is always difficult. The crew needs to shake down, find its rhythm and get used to working together. For that reason it's usually prudent to schedule an easy first few days of work, so that useable footage is in the can and the film is into its stride. But the progress reports and cost statements at the end of the first two weeks on *Convoy* began to alarm me. Either we had been remiss in our preparation of the picture; the production had been struck by some logistical act of God of which I hadn't been made aware, or Peckinpah was working in a manner and at a pace contrary to what we had agreed.

I flew out to Albuquerque, and found the situation to be even worse than I had feared. Peckinpah, not for the first time, was determined to eliminate any lingering authority on Sherman's part. Years before, during the making of *Straw Dogs* (1971) in England, he tried the same stunt on producer Dan Melnick, who had helped Peckinpah out of a career hole a few years previously by hiring him to direct an ABC-TV play. Melnick is a very good producer, concealing considerable strength under a cool exterior. Though not as crazy in those days as he would become, Peckinpah had still managed to cause the temporary shutdown of *Straw Dogs* two weeks into the shoot, on account of his unmanageable drinking. But Melnick deftly held the production together. Perhaps it helped that on *Straw Dogs* Sam was out of his usual milieu, shooting on the very south-west tip of England in St Buryan, Cornwall, with a British crew. Now, with *Convoy*, he was fighting on his own ground: the maker of great Westerns was in the desert land of New Mexico, surrounded by his personal coterie. All Sam's cronies would do anything he wanted – even wage war against the producer and threaten the integrity of the production, if Sam told them such efforts were necessary in order to make a Sam Peckinpah picture.

It had reached a point where Peckinpah was making it intolerable for Bob Sherman even to walk on the set, for Sam would then claim that his work was being interrupted, his concentration destroyed. If Bob was present, Sam would point his camera up at the sky and all meaningful work would cease. Another Peckinpah trick was to pack off one of his cronies with one of his many cameras in order to shoot material that wasn't in the script but which Sam thought might come in handy later. This 'rogue unit' material was never included with main unit rushes, and so Sherman was never shown it. It wasn't that Peckinpah was shooting anything necessarily improper. It was just another knife in the producer's back. Peckinpah blankly refused to accept that Sherman had put this project together, cared about it deeply and was doing everything he could to help the director and make the picture a success.

Sam's motive in running Bob off the set could have been sheer anti-authority or, as likely, the fact that he wanted to shoot a great deal more footage than we had budgeted. On the straitened budget of *Cross of Iron* he had been confined, as far as possible, to one or two cameras. But he had always liked a multi-camera situation. Garth Craven, a film editor on several of Peckinpah's pictures, quoted Sam as saying that if you shoot enough footage you are going to find a few good moments – enough to stamp the director's style upon the picture. 'Sam's films were discovered in his editing room,' Craven has said. There is a bravura quality that comes by those means, but I think that by 1977 Peckinpah had lost a lot of his old confidence.

At times he was shooting with half a dozen cameras and still following up with a single camera for close-ups and two-shots. I suppose this way he figured he would get what he needed to 'discover the film', but it was a hopeless extravagance. We had budgeted for double the amount of stock another director would have needed, and we were already exceeding those numbers. Moreover, Garth Craven wasn't able to start assembling the picture as shooting proceeded (always an invaluable aid to getting an early sense of what one has), since Peckinpah would want to be in the cutting room to select which of the many camera angles would be used.

One special complexity of *Convoy* lay in filming the trucks. Marshalling a hundred vehicles into a long drive-by scene was a task riven with problems, particularly as one truck halfway down the line would almost inevitably pick its moment to break down. There is an analogy with the difficulty of shooting at sea. For a ship to sail past a camera mounted on a floating barge is a lengthy procedure even on take one, but it is made interminable for take two because the ship has to slow down, turn round, sail back to its starting point and once more proceed past the camera. Such a manoeuvre will take twenty minutes each time, eating money with each second – and this is not to mention the possibility of shifting sea conditions, or a barge drifting loose of its moorings . . .

One of the first days of *Convoy*'s schedule to be blown out came about when Burt Young, driving the leading truck, took a wrong turning. That doesn't sound too terribly serious, but then, of course, the entire convoy followed Burt. On New Mexico's endless roads it was not uncommon that there be no turn-off for twenty-two miles, or for any such turn-off to lead only to a dead-end eighteen miles later. Turning round a hundred trucks is not the work of five minutes, and so our convoy was only on its way back by lunchtime. Meanwhile a second unit was perched on top of a water-tower, baking in the sun and waiting to grab a shot that should have been in the bag by 8:30 a.m. For this debacle Bob Sherman received a completely unjustified tongue-lashing from Sam, who had spent the day comfortably snoozing in his Winnebago.

Soon after, still trying to be supportive, Bob had to endure more wasted time when Peckinpah spent a week shooting the scene of a brawl in a bar which had been scheduled for one and a half days. Everyone knew it was a truck movie before it started, so excuses about normal production difficulties were not the answer, but this was a straightforward fight scene.

Sam put on a slight veneer of responsibility when I showed up in Albuquerque. As president of EMI Films Inc. I was the money, not a disposable producer. He could have been concerned that I would stop the picture and cut our losses – which might have been the sensible thing to do, and probably would have happened if the financiers had been one of the majors. But EMI's modest production fund would have been severely dented if I had sent everybody home. Even more to the point, I had pre-sold this picture and EMI's new face would have been very red-cheeked. I imagine Peckinpah's only concern was that if the picture were closed down it would, correctly, be blamed on him and he would never work again.

I sat down with Sherman for several hours to review the situation. He had been cruelly treated – I never knew the half of it. He was very hurt, and reluctantly came to the view that I had already reached, which was that he could never assert any authority over the director. We had reached the situation I had dreaded. I was running an American film company with two big pictures in production. It was not going to be easy to keep an eye on the office, future productions and what would become *The Deer Hunter* if I were to end up as hands-on producer of *Convoy*. But there was no choice. I knew the project backwards and only someone with absolute control of the money could deal with this situation. This was against my new structure for EMI. I had publicly told the press in Cannes before the British Lion takeover that my plan was no longer to produce films, but instead to concentrate on producing producers. Here, only a year later, I found myself back on the floor taking control on one of our first major projects.

I told Bob that his producer credit would remain and his fees and profit share wouldn't be affected – after all, he had done nothing wrong. Sherman stayed near by in New Mexico throughout the shooting in case he could be of any help. He went on to produce a couple more pictures in the mid-1980s, and he made several hundred thousand dollars from the profits of *Convoy*. But I suspect that in every other respect the endeavour must have broken his heart.

I had worked on other down-and-dirty pictures. I knew something about cost control, and I knew that I would be responsible if

Convoy failed. In other words, I had been around the block rather more often than Bob Sherman, and so I had to believe that I would be tougher than him and harder to fool. Mercifully, Peckinpah didn't try the same stunts on me as he had tried with Bob, but he still dreamt up a lot of imaginative little needles with which to prick us.

A stock trick of his was to demand, at the last moment, that a certain crew member play a small and hitherto unscripted role in the picture. Sam knew that any time one of the crew appeared in the picture, they would be paid extra – in other words, another amusing little dig at the production office for him and his retinue. On *Convoy* he got Garth Craven to play a bit-part, though Garth was modest enough to edit himself out as soon as the rushes reached the cutting room. Bobby Visciglia was a canny and good-natured property master who had worked on many of Sam's films and become a sort of amanuensis deployed to deal with many of Sam's needs, normally outside the remit of the props department. (Since *The Getaway*, for instance, he had provided his director with an on-set drinks-tray service.) Bobby duly got his face into *Convoy*, playing an ice-cream salesman.

So it was that, in a moment of false bonhomie, Sam asked me if I too would do a small part. The game he surely had in mind was that I would be in front of the camera and he would be behind it, giving me orders – an absolute power-trip on his behalf. No one in charge of a picture can afford to put themselves into that kind of vulnerable position, so I politely told Sam that I was the boss, not a bit-part actor, and that he should go fuck himself.

In the days when Sam was dependent on alcohol, he probably would have attacked me physically – and, although small of stature and prematurely aged, he could be a dangerously erratic assailant. But Sam did occasionally exhibit a sense of humour and, for a moment, he might have been amused by how easily his stratagem had been spotted. Or perhaps his post-*Killer Elite* reliance on cocaine had somehow made him less aggressive, even if rather more paranoid.

Peckinpah was by no means the only offender in the industry: drugs were all over Hollywood productions in the mid-seventies. They may have been less in evidence on studio-bound pictures, but once an actor or crew member got away to a location far from home, domestic restraints ceased to exist. Love affairs on location are frequent, whether with fellow crew members or locals, but sexual escapades were not the problem on *Convoy*. Drugs were, and when one particular small-part actor joined the production unit for a few weeks, it became plain that Sam had tapped into a new and abundant supply.

I gathered from the tone of one or two of his remarks that Peckinpah felt himself diminished by doing a 'truck movie'. Since *The Wild Bunch* (1969) – which *Time* magazine called 'Peckinpah's most complex inquiry into the metamorphosis of man into myth' – a number of his films had been hailed as masterpieces, and he had certainly entered the critical pantheon of Great American Directors. Some of his films carried powerful messages about the violence of the world and of individuals, the difficulties of taking a stand or questing for personal freedom. Sam's own political position I found hard to pin down. He seemed to me at first a sort of left-wing fascist – if that's not an impossible concept. I eventually came to the view that he was not so much socialist as anti-social: the sort of anarchist who couldn't see beyond the destruction of society. *Convoy* was a film about protest – but a protest about gasoline prices rather than anything more lofty. And yet Sam was determined to insert some 'political' aspect into the picture, even though the script simply wasn't designed to support such aspirations.

One morning, while I was in my office at the Hilton hotel engaged in a telephone call to EMI in London, there was a frantic knock on the door. An assistant director rushed in. It appeared Sam had locked himself in his caravan, flatly refusing to come out. Katy Haber, the only person he might listen to when in a filthy mood, couldn't get him to budge. I raced to the location where a hundred trucks were standing idle and five camera crews were lolling about, drinking tea. Katy had by now extracted an explanation of sorts: Sam had told her that he would not be starting work until Bobby Visciglia had been paid.

This was madness. All the crew were paid by direct credit to their bank accounts, and Bobby hadn't complained of any error in this process. I racked my brains for what Sam could mean. Perhaps the voucher for Bobby's walk on as an ice-cream salesman hadn't been presented? But that only amounted to $25. Katy, who had kept a discreet silence as she always did around Sam, finally whispered to me that it was really nothing to do with money. It was that Sam had completely blocked, dried up, and hadn't the faintest idea how to shoot the sequence that had been scheduled for the day. Clearly, he was unlikely to work this out while sitting in his trailer. This was the situation I had walked into and it was up to me to sort it out.

I banged on the window, which he opened. Taking care that the crew did not overhear, I told him, 'If you don't start work now, immediately, I will have this trailer dragged away with you in it. You can imagine the consequences if you make me do this.' In truth I was dreading the thought that the picture would be further delayed by the director walking off, but Sam responded quite meekly and stepped out into the sun, smiling to the crews as if nothing unusual had happened. Sometimes he did respond to a hard-line approach.

For a while, the production got onto a more even keel. Less film was exposed, and yet more useable material emerged from those rushes. It was still a cause of concern that Sam was being cruel to Ali MacGraw, something I suspected he was doing in order to rile her husband, Steve McQueen. McQueen visited the set disguised with an enormous bushy beard which he had grown for his ludicrous production of Ibsen's *An Enemy of the People* (1978). But he and Ali were going through their marital difficulties, and they were left well alone.

Peckinpah, *Convoy* and a Blizzard of Cocaine

James Coburn had been one of McQueen's co-stars in *The Magnificent Seven* (1960), was also an old friend of mine, and had been in several of Peckinpah's pictures, including *Pat Garrett* and most recently *Cross of Iron*. He came on to *Convoy* to do some second-unit directing and pick-up shots. Jim's sweetness of character brought a breath of fresh air to this tense enterprise. I don't remember paying him other than his expenses, simply because he was looking for experience behind the camera and a route to obtaining a Directors Guild card, and probably would have paid us if I had asked. It never occurred to me that we might therefore have been breaching the Guild rules, and I might have laid myself open to a trap by using a non-DGA director. Mercifully Sam didn't wake up to that one.

Production ground onward, and we were gradually getting the picture in the can. Technicians came and went: even hard-nosed first assistant directors who had been on all sorts of tough locations couldn't stand Peckinpah for very long, and quit. Some of these people had worked for Sam when he was at his best, and they wanted to support him as much as possible in the present doldrums. One said to me as he left that he couldn't help somebody who wouldn't help himself. Occasionally Sam wouldn't come out of his trailer until he was dragged out; and then sometimes he would make very strange decisions. But with five cameras shooting we usually scraped by, even though this put a lot of pressure on a harassed script supervisor and on the editor, who had to make a very quick judgement of the rushes as to whether we were sufficiently covered or not. Sam often couldn't remember much of what he'd shot, which made him even more frustrated and furious.

Kris Kristofferson was a problem in his own right. A hugely gifted singer-songwriter, with an undeniable outlaw/cowboy presence on screen, he nevertheless struggled at times with what were relatively straightforward directions. For instance, there was a particular night shoot where Kristofferson's job in the scene was simply to step out of a tent, walk round it, and exit the frame. It was dark, admittedly, but the scene was lit. Still, eight times the scene was run and in each take Kristofferson managed to trip over the guy-rope of the tent. He just couldn't seem to handle that particular obstruction. Comic though the spectacle might sound, it wasn't very funny at the time, and eventually we resorted to having Kristofferson do nothing more strenuous than appear at the flap of the tent before we cut away to something less accident-prone.

The production was approaching a deadline, and it was two weeks behind schedule. Kristofferson's contract gave him a definite stop-date: for a full four weeks after that date he would not be available to work on the film because he was committed to a major thirty-day concert tour. So I sat down with Sam and the senior crew members, the idea being to prioritise the remaining work. I told Sam that we had only two weeks left with Kris, and I asked him to list the necessary material in order of importance. I advised him that I would be doing the same. Sam came up with pages of shots that he considered essential, the sum of which looked to me like eight weeks' work. I gave him my list and told him that after two weeks I would be wrapping the picture – not only because our star was decamping, but because EMI was not willing to plough yet further over budget. Peckinpah said it couldn't be done. I told him to do his best. At the end of the two weeks, Sam brought forth another wish-list, which would have stretched the shooting out a further five weeks. I told Sam to go home, and advised him that we would reassemble for one week to shoot the essential climactic scene where the sixteen-wheeler driven by 'Rubber Duck' plunges into the river.

A skeleton crew duly reconvened, Katy Haber conspicuous by her absence. (Peckinpah had fired her, and she was back in England, having been shopped to the immigration police by one of Sam's cronies because she had no current work permit.) We shot the big scene and some other essential material with Ali MacGraw, as well as many of the essential insert shots – detailed close-ups of feet on accelerators, hands on steering wheels et cetera. On 27 September 1977, finally, the production wrapped.

Peckinpah, though, was livid, outraged that his demand to go on shooting for several more weeks was not being acceded to. He threatened to take his name off the picture. 'Not this picture,' I replied. 'Not now or ever.' What I had already sold around the world was a Sam Peckinpah picture, and I had stated in his contract that if Sam shot for more than five weeks then the film would be described as 'Directed by Sam Peckinpah', even if he never finished it. Of course he could feign illness, but once he had worked five weeks and been paid then what we had was a Peckinpah film, who-ever finished it off.

When a disagreement between director and producer and/or financier escalates to such enmity that the director seeks to remove his name from the picture, there is a convention in Hollywood that a pseudonym is used. (The same pseudonym will crop up when a director is ashamed of having made a ghastly movie.) The picture is then credited as 'Directed by Alan Smithee'. Since the mid-1960s the non-existent Mr Smithee has amassed sixty or so credits, his body of work including *Iron Cowboy*, *Let's Get Harry*, *Blood Sucking Pharaohs of Pittsburgh* and *The O. J. Simpson Story*, shot in 1994 and so lacking the unhappy denouement. None of these productions reflected well on their makers, and I couldn't face United Artists or Sam Namba with 'An Alan Smithee film'.

The Directors Guild of America and the Writers Guild of America (DGA and WGA) are very powerful unions. By comparison, pro-ducers, the third branch of filmmaking aristocracy, have never had any negotiating power. This stems from the days when the studio system was in full bloom and producers were, in the majority of cases, studio employees. Thus the major companies (MGM, Fox, Warners, Columbia, Paramount, United Artists, Disney, Allied Artists) who formed the Motion Picture Association of America (MPAA) became the negotiator between employers and the unions. As time went on and the studio contract system collapsed, not only stars and directors but also producers became independent. One day producers woke up to realise that they had no representation at all with the guilds whose members they employed. The MPAA had blindsided the producers.

These power relationships acquire a particular definition when a picture finishes shooting and goes into post-production – editing, music scoring, sound mixing and finally, after the laboratory has balanced the colour negative, a viewing of the first married print of sound and picture. DGA agreements give the director a minimum of six weeks to produce his own first cut: in theory he can deliver anything he likes, and is completely free to work with the editor in any way that he sees fit. The producer and the studio are effectively barred from the cutting room for this period.

Not wanting to risk breaking any rules, I gave Sam two months before asking to see his first cut of *Convoy*. When the clock ran out a screening was duly set up, and I was surprised by the number of people there – presumably friends of Sam's – who were not connected to the production. Lights dimmed, and we watched what was clearly an unfinished picture. Worse than that, there was one amazing shot of Ali MacGraw running across the screen upside down. Obviously this was Sam's pathetic attempt to prove that without more shooting and more money paid to his account, we might as well throw away the picture. I had spent a few years in cutting rooms, and had a good grasp of the general principles. I had seen the *Convoy* rushes and knew we had enough material. I reminded Sam that shooting was over and I gave him a further four weeks to put together a cut.

Awful memories of this period have survived the passage of time. On one occasion Peckinpah turned up an hour late to a meeting with me, kicked open the editor's door and loudly proclaimed, 'To be or not to be, that is the question.' He then fell flat on his face and passed out for several hours, or so I was told – I didn't wait around for him to come to. There was also an assistant editor whose main job was to replace the bobbins on thousand-foot rolls of film which Sam had taken from their cans and thrown all over the cutting-room floor. He always forgot in which can he had hidden his cocaine stash, and the search grew more frantic with every wrong can he opened. Cutting-room personnel tended to remove themselves during these outbursts. Perhaps Sam didn't believe I was serious in my deadlines, or didn't believe I knew what he was doing, but things certainly got worse and worse. Three months after we finished shooting I informed Sam that he had had more than enough time for his cut and my patience was at an end: he was off the picture.

I had carefully documented the events of the preceding weeks, because Peckinpah's next move was completely predictable: he went to his union, the DGA, and lodged a complaint. The president of the Guild at that time was Robert Aldrich, a formidable director of some tough pictures – *Kiss Me Deadly*, *The Dirty Dozen*, *The Longest Yard* and a number of Westerns such as *Ulzana's Raid* that were slightly in the style of Sam Peckinpah. Aldrich stormed into the meeting, and at sixty years of age he was a heavy guy physically, very authoritative. Immediately he gave out the aura that he would not be taking any shit from any little Limey producer. Getting straight to the point, he said, 'You can't take the picture away from Sam. He is one of our great directors.' I answered, 'He definitely was once, and I hope he will be again. But if you want to see why I'm doing what I'm doing, come and take a look at his cut.' He declined, and this unreasonable stance annoyed me. I said, 'You don't want to see it because you know Sam is a madman, coked out of his skull, and you can't defend him if you see the evidence. This is a truck movie, one in which it's hardly appropriate for Ali McGraw to be running across the screen upside down. The Sam you knew is not the man I had in Albuquerque.' Aldrich grumbled and left it at that. The DGA rarely concedes, but this complaint, perhaps tellingly, had come to nothing.

I now had an enormous amount of film on my hands, a picture

to deliver as soon as possible, and Peckinpah's editor had already quit. I ordered all the selected takes to be reprinted and called up Graeme Clifford, the brilliant editor who had cut *Don't Look Now* and *The Man Who Fell to Earth* for Nicolas Roeg. It's a rare thing for a film editor to have carte blanche: competent directors know what their finished film should look like, and they sit at the editor's side throughout the whole process. Yet it was not ever thus. Under the old studio rules, the director would leave his picture the day he finished shooting, and the final result would be put together by the editor under studio supervision. *Convoy* was essentially finished under the old system: a working day-to-day collaboration between editor and producer. The producer/composer Chip Davis, who had penned the music for C. W. McCall's hit song, put together our score. It took us three weeks to get a rough cut, and four weeks after that we started sound mixing.

Katy Haber, whose efficiency while working with Peckinpah had much impressed me, came back to help with post-production. (Thereafter she worked for EMI until I left, whereupon she joined up with me for the experience of *Blade Runner*.) It's perhaps in light of all that had gone before that I recall the post-production period of *Convoy* as one of the happier experiences of my life. From time to time, though, I was distracted by rumblings of trouble on the production EMI had running concurrently, and to which we now should turn.

13

A National Anthem: *The Deer Hunter*

My enthusiasm for *The Man Who Came to Play*, Quinn Redeker and Lou Garfinkle's script about the Vietnam War and Russian roulette, had never dimmed. The screenplay had struck me as brilliant – but it wasn't complete. The trick would be to find a way to turn a very clever piece of writing into a practical, realisable film. Disappointed by the early reactions I received, I had put the script away in my drawer, knowing that I would have to wait until a satisfactory outcome of negotiations with EMI or Rank put British Lion into a strong enough position to produce the picture. Given that the original outlay was a mere $19,000 we could afford to put this script on the back burner. Once the deal with EMI had been completed in August 1976, it was time to dust off *The Man Who Came to Play* and try to revive it. With EMI's name and money behind me, my approach to the studios would be quite different, as I would be asking them for only half of the budget. But in order to excite the studios and get us on the map, it would be necessary to find a big star. And before that, we needed a complete and workable draft of the script.

I consulted various Hollywood agents in the hope of uncovering a good writer, ideally one with some directorial experience, who could work on the Redeker/Garfinkle pages. Michael Cimino was represented by Stan Kamen at the William Morris Agency, and had written three pictures, two for Clint Eastwood, who allowed him to direct *Thunderbolt and Lightfoot* (1974), which Cimino did competently enough. Cimino had also shot quite a few visually pleasing

TV commercials, and he was confident that he could meet the brief of further developing the principal characters in *The Man Who Came to Play* without losing the essence of the original. I decided to go with Cimino, and reasonable terms were negotiated with Stan Kamen.

As soon as Cimino was hired we called him into a meeting with Garfinkle and Redeker at the EMI office on the corner of Dayton and Rodeo. Cimino did little to endear himself to the writers by questioning the need for the Russian roulette element of the script ... Quinn made a passionate case for it, ending up on his knees, literally, though even this didn't seem quite enough to sway Cimino. It was becoming clear that he had other ideas for the picture.

Over the course of further lunches on the office roof-garden, Cimino and I discussed the work that was clearly needed at the front of the script, and he believed that he could develop and enrich the stories of the main characters in about twenty minutes of film. Off he went to do the work.

At some point a curious rumour trickled back to EMI's offices to the effect that a writer I had never heard of was working on *The Man Who Came to Play*. It appeared that Cimino had engaged Deric Washburn, with whom he had previously worked on the script of *Silent Running*, a 1971 picture directed by effects wizard Doug Trumbull. Whether Cimino hired Washburn as his sub-contractor or as a co-writer was constantly being obfuscated and there were some harsh words between them later on, or so I was told. In any event, down the line Washburn would share an equal writing credit with Cimino. (In consequence of a Writers Guild arbitration process Lou Garfinkle and Quinn Redeker received mere story credits, which did them less than justice.)

A certain lull arises during the writing process of a film. The script isn't finished so neither casting nor financing can proceed. But then no one knows if the film will actually be made, although everyone acts as though it will. In the spring of 1977 both *The Man Who Came to Play* and *Convoy* were in this limbo, although *Convoy* was a little further advanced. Everyone at this stage was on their best behaviour, but Cimino's curious script-writing deception had raised a red flag.

My wife, Ruth, and I made a habit of inviting groups of people out for Sunday lunch at our Malibu beach house. In Hollywood, Sunday lunch is strictly a business activity, and on this particular day we had the company of Sam Peckinpah, with Katy Haber and Michael Cimino, over a fantastic feast. For pleasure I had invited our friends Lee Remick and Jim Coburn, and the sunshine, surf and red wine made for a very relaxed atmosphere. Then Cimino, a great admirer of Peckinpah, decided to put on something of a display of machismo. He jumped to his feet and declared that he was going for a swim. Then he ran off down the beach and, above the high-tide mark, stripped off his clothes before leaping into the water. Looking back, I suspect it was Sam, who had not declared any admiration for Cimino, who egged Katy on to what happened next.

As a naked Cimino gambolled in the bitterly cold Pacific Ocean, Katy darted down to the edge of the water, grabbed Cimino's clothes and was back on our deck in a flash. A very happy, well-fed-and-watered gang of Hollywood people patiently awaited Act III. Because the Pacific is so frigid (a fact that many seem surprised by), Cimino did not spend too long in it. Once he was satisfied that he had demonstrated to his audience his powerful masculine ability, he scuttled out of the water heading to where he had left his clothes. We all engaged in busy conversation, pretending not to look at him, though the effects of the freezing temperature of the Pacific Ocean were most certainly apparent. Cimino couldn't assume that we had his clothes. Finally he took the only course left to him, which was to rush back up the beach, naked, and into the house to borrow a towel. Everyone else was much amused, and in fact Cimino appeared to take this practical joke in good spirit. The new script (newly titled *The Deer Hunter*) was delivered to me a few days later, and to a great extent it broke fresh ground for the project.

The Redeker/Garfinkle protagonist, Merle, had been an individual who had sustained a bad injury in active service and had also been damaged psychologically by his violent experiences, but was nevertheless a tough character with strong nerves and guts. The effect of the Cimino/Washburn work was to distil these three aspects of personality and separate them out into three distinct characters – three old friends who had grown up in the same small industrial town and worked in the same steel mill, and in due course would be drafted together to Vietnam. (The mercenary Keys figure, meanwhile, slipped out of the picture . . .) If Redeker and Garfinkle's script had been more in the way of an adventure yarn, Cimino and Washburn had in mind a statement on national themes. That said, Cimino was not going to be able to manage without the motif of Russian roulette, which in its terrible sense of jeopardy seemed not only a tremendous dramatic engine but also a kind of metaphor for a nation's involvement in war.

Cimino and Washburn had added insights into the work done by our three heroes in the steel mill, into their leisure pursuit as hunters, and into the social aspect of the community among whom they lived. These elements thoroughly defined the relationships between the three buddies who go to war and those who stay behind. Obviously we needed strong characterisation of the three main characters going through this brutal experience: we needed to know enough about who these men were before they joined the army, in order to understand in due course how one would survive intact, one would suffer terrible physical wounds, and the third would be crippled mentally.

In the early part of the script a wedding sequence covered a few pages and offered us an opportunity to observe a working-class second-generation Russian immigrant community maintaining its ethnic traditions in an American environment. My sense was that the depiction of the steelworks environment and the wedding party might run for as long as half an hour of screen time, rather than the twenty minutes Cimino had originally pitched. But I didn't see this as a great problem – the editing process would surely weed out any overage. Above all, I thought the draft was good and ready for principal casting, and it was time to turn the focus onto our foremost task, that of getting a major movie star attached. However compelling the script, the studios would not come in unless there was this sort of marquee-value insurance.

People often question the size of movie stars' earnings, but it should be realised that producers only pay out as much as they do in the belief that the actor is worth the money. Worth can mean that he has just come off a big hit and is basking in the temporary affections of the public, or it can mean that he consistently delivers performances that appeal; in other words, and in the manner of, say, Clint Eastwood, he is a reliable box-office attraction. Actors' agents and their managers have no intention of letting their clients be hired out for less than their perceived box-office worth, although sometimes a star might insist for artistic reasons on doing a minor film for less or no money. Such charity is considered risky, though, because it can set a sort of precedent, and so dilute the star's perceived value.

The Deer Hunter was probably the most difficult film I had ever tried to sell: a gruesome-sounding storyline and a barely known director. We still had to get millions out of a major US studio as well as convince our markets around the world that they should buy it before it was finished. I *needed* someone of the calibre of Robert De Niro.

Thirty-four-year-old De Niro had become one of the hottest stars of the day by way of *Mean Streets* (1973), *The Godfather, Part II* (1974) and *Taxi Driver* (1976). His name alone would attract buyers in the foreign territories, for it had become clear that the likes of De Niro and Al Pacino, with their Italian backgrounds, didn't seem as foreign to the rest of the world as WASP Americans of the Robert Redford variety. (Blond, blue-eyed stars speaking in dubbed Portuguese present something of a credibility problem.) And quite apart from the issue of numbers, De Niro was the right age, apparently tough as hell, and immensely talented.

I turned to a long-time friend: De Niro's agent Harry Ufland, a man with a sharp tongue and tremendous energy. His relationship with his client was very close, and if Harry liked our script we would be halfway there. But De Niro's most recent works had been two big, sprawling pictures, Bertolucci's *1900* (1976) and Scorsese's *New York, New York* (1977), and I was aware that he was looking to take some time off. Up to a dozen scripts were landing on Ufland's desk every week, but for the time being De Niro was passing on everything.

Ufland did like our material – but he realised that there were some risks in it for his apparently fireproof star, and he was determined to break new ground in terms of remuneration. De Niro had never earned more than $1 million for a picture, but to me he was certainly worth Harry's asking price of $1.5 million. In addition he was to have a percentage of the profits, but this would have to be based on EMI's distribution accounting system, which was different from those of the Hollywood majors, and in most respects more beneficial. De Niro himself would later admit that his rationale for choosing *The Deer Hunter* was because the script struck him as both simple and real. Once Harry had examined our distribution and profit-sharing methods we were in a position to strike a deal and I was left with a very short time to bring in a US partner to contribute half the budget.

While I was doing this, De Niro met with Michael Cimino and was reassured. Whether or not he checked in with the last major star Cimino had directed – Clint Eastwood in *Thunderbolt and Lightfoot* – I do not know, but I had certainly done so, and Eastwood gave Cimino a clean bill of health. In retrospect, it doesn't surprise me that Cimino would have caused no trouble to a major star who was also the producer of the picture as well as a more-than-competent director. Eastwood's presence would surely have required Cimino to mind his manners. As it transpired, Cimino would never again subject himself to that same set of shackles.

My policy for the new EMI in America was to work with as many different major studios as possible within the first year. I set up *Convoy* with an old friend, Mike Medavoy at United Artists, and we had two pictures left over from British Lion with Columbia. Paramount was handling the Agatha Christie films, and I had sold *The Driver* to 20th Century Fox. With uncommon insight, I divined that a picture about Russian roulette in Vietnam might not go down too well at Disney. So this left Warner Brothers and Universal as uncharted territory. Oddly enough, it was Universal, whose recent output had been on the lighter side – certainly nothing like *The Deer Hunter* – who declared an interest. The studio hadn't won a Best Picture Oscar for decades but head of production Ned Tanen wanted to engage in something more serious and *The Deer Hunter's* script was certainly that. Our budget was $8.5 million; Ned agreed to put up half of that and we were off to the races.

EMI's London office rounded up its usual contributors in the rest of the world: Italy was a slam-dunk thanks to De Niro, but our Japanese distributors, although they had paid a great advance for *Convoy*, were very skittish about *The Deer Hunter*. Perhaps they saw in it a disparaging treatment of their fellow Asians; but then in other territories, too, we were meeting with more resistance than we had grown used to.

Still, with my star now signed up, I took out a full-page advertisement in *Variety* depicting De Niro wearing a pair of dark sunglasses and carrying a hunting rifle. This was to be a De Niro vehicle and I wanted Hollywood to know about our latest coup. It was also to reinforce the fact that EMI Films Inc. was now a name to be reckoned with among the Hollywood big boys.

We soon discovered that Robert De Niro could give more to *The Deer Hunter* than his good name, as if that were not enough.

He lived in New York, seemingly knew the work of every actor in the city, and so was able to contribute inspired casting ideas. It was De Niro who delivered to us Meryl Streep, hitherto seen briefly in Fred Zinnemann's British production *Julia* and in the eight-hour mini-series *Holocaust*. And with Streep came her lover John Cazale, who had the distinguished record of acting only in movies nominated for the Best Picture Oscar: *The Godfather, The Godfather, Part II*, Coppola's *The Conversation* (1974) and Sidney Lumet's *Dog Day Afternoon* (1975). But *The Deer Hunter* would be Cazale's final work, for he was suffering from bone cancer.

Although we couldn't get the customary insurance, all the medical advice we received suggested that Cazale's condition would not affect his work, nor was it likely to reach a crisis-point until well after we had finished shooting his scenes. It was important to Bob De Niro and to Meryl that we took this risk, which would be lessened further by shooting out of continuity and having a fallback plan if illness suddenly forced Cazale off the picture. To this end I asked Cimino to rough out a back-up piece of script, a request he pooh-poohed until I insisted, pointing out that our insurers had every right to make sure that we used good faith in containing any potential damage. Luckily we didn't need the back-up, and Cazale's excellent performance in *The Deer Hunter* would be a fitting memorial to a brave man. Rounding off the principal cast were two excellent but as yet unheralded actors, Christopher Walken as Nick and John Savage as Steven.

De Niro performed another unusual function for us. Prior to production he and Cimino were scouting locations for the steel-mill sequence intended to open the picture. De Niro was very struck by the personality of a mill supervisor who showed them round, and drew Cimino aside to suggest that they offer Chuck Aspegren a part in the picture as one of Michael's friendship group. Chuck was astounded by the offer, pausing only for a moment before replying: 'If you're fool enough to ask me I'm fool enough to take it . . .' De Niro was determined to bring an air of authenticity to his character and while at the steel mills he ate, drank and played pool with the workers. He wanted to get as close as he could and even asked if he could work a shift at the mill – an offer that was, not surprisingly, declined by the management.

De Niro further took it upon himself to rehearse a lot of the early scenes with his fellow cast members. His intention was not to interfere with the director's function but rather to use these work-shops as a bonding process, so that by the time cameras rolled the actors playing GIs and those left behind would not just be acting buddies but would have become truly close. The quality of this device shows most clearly in the sequences leading up to Vietnam, and after De Niro's character Michael returns to the US.

The preparations appeared to be proceeding as usual: locations were being sorted out, the budget was locked at $8.5 million, and we were edging towards principal photography – or so I thought from my chair in the Rodeo Drive office, until my appointed producer Bob Relyea asked to see me.

I had hired Bob to produce *The Deer Hunter* because he was an experienced campaigner who had risen through the ranks. If he was not necessarily a creative contributor to a movie, he was nevertheless an accomplished boss of a production, who knew picture-making backwards. I had met him first when he was producing *Bullitt* for Steve McQueen's company, and he would later be head of production at two Hollywood studios. I was confident that Bob's towering physical presence and reserves of experience would extract the same sort of respect from Cimino as Clint Eastwood had received.

But now in our meeting he appeared grave, and clearly found it difficult to disclose what was going through his mind. He eventually told me he didn't want to produce *The Deer Hunter*, and that this was his irrevocable decision. For a man of Bob's integrity to quit a picture at this stage of pre-production was a serious blow, made the more alarming because he would not elaborate his reasons. I'm sure that if there had been personal, family or health considerations he would have told me at the time. But still to this day he will not speak of the matter.

I have long since concluded that Bob must have detected something in Cimino which he believed might lead to the gravest production difficulties. Had he learned that Cimino was planning to turn the proposed twenty-odd minutes of character establishment into a sequence running a little over an hour? Did Cimino make it plain that he would not accept the authority of the producer? Did Bob foresee his reputation in Hollywood to be seriously at risk? Whatever were Bob's reasons, Cimino at this point found himself free of any day-to-day supervision.

Suddenly EMI's production capacity was looking very stretched. I was the only experienced producer on staff. Barry Spikings had not worked as a hands-on producer on a major theatrical film and was, in any case, busy running the London operation. It was too late to bring a new producer onto the picture and nearly all my time was committed to dealing with Sam Peckinpah in New Mexico. Our best hope was John Peverall – an experienced British production manager for whom I had great respect. John is a straightforward Cornishman who had worked his way up to become a production supervisor, and we employed him as EMI's watchman on certain pictures. Budget and schedule were John's area of expertise for us, and with Relyea's departure he was a natural successor. He already knew the picture and grasped the opportunity to be elevated to producer status. I left the location shooting of *Convoy* briefly to visit Pittsburgh and check out *The Deer Hunter* unit. Progress at this stage was a little slow and a little over budget, but Cimino assured me that he would pick up speed as they went along. Little did I realise what a mess I had dumped John Peverall into.

Whether I was too busy on *Convoy* or optimistically lulled by Michael Cimino's assurances I don't know, but I certainly woke up very late to the realisation that there were nasty parallels between EMI's two major productions in America. *Convoy*'s producer had been chased off the picture by a director who didn't want to make the script he had agreed to. And it became clear over the weeks that followed that Cimino was making a film destined to go severely over budget because of the tremendous weight he was placing on the Russian–American community sequences.

Studios don't pay much respect to most producers. Directors, in many cases understandably, are treated as stars. I have seen cases where a young studio executive will assure a director that if he has any trouble with the producer he can come to the studio to sort it out. Consequently some directors become their own producers, and when that happens there is a risk of chaos. Cimino had been hired to direct *The Deer Hunter* but it seems that he had plans for a picture which EMI didn't know about. I was later told that he had always intended to ignore his contractual commitment to shoot a film between two and two and a half hours long.

One uneconomical aspect of the opening sequences was the selection of locations in seven different cities to provide the images for Clairton, the town in which the story is set. St Theodosius Church in Cleveland, a replica of St Theodosius in Moscow, is gloriously rich. There were no studio sets. Everything was on location, even though the bar and the trailer home had to be built.

The famous wedding scene was designed to place the main characters firmly in their correct ethnic setting. As indeed it does – but it takes fifty-one minutes of screen time before they then go hunting. It is gorgeous to look at, but I was reminded of Bob Evans's terse dismissal of Peter Collinson's 'Blue Danube' sequence in *The Italian Job* as 'directorial masturbation'. If it were practical to spend a few million dollars on a magnificent documentary about the lives and behaviour of Pennsylvania/Ohio steel workers, the first hour of *The Deer Hunter* would do the job better than anything else. I have to presume that Michael Cimino had always planned to extend this prologue to one hour, and that the plan was to be advanced by stealth rather than straight dealing.

Animal lovers will be relieved to know that the first deer seen to be shot was not actually harmed. In spite of his gruesome close-up, he had merely been hit by a tranquilliser dart and so woke up a little while later – albeit with a headache. The stag which Robert De Niro doesn't shoot at the end of the picture was an extremely well-trained creature who had made a living for several years appearing in TV commercials for the Connecticut Life Insurance Company.

Keen drinkers, meanwhile, may be pleased to learn that all the amateur extras lined up for the crowded wedding-dance sequences were rewarded with real liquor and beer. This was designed to relax them, and certainly worked on one of two of the main cast. How they stood it over so many days of shooting is a tribute to their stamina. The community around St Theodosius showed wonderful warmth towards the film unit and I think that they must sometimes look back at their DVD with great affection. The wedding sequence, to some long and indulgent, must to these parishioners be a treasured memory in their life.

The production manager asked each of the Russian immigrant extras to bring to the location a gift-wrapped box to double for wedding presents. They figured that if the extras did this, not only would the production save money and time, but the gifts would also look more authentic. Once the unit had wrapped and the extras had disappeared, the crew embarked on disposing of all the empty boxes. To their amusement they discovered that the boxes actually contained real presents from china to silverware. The extras had treated our shoot as if it was a real wedding and had felt obliged to bring a present. Who got to keep all these wonderful offerings is a mystery I never quite fathomed.

The cut from John (George Dzundza) playing a Chopin nocturne for his buddies in Walsh's bar to the sounds of helicopters and bombing in Vietnam is beautifully effective. With this stroke *The Deer Hunter* rejoined the narrative of the original *The Man Who Came to Play*. Cimino shot the brutal Vietcong Russian roulette scenes brilliantly and more efficiently than any other part of the picture. They were shot in real circumstances, with real rats and mosquitoes, as the three principals were tied up in bamboo cages that had been erected along the River Kwai.

The woman tasked with casting the extras out in Thailand had her toughest brief in finding a local to play the vicious individual who runs the Russian roulette game. The first fellow they hired turned out to be incapable of giving Robert De Niro a slap in the face. Mercifully our caster knew a local Thai man with a particular dislike of Americans, and she pulled him in; and this proved to be one of the picture's luckiest breaks. After all, the degree of 'bad' personified by a bad guy in a movie is critical, and this particular amateur was unforgettably unpleasant on screen. It was De Niro who suggested that Chris Walken should get a real slap from one of the guards without any forewarning to Walken. The reaction on Chris's face was for real. But our three main actors were in perfect balance and the more demanding the scene the more their talents shone.

Some sequences were fraught with danger. After the three escape from the Vietcong they float down the fast-flowing Kwai on a log which hooks onto a fragile bamboo footbridge across the river. The US helicopter tries to rescue them and in the confusion the Thai pilot inadvertently hooked one of the choppers' skids under this fragile bridge, nearly tipping De Niro, Walken and John Savage into what might easily have been a watery grave. There were no stuntmen performing these dangerous feats. The bravery and professionalism of these three actors was truly exceptional.

There is a now-legendary story of De Niro's desire for realism. After Michael has returned from his tour of duty in Vietnam he goes hunting but can't bring himself to kill the noble stag. He returns to the hunting lodge to see Cazale's Stan brandishing a pistol. By now disgusted by gun machismo, De Niro snatches the revolver and rams it into Cazale's face. He offers to play Russian roulette. To give this scene an extra burst of energy De Niro proposed to Cimino that there should be one round in the gun. Cazale agreed, and there was no danger because the gun was never fired.

The first scenes shot upon arrival in Thailand were the hospital sequences between Christopher Walken and the military doctor. Steven's legs have been amputated and he has been sent home. Nick (Walken) is as if struck dumb, traumatised by the horrors of imprisonment. It is widely thought that Walken's moving performance in this scene was the spur that would earn him an Academy Award.

Shooting in Thailand had not been easy from the beginning, and because I had my ongoing battles over *Convoy* in New Mexico I asked Barry Spikings to go out and use his authority to speed up work and try to staunch the expenditure that had us running fifty per cent over budget. Barry was certainly thrown in at the deep end, and he hadn't faced this sort of problem before.

John Peverall, elbowed to one side by the arrival of Spikings, was understandably resentful, and further felt he could see Cimino skilfully manipulating Spikings, who was clearly impressed by the director. Any producer capable of forging a warm relationship with a director hopes that this will result in an opportunity to work with that director again. (In fact, Spikings would play a part in the *Heaven's Gate* drama when United Artists were constantly threatened by Cimino in the early stages that the production could be transferred to EMI if UA did not want to foot the mounting bills.)

There was some genuine bad luck in the making of *The Deer Hunter*. The Thai army were renting us the military equipment and personnel and one day they simply didn't turn up for work. It seems there was some trouble on the Cambodian border and it was more important for the army to be at battle stations than on location. Then we encountered the weather problems common to every location picture. It can really hurt when you don't have any interiors as wet-weather back-up cover.

The tense Russian roulette sequences had been written by Redeker and Garfinkle. Cimino shot them with great energy. After the exhausting POW sequence, the final scene in the gambling den between Chris Walken and Robert De Niro was the most testing of all. Mike and Nick are matching one enough click for click, Mike desperate to bring his friend back home. But for the film to reach its dramatic conclusion, one of them must die. The hubbub of gamblers placing bets, counterpointed by the concern and love projected by Mike to Nick, lead to the climax which was to be shot in one take entirely improvised by Walken and De Niro. Cimino simply said, 'You put the gun to your head, Chris, you shoot, you fall over and Bobby cradles your head.' Pretty sparse direction, but perfect for such an emotional scene, carried off by actors of this calibre.

Cimino handled his actors well, it is true; but many of the crew disliked him, feeling that he didn't respect their abilities. A major exception was the cinematographer Vilmos Zsigmond, who had lensed *Deliverance* (1972), *Close Encounters of the Third Kind* (1977) and many others, and went on to photograph *Heaven's Gate*. Zsigmond acknowledged that Cimino was a difficult person, but also a talented one – and Zsigmond always liked to work with talented people. He said he could surmount any personality problems because he only looked at the man as an artist.

Undoubtedly Zsigmond gave *The Deer Hunter* a distinctive look, and this was no easy task. The insertion of the hunting scene gave us a good title, and set the scene for De Niro's later catharsis when he cannot bring himself to shoot the stag. But it also posed us some logistical problems because, as every American knows, the stag-hunting season starts early in the year. Therefore the picture had to have a 'winter' look; and Zsigmond and our art department then had a few problems to overcome. Pine trees are fine all year round, but any deciduous trees at the location had to be defoliated, each leaf plucked by hand. Vilmos had to soak the colour out of his exterior shots, and this is plain to see when the movie cuts from the rich interiors of the wedding to the street scenes. (Part of this desaturation process happens in the exposure of the film, a further part in the laboratory processing.)

Another enforced deterioration was essential in order to match footage Cimino would shoot to be inter-cut with library images of the evacuation of the US embassy in Saigon. Vilmos had to go against all his better instincts and shoot certain images so murkily that the geographical differences wouldn't be noticed.

As the production progressed, I, as president of EMI Films, learned the hard way how deceitful Cimino had been. He had taken half a dozen pages of character set-up and turned them into sixty-six minutes of screen time. We had been manipulated. Cimino was selfish. But then again, directors often have to be selfish to preserve the integrity of the picture they want to shoot. Selfishness, in itself, is not necessarily a flaw in a director, unless it swells into ruthless self-indulgence combined with a total disregard for the terms on which the production has been set. The ingredients of script, schedule and budget are the boilerplate of the agreement between producer and director. It had become plain that both Peckinpah and Cimino were cut from the same cloth when it came to respecting that boilerplate.

It is fabled that whenever financiers asked Jean-Luc Godard for a script on which to base their budgetary calculations, he told them they'd see just such a script the moment the picture was finished . . . A reasonable and amusing ploy, perhaps, on budgets of £40,000 a picture; but by 1977 the art or science of filmmaking in America had reached a stage where the then medium-high budget of $8.5 million demanded different disciplines. Neither Cimino nor Peckinpah cared for such disciplines. But I did – I had to. I should have seen the red flag being hoisted when Cimino expressed admiration for Peckinpah at that Sunday lunch back in Malibu. As it was, a terminal clash between Cimino and me was now on the cards.

The raw footage of EMI's by-now $13-million baby was returned to Hollywood into the hands of the talented and respected film editor Peter Zinner. He had a monumental task before him, as there was an unusually large amount of footage to sort through. What neither Zinner nor EMI realised at this point was that Cimino had an ambition to make *The Deer Hunter* the same length as *Gone with the Wind*, which ran to three hours and forty-two minutes when it was first unveiled in 1939. Under the Directors Guild of America's rules the cutting room is virtually barred to producers until the director has completed his first cut. This is not a rule I disagree with. After the arduous months of preparation and shooting, a director at least should have some leisure to put the movie together the way he wishes. As far as I was concerned I had enough to do on *Convoy*, which didn't finish shooting until the end of September 1977, and was happy to be left with no further shooting costs on *The Deer Hunter*.

Spikings flew over to Hollywood and sat with me to see the first cut. We were both thrilled by what we saw and knew that within the three and a half hours we watched there was a riveting film. In that respect Cimino had done his work well, no question about it. We had anticipated a picture of some two hours in length, but after this screening it was clear it would be fifteen or thirty minutes longer than that. The other US pictures were 'money' pictures but *The Deer Hunter* felt as if it could do something beyond the financial needs of EMI's pre-selling system.

Universal, our American partner, saw the cut and were less than enthusiastic. This was disappointing but, on reflection, not so surprising: *The Deer Hunter* was a United Artists sort of picture, whereas *Convoy* was more in the style of Universal. I'd muddled and sold the wrong picture to each studio (though I have to say that United Artists never complained about *Convoy*, which made us all some pretty good money). But the worst thing for a producer at this stage of a picture is to feel that the distributor isn't going to get behind the release of his film. The producers or directors with clout can force a distributor to spend enormous (often wasteful) amounts of money on advertising and promoting a release, but this is only possible if they have an ongoing and important relationship with the studio. There was no certainty that EMI would do another picture with Universal, and although our relationship was cordial and respectful it didn't seem likely that I could generate much enthusiasm within their sales department.

I decided to call up my friends Mike Medavoy and Arthur Krim at United Artists. I set up a meeting with the pair and told them that the people at Universal were soft on *The Deer Hunter*. I put it down to a cultural difference, and asked them if they would sneak a look at the picture to see if UA might be interested. I told Cimino what I was doing and this was no problem for him because he, too, didn't want a less than enthusiastic distributor for our film.

Krim and Medavoy saw the rough cut and were bowled over by it. The next day I talked to them along with Bill Bernstein, their head of business affairs, and reminded them how EMI operated: fifty per cent finance from their US partner against distribution in the US and Canada. I made an adjustment here. Our deal with Universal had been fifty per cent of the *budget* of $8.5 million, so they contributed $4.25 million. I was now asking UA for $6.5 million, which was half of the actual cost rather than the budget. We settled for an advance by UA to EMI of $6 million – if I could get the picture back from Universal.

Everyone at EMI was thrilled by my negotiations. I had found an enthusiastic distributor and had increased our advance against US distribution by $1.75 million. I went back to Ned Tanen at Universal. I told him how worried we had been by his company's lukewarm feelings for the rough cut. I told him that I understood that the picture had turned into something much tougher than any of us had expected and that because EMI was in the movie business for keeps the last thing we wanted was a dissatisfied partner. I told him that I had spoken with my principals in London and they were big enough to offer Universal its money back to spare us both the embarrassment of an uncomfortable relationship. Ned was pleased by this and said he would get back to me.

ORGASMA MASK: SHOWS EYES & MOUTH.

1 The following pages showcase the brilliant work of *Blade Runner*'s 'visual futurist' Syd Mead, beginning with a number of pre-production sketches. Sketch for an 'Orgasma' mask to be worn by the replicant Zorah.

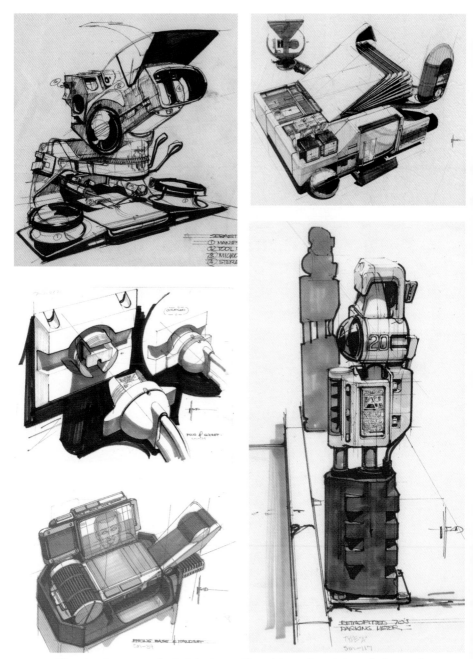

2–6 Chew's microscope; the Voight-Kampff machine; a futuristic wall plug; a phone with video function built into the handset; a 'retro-fitted' parking meter.

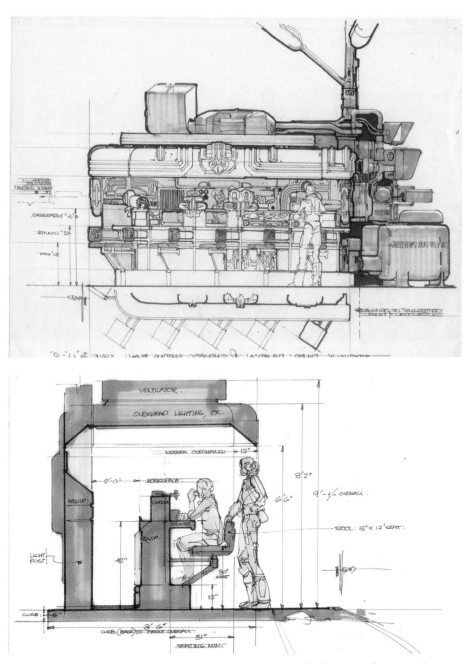

7, 8 Sketches for an elaborate automated tea room, which eventually inspired
the sushi bar in *Blade Runner*.

9, 10 Scene paintings by Syd Mead: the cityscape of Los Angeles, 2019; Zorah's nightclub dance (never shot).

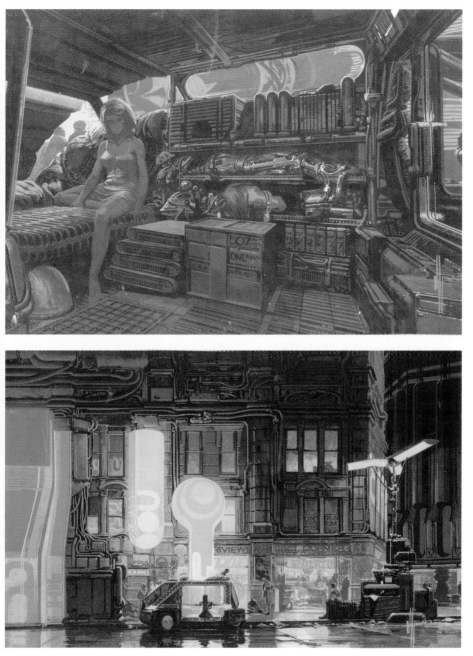

11 Pris in the back of J. F. Sebastian's cluttered truck.
12 Street scene, Los Angeles, 2019.

13, 14 *Blade Runner*'s fearsome replicants: Daryl Hannah as Pris; Rutger Hauer as Roy Batty.

15 A photo of Sean Young inscribed to Michael Deeley.
16 *Blade Runner* director Ridley Scott.

17 Ridley Scott and Harrison Ford in conference.
18 Production Executive Katy Haber and MD on the *Blade Runner* set.

I reported to UA these optimistic expectations and looked forward to the support of a new distributor. By now, I had my first stirrings of hope for a couple of Oscar nominations. I was sure that we needed Oscars to overcome the revulsion some might feel towards the Russian roulette sequences. UA were the kings of Academy Awards and in recent years had collected more Best Picture statuettes than any other studio. Moreover, United Artists' name gave legitimacy to difficult or dangerous works – *One Flew Over the Cuckoo's Nest* (1975), *Rocky* (1976) and *Annie Hall* (1977), an historical three Best Picture Oscars in a row for one studio.

I soon heard what had happened when Universal's film management met to decide whether to take back their money and give EMI back its film. There was one missing factor of which I had not been aware. Universal had, as was their custom, made a deal with CBS whereby the TV network acquired three runs of *The Deer Hunter* for $3.5 million. Tanen was canny and very up to speed with Hollywood thinking and behaviour. He reasoned that with a guarantee from television a couple of years down the line their risk was only $750,000 plus distribution costs. Since they had not guaranteed any level of advertising, they could open the picture as minimally as they liked and slowly increase their advertising, promotion and print costs as and when the reviews or the business justified it. Tanen pointed out to his colleagues that this TV guarantee reduced their risk, but his main thrust was that 'If Universal walks away from the picture and it's a success the studio will look like idiots. If we hang on to it and it's a success it becomes a bargain.'

Ironically, if Universal had known then what it found out later, their decision would most likely have been different. When it came time for TV screening, CBS opted to cancel their $3.5 million acquisition on the contractually permitted grounds of the film containing too much violence for US network transmission.

Still, these were only my problems with Universal. EMI had problems of its own.

14

Low Grade

In the history of British post-war entertainment there are few more significant set of siblings than the three Winogradsky brothers, Ukrainian Jews whose family fled the Tsar's pogroms in 1912 and found sanctuary in the East End of London. The youngest of the three boys, Leslie Grade, became a gentlemanly and much respected talent agent. The eldest, Lew Grade, certainly created an image of himself as an honest and hard-working company chairman whose word was his bond. But the image was undermined in 1982 when his company ACC was unravelled, after its sale to the Australian corporate raider/entrepreneur Robert Holmes à Court. Previously Lew had pushed out the competition to become the boss of ATV, one of the first regional television stations in Britain, which then became successfully involved in TV films and series in the 1950s and 1960s. But the trouble started when Lew's ambition to take on Hollywood propelled him into film production.

The third Winogradsky brother, Bernard Delfont, had worked mainly in live theatre management before he became a director of EMI in the early 1970s, taking charge of their entertainment division which included cinemas, bingo halls and film production and distribution. Bernie was sly, as I was later to discover. Sir John Read, EMI's chairman, found likewise when he woke up one day to find that Bernie had taken over his job. In any event – they were forces to be reckoned with, the Grades.

★ ★ ★

In the early months of 1978, while we were in post-production on *The Driver*, *The Deer Hunter* and *Convoy*, I was setting up the next batch of EMI pictures to be made in the US. By now I knew that the sales we had made on those three pictures, plus *Death on the Nile* and *Warlords of Atlantis* in Britain, had assured net profit on our first slate. In Hollywood the buzz was very good, and EMI had rapidly become a big name in this small town.

One Sunday afternoon, Lew Grade called me at home and we had a curiously oblique conversation. Ostensibly, his purpose was to find out the financial terms of the deal I had made with Kris Kristofferson for *Convoy*; but Lew could have had his assistant call mine for this information. Then Lew steered the conversation round to our distribution in America, where we were working with a different major for each of our five films. I reminded Lew that EMI wouldn't green-light a production without at least half of the budget committed against US distribution, and for this guarantee we gave away a share of profit. In return we couldn't lose a penny on any picture, and we could already see net profit on the first five we had made.

However, Lew argued that if EMI had its own distribution set-up in the US then we would not only keep all the profits but also make money from the distributor's fee, currently being nabbed by the major. Patiently I reiterated that our method was a stop-loss technique. If we couldn't lose we might make plenty of money, but if we gambled without the US guarantees we could lose big-time – as Lew surely knew from his experience of making a number of old-fashioned pictures that had proved ill suited to the US market. But we agreed to disagree, and I thought no more about it.

On 20 June 1978 some enterprising soul took out a full-page advertisement in the *Hollywood Reporter*, touting an unmade script and hoping to draw the attention of the ten Hollywood 'studio heads', who were named as: Alan Ladd Jr, Danton Rissner, Michael Eisner, Roger Corman, Ned Tanen, Richard Shepherd, Robert Shapiro, Mike Medavoy, Daniel Melnick – and Michael Deeley. By such symbolism it was apparent that EMI Films was playing in the major league. The prideful glow was to prove short lived.

The following month Bernie Delfont announced that he would like to meet Spikings and myself at the Beverly Hills hotel. Spikings and I went to the meeting full of confidence. After the usual beat-

ALAN LADD JR.
DANTON RISSNER
MICHAEL EISNER
ROGER CORMAN
NED TANEN
RICHARD SHEPHERD
ROBERT SHAPIRO
MIKE MEDAVOY
DANIEL MELNICK
MICHAEL DEELEY

Suppose you spent 7½ million dollars of a 10 million dollar picture,
and with only two more weeks of principal photography
your star gets kidnapped and held for ransom,
what would you do?

212 249-7334
call for a **SWEET DEAL.**

Some enterprising soul took out this full-page advert in the *Hollywood Reporter* of 20 June 1978, so pitching direct to the heads of the ten major Hollywood studios – which, by his reckoning, included EMI Films Inc. and myself as its president.

ing about the bush, Bernie got to the point. 'Well, boys, it's over. EMI won't be able to finance any more films.' We were aghast. The financial buzz on *Convoy* and *The Driver* was very promising world-wide and *The Deer Hunter* was attracting word-of-mouth. We had five more pictures in mind.

I knew that EMI's hardware division (manufacturing body-scanning MRI devices) was having appalling quality-control problems and was haemorrhaging money. But we also knew our small film division had a forecast profit approaching $20 million. Spikings and I left the meeting determined not to let EMI's finan-cial woes interfere with our production plans, and within a few days we had worked out a solution – after discussions with two banks and one of our major US distributors.

We then met Delfont in London and proudly pitched our plan. Put simply, we proposed to re-create British Lion Films and finance it based on our present film income and forecasts with off-balance-sheet funds that the bank would provide: a neat solution that required no further cash from EMI. Delfont purported to consider this feasible scheme for a few days and then turned us down. 'No,' he said. 'EMI is out of films and you are both out of EMI.'

For me, it had been an arduous six years. I was ready for a break. Also, in my heart, I wasn't wholly certain that the brilliant first batch of EMI pictures could be repeated the following year. I had no scripts of the same quality on the horizon. Also, my contract would ensure me more than $500,000 in severance pay. Added to which, I had been producing films for over twenty years and had acquired substantial assets.

If leaving EMI wasn't a problem for me, it was for Spikings, who was being paid on the EMI London executive scale of about £20,000 a year. We did have profit shares in pictures made under our supervision, but that income would only be realised years into the future. Spikings was anxious to move to Hollywood, and sug-gested that we set up an independent production company of our own. Although we had had an excellent relationship, I declined. I felt it was time for me to have a simpler life, concentrating on one project at a time and answerable to no one but myself. But while I still had any clout as president of EMI Films, I felt obliged to do everything I could to help Spikings, whom I thought was being treated unfairly in financial terms.

I met with Delfont and argued Spikings' case as strongly as I could. Delfont expressed astonishment, having assumed that Spikings and I would carry on working together in some form of partnership. Thus corrected, Delfont told me he would consider what I had said. I went back to Beverly Hills and day-to-day EMI business. I negotiated the settlement of my contract and was set to leave the company in March 1979.

Meanwhile – as I later learned – back in London Delfont was cross-examining Spikings to determine where his loyalties might lie. Satisfied at last, he offered Spikings a job handling both his own and my responsibilities. So Spikings was saved financially, and with good prospects for as long as EMI prospered.

Soon, though, some facts began to emerge which graphically

This introduction to HM Queen Elizabeth II was on the occasion of the royal premiere of EMI's production of *Death on the Nile* in 1978.

illustrated the extent of Delfont's dishonesty. He had told us that EMI's financial difficulties had forced them out of the film business. This was a barefaced lie. Ironically, the half-year results to 31 December 1978 produced this headline in *The Sunday Express*: 'Movies Put New Life into EMI'. The trade magazine *Screen International* headlined 'Entertainment Gains Offset EMI's Losses'. If Delfont was planning to expand its film division, why had he fired us? The answer lay with his elder brother, Lew Grade.

When Grade's financial backer, General Cinema Corporation, pulled out of his production programme, Grade had to find another investor. This was not easy because his films were old-fashioned, costly and didn't work in America. (Of *Raise the Titanic* (1980), a typical Grade production which went horribly over budget and performed miserably at the box office, Grade wound up admitting that it would have been cheaper to lower the Atlantic.) Finally, Grade did find a partial backer, but there was a condition attached: he had to bring in as a partner a company of substance with a proven record of worldwide film production and the capacity to add five or six major pictures each year to Grade's production slate.

I knew that Grade had been complaining for years that the US majors were deliberately sabotaging the release of his films. They were afraid of competition from the self-proclaimed 'World's Greatest Showman' – a piece of puffery much diminished by General Cinema's defection. Grade's solution for the failure of his films was to have his own distribution system in the US which he could rely upon to treat his films with the 'respect he deserved'. Who better to co-operate with Grade than his younger brother? Grade knew that EMI's first film programme was financially very promising – *The Driver* had made a twenty-five per cent profit in pre-sales before it had even finished shooting. In addition, EMI's UK cinema chain would be another benefit to assure the release of Grade's films. So Grade had to persuade Delfont, and I suspect he did no more than adapt what he had gleaned from his fact-gathering conversation with me: namely, that if EMI acted as its own distributor, then it could mop up all of the net profits rather than the more measured slice assured at present.

These simple mathematics were appealing to a man such as Delfont, who never understood the movie business, because they addressed only profitable pictures and did not deal with the risk of losers – about which Grade knew plenty but which Delfont had not experienced recently. Under my control EMI Films Inc. took few risks beyond the script costs. We wouldn't make a picture without it being pre-sold in America and the major foreign markets.

Grade's faith in his ability to succeed where none had done before astonished me. Bigger companies than Grade's – such as the Rank Organisation – had taken the appalling risk of setting up a full-scale film distribution company in America, only to fail. Grade had done a good job producing television series such as *Robin Hood, The Saint* and *The Avengers*, but there he had control of a major UK television station, guaranteeing a network sale in Britain. And he had always ensured that he had pre-sold his series to an American network before shooting. Television was not a cutting-edge medium, so it suited his old-fashioned style. But what possessed him to abandon the pre-sale method which had worked for him just as well as it had for me? The answer seems to be desperation. Grade believed his big motion pictures such as *March or Die* (a turgid Foreign Legion adventure) and *The Medusa Touch* (a silly horror movie starring Richard Burton) had failed only because of poor distribution in the US. It happened so often that he seemed to have become paranoid.

Delfont put EMI money into the new company, Associated Film Distribution Inc. EMI would finance movies based, presumably, on Barry Spikings' judgement. I have no doubt that Spikings himself was entirely aware of the risks involved, but his choices were limited and he may have taken the view that he would ride his luck and try to beat the odds. At least he would be spending time in Hollywood, which is what he wanted. And even if AFD failed, surely it would take at least three or four years to fall apart?

What Grade did to his own shareholders was not my concern, but since I had spent a painstaking three years solidly establishing a reputation for EMI in Hollywood, I was of course saddened by what was going to happen. Back in London, Barry Spikings was now solely responsible for EMI's film programme worldwide.

It was by no means a happy period for British film and filmmakers. Mrs Thatcher's government would soon be credited with the destruction of the British film industry. Even the legendary Cubby Broccoli temporarily moved his Bond franchise to Paris because it was deemed too expensive to make motion pictures in Britain. Mrs Thatcher didn't give a damn about cinema. She ignored the arguments for providing some sort of support on the grounds that films have a value beyond the employment factor. The ability to produce entertainment with a cultural impact serves British interests, including the tourist industry. Under her rule the Eady scheme disappeared and the NFFC vanished. France, Germany, Italy, Canada, Australia – they all had incentives in one form or another, whether tax breaks or grants. Under Mrs Thatcher's reign, such practices were held to be inappropriate for Britain.

Once I was out of EMI I would be too absorbed in *Blade Runner* to take much note of what was happening inside the new Grade/ Delfont US distribution business, though from time to time I did hear some uneasy rumbles. My former chief financial officer, John Chambers, has always kept in touch and I heard from Peter Beale, managing director of EMI Films Ltd from August 1979 until he left under rather unhappy circumstances. Peter had recommended to EMI an investment of fifty per cent of the modest budget of a picture called *Chariots of Fire* in return for worldwide distribution and a share of profits. He had also recommended an investment in Richard Attenborough's *Gandhi*, for which EMI would handle distribution in Britain and sales throughout the Commonwealth. But these recommendations were the scene of early creative differences between Peter and his then boss, Barry Spikings.

David Puttnam was so enraged when Spikings turned down *Chariots of Fire* that he sent what he described as the most vicious letter he had ever written to EMI's leaders, demanding that they remove Spikings promptly. This didn't happen until a few months after March 1982, when Puttnam was to stand on stage to receive the Best Picture Oscar for *Chariots*. The film also made an impressive amount of money. I don't think Puttnam would have been so cross if there hadn't been a lot of talk coming out of EMI's London office about how keen the company was to make British pictures. There was a great deal of anger in London because all EMI's focus was now on America in order to feed Grade's folly.

It might have seemed a good opportunity to redress the balance when British producer Don Boyd brought EMI *Honky Tonk Freeway* (1981) together with British director John Schlesinger. But under the old British Lion/EMI formula this film would not have been made because no US major would have put up half the budget with overseas pre-sales amounting to only $1.5 million on a film with a production cost of $22 million – not to mention prints and advertising. *The Jazz Singer* (1980), a project much favoured by Delfont, was a disappointment for EMI and Allan Carr's *Can't Stop the Music* (1980), reported to have cost more than $20 million, took at the US box office around a tenth of that.

The Grade brothers now planned to set up a joint international sales division under Lew Grade's overseas sales manager. Lew had had some of the same problems selling his product outside the US as he did inside and he saw the advantage of exploiting EMI's reputation in overseas markets where its five-film programme had achieved such success. This time, however, Peter Beale appealed directly to Richard Cave, EMI's chairman/CEO, who stopped the brothers in their tracks.

As EMI was shooting itself in the foot, Grade was having his own problems, the most striking of which was the complete failure of his $35-million *Raise the Titanic*, which grossed less than twenty per cent of its budget in the US. Associated Film Distribution Inc. couldn't go on and in 1981 it was closed down, its product handed over for US distribution to Universal Pictures. Early in 1982, Grade was kicked out of his company and went to work for ex-boxing promoter Jerry Perenchio (one of my financiers on *Blade Runner*). Grade and Delfont's foray into the US film distribution business is reputed to have cost between $90 and $100 million and there were bitter accusations flying around when Holmes à Court's people examined Associated Communications in detail.

Post-Spikings, Verity Lambert, a successful and popular British producer of TV drama, was recruited to manage EMI Films Ltd, and she made pictures on modest budgets from London. But to watch, even from a distance, Grade and Delfont butchering the promising infant EMI Films Inc. was heartrending. Spikings and I had put so much blood and sweat into first British Lion and then EMI that to see it crash for such ill-informed and selfish reasons made me feel that all that hard work had been squandered. I'm certain that if our financial plan had not been kicked out, EMI Films would have become a name to be reckoned with even into the twenty-first century. The cheap, self-serving manipulation of the brothers Grade robbed the British film industry of the opportunity EMI had created for a glorious future.

"You can stop smiling now Barry."

Director and occasional cartoonist Alan Parker drew this for *Screen International* after it was reported that Barry Spikings was exiting EMI Films.

15

Power, Vainglory and Michael Cimino

As I faced up to the extent of Grade's and Delfont's shenanigans, I still had to deal with recurring post-production problems on *The Deer Hunter* which needed to be resolved quickly if we wanted the picture to qualify for Academy consideration before the end of 1978.

Universal set up various previews of the film, sometimes different versions thereof. Audiences were generally stunned by the picture's power, but there were always some walkouts. Women rarely got much beyond the first ten minutes in Vietnam, and the reactions of war veterans were mixed. Many found it authentic. Some were shocked, others were angry.

Meanwhile, both Universal and I were beginning to focus on the question of length. The first sixty-six minutes were much appreciated, but it seemed to us that it was far longer than necessary to establish the milieu and relationships between the principal players. I didn't think much of Cimino's determination to work on an epic scale for scenes that were, in essence, of an intimate nature. Moreover, the picture had been contracted for the shorter length.

But Universal and EMI had other concerns too. A picture under two and a half hours can scrape in three shows a day but at three hours you have lost one third of your screenings and one third of your income for the cinemas, distributors and the profit participants. I was running a business that was relying on income: thus was the beginning of yet another conflict between Cimino and me. A two-and-a-half-hour version of the picture was tested and had a better response. But it was while the atmosphere between Cimino and me worsened that Delfont dropped his bombshell that I was to be out of EMI in less than six months.

Cimino then declared war on me. His essential aim was to make sure that I didn't use my experience and prerogative as president of EMI Films to deliver what I regarded as a more effective length. In Spikings – who had been friendly and cooperative with him during the few weeks he spent in Thailand – Cimino saw someone to help him achieve his end. Spikings and I had been in a very effective partnership for seven years: we had never quarrelled. But now our interests lay in different directions, as he came under the strong influence of Cimino.

I remember Spikings suggesting to me in January 1979 that I shouldn't go to the Golden Globes press conference (*The Deer Hunter* had been nominated) because Cimino had announced that if I showed up then he would absent himself. Of course that was nonsense, because Michael Cimino never missed an opportunity to show off to the press. Spikings simply couldn't see this and empowered Cimino's efforts to treat me as a lame-duck president. Cimino further solicited Spikings to obtain himself a producer's credit on the picture, though Cimino had performed none of the traditional producer's functions – rather the reverse, and most unhelpfully so.

I assume it was Cimino too who was behind the alteration of the order in which our credits appeared. These were to have been: *Produced by Michael Deeley, Barry Spikings and John Peverall.*

The moment de facto control of EMI Films passed to Barry Spikings, Cimino was added as a producer and the order in which the credits appeared was changed to: *Produced by Barry Spikings, Michael Deeley, Michael Cimino and John Peverall.*

The final absurdity was that there appeared from nowhere at the last minute on promotion and advertising material the words: *A Michael Cimino Production.* Certainly *The Deer Hunter* was never that. And yet, though Cimino had been hired simply to revise an existing script and direct the end result, he finished up with the following roster of credits:

A Michael Cimino Film
Story by Michael Cimino
Directed by Michael Cimino
Produced by Michael Cimino
A Michael Cimino Production

During production Cimino had passed me his pet project, a script entitled *The Johnson County War*. But I declined it as an EMI project. As Cimino basked in the buzz that *The Deer Hunter* was creating, United Artists (now under new and less experienced management) entered into negotiations with Hollywood's flavour of the month. Given Cimino's determination to have complete control with no restraints of any sort on the production of what became *Heaven's Gate*, I later realised that part of his strategy had been to wangle a producer's credit on *The Deer Hunter* to demonstrate to UA his qualifications to run unfettered the production of *Heaven's Gate*.

Universal's indifference towards *The Deer Hunter* continued even as it was still being assembled by Peter Zinner under Cimino's watchful eye. Long after the movie was released Cimino would contend that he had to guard *The Deer Hunter*'s negative from Universal's scissors, and that he threatened to kidnap the working print if they edited it without his consent. These comments are complete nonsense. I would have had Cimino banned from the cutting room if he had made such threats: having barred the irritable Peckinpah from his Moviola, I would have quite happily done the same with this weasel.

Other concerns were mounting beyond the matter of the film's length. The haunting guitar theme 'Cavatina', written by

Stanley Myers, was creating one such problem. Myers was a talented composer of more than a hundred films, including *Conduct Unbecoming* for me, but we were all somewhat surprised and disappointed when we discovered that this theme wasn't an original piece of music: it had previously featured in a film called *The Walking Stick* (1970). Whether Cimino knew this and decided to let the producers worry about it I do not know, but the problem was solved by our payment to the original purchaser of a chunk of money.

At this point a most unlikely white knight rode to the rescue. Allan Carr was in every respect a larger-than-life character. Physically he was enormously fat. Unable to restrain his huge appetite for food, he had his teeth wired together and was fed by a tube: a brave and desperate act, and though it worked for a while he continued to have problems with obesity until his early death in 1999. Yet being overweight didn't slow the man down: in 1977 he was busy preparing the romantic musical *Grease* with director Randal Kleiser. His energy was amazing, and by combining it with his business acumen and his great networking skills he had achieved early success managing the careers of Ann-Margret, Peter Sellers, Tony Curtis, Peggy Lee, Paul Anka, Herb Alpert and many more. Now he was living in Hollywood, where his lavish parties and social activities had an old-fashioned mogul look to them.

Exactly how Allan Carr came into *The Deer Hunter*'s orbit I can no longer remember, but the picture became a crusade for him. He was determined by any means possible to persuade Universal that they were sitting on a masterpiece. He nagged, he charmed, he threw parties, he created word-of-mouth – everything that could be done in Hollywood to promote a project. Because he had no apparent motive for this promotion, it had an added power and legitimacy and it finally did start to penetrate the minds of Universal's sales people that they actually had in their hands something a bit more significant than the usual.

Carr's activities in Hollywood were influential in positioning *The Deer Hunter* for Oscar nominations and Universal was reluctantly coming round to the view that the film might be special. To qualify for the 1979 Academy Awards, a picture had to be released for at least one week in 1978 in both New York and Los Angeles. This is often convenient in that the Christmas holiday period is a lucrative time at the box office. However, the qualifying release strategy for *The Deer Hunter* was more sophisticated. We decided to release it for only one week in December in one theatre on each coast. This should and did guarantee totally sold-out business because the buzz by then was strong. People just couldn't get into the theatre and anticipation grew for a wider release.

This strategy stimulated the energy and excitement which culminated in nine Oscar nominations. Universal widened the distribution to include major cities building up to full-scale release scheduled for immediately after the awards. The Academy recognition was, for me, an absolute thrill.

By this point Cimino was using Carr's parties and his enhanced reputation to seduce the executives at United Artists. Steven Bach and David Field, the heads of production at UA, were seriously considering Cimino's screenplay, soon to be called *Heaven's Gate*, after they saw *The Deer Hunter* in a private screening in LA. They were impressed. Bach would later say that he found the movie 'absorbing, repellent, romantic, touching, brutal, confusing, stirring, annoying, technically sure, structurally shaky, and long'. But most of all he found it impressive. In Bach's words, UA thought the film was poetry.

I was now sidelined and Delfont moved into the vacuum to claim credit. In November 1978, EMI threw a party at the prestigious 21 Club before a screening of *The Deer Hunter*. There was a glittering turnout. Just as my invitation to the pre-Oscar nominees' lunch conveniently failed to reach me, I, president of EMI Films Inc., wasn't told of the New York event. However, Cimino made certain that among the crowd was Steven Bach, whom he was carefully reeling in as his next victim.

The Deer Hunter was eventually released for its one-week run in December 1978. The critical reviews were mostly enthusiastic. It was hailed as the most important picture since *The Godfather*. As the press began to take an increasing interest, every magazine and periodical in New York and Hollywood wanted to interview the man responsible: Michael Cimino. As these interviews began to appear in the *New York Times*, *Esquire* and *Time* I was amazed at what the man was saying. In an interview with the *New York Times*, Cimino began by stating that Francis Ford Coppola had dropped by his suite at the Sherry Netherland to say 'You beat me, baby!' referring to the fact that *The Deer Hunter* had been completed in advance of Coppola's own Vietnam war epic *Apocalypse Now*. Cimino told reporters he was thirty-five and we knew from the insurance data he was just short of forty.

Cimino basked in the glory of his new-found celebrity and told the press, who were hungry for his comments, that *The Deer Hunter* was 'extremely personal', claiming that he himself had been 'attached to a Green Beret medical unit'. Possibly some interviewers inferred that this unit was in Vietnam, but then whenever a Vietnam-related inaccuracy was exposed Cimino would usually switch to the position that literal accuracy was never intended. In *Final Cut*, Steven Bach's hugely absorbing journal-cum-postmortem of the *Heaven's Gate* debacle, Bach records how he duly learned that Cimino had never even served in the regular army, let alone Vietnam, merely enlisting himself in the reserves in New Jersey and Texas. Some determined journalists, such as Tom Buckley of *Harper's*, weren't seduced by Cimino and suggested that *The Deer Hunter* didn't hold a mirror up to nature so much as it 'holds it up to Cimino'. Some argued that Cimino's ignorance of the war was perverse to the point of being megalomaniacal. Buckley said that the movie didn't examine cruelty, it exploited it.

However unfounded Cimino's claims may have been, I was

quick to defend the director's comments on the nature and motives of the picture. *The Deer Hunter* wasn't really 'about' Vietnam. It was something very different. It wasn't about drugs or the collapse of the morale of the soldiers. It was about how individuals respond to pressure: different men reacting quite differently. The film was about three steel workers in extraordinary circumstances. *Apocalypse Now* is surreal. *The Deer Hunter* is a parable. Some reviewers focused on the issue of whether there had or hadn't been truth in the central theme of Russian roulette. For a while in press meetings Cimino darkly hinted at evidence of this horrific practice, but in truth we never had a jot of proof. My own view is that it didn't happen, although worse atrocities were committed on prisoners, much as the Japanese had perpetrated during World War II. It doesn't matter. Garfinkle and Redeker had invented some appallingly dramatic sequences, Cimino had mounted them brilliantly, and the gifted actors created a gripping reality on the screen.

Men who fight and lose an unworthy war face some obvious and unpalatable choices. They can blame their leaders (Hitler, say, or General Westmoreland and Presidents Johnson and Nixon) or they can blame themselves. Self-blame has been a great burden for many war veterans. So how does a soldier come to terms with his defeat and yet still retain his self-respect? One way is to present the conquering enemy as so inhuman, and the battle between the good guys (us) and the bad guys (them) so uneven, as to render defeat irrelevant. Inhumanity was the theme of *The Deer Hunter*'s portrayal of the North Vietnamese prison guards forcing American POWs to play Russian roulette. The audience's sympathy with the prisoners who (quite understandably) cracked thus completes the chain. Accordingly, some veterans who suffered in that war found the Russian roulette a valid allegory.

For my part I thought the Vietnam War was doomed, foolish – even impertinent. I had seen the French, who believed that they still had colonial rights in Indochina, thoroughly wiped out there. Perhaps because I had fought in a British Army unit 'fighting communism' I felt for the veterans who came home to a hostile public. I still do. So anything which steered American wrath at a humiliating defeat away from the scorned veterans seemed a valid endeavour – as well as the premise for a riveting drama. *The Deer Hunter* surely wasn't a work of history – but in the context of the late 1970s I rather hope it was somehow therapeutic.

I paid little heed to the press row over whether Michael Cimino was a narcissist and a megalomaniac. I had seen enough on my own watch, and simply counted the box-office receipts. The Oscars rolled around in March, concluding my involvement with EMI and gifting me with a coveted statuette for my trophy cupboard. But my *Deer Hunter* experience had been tainted by ill feeling. Certainly it was not the picture I was ready to retire on. The next one, as it happened, would be a monumental challenge all of its own, but undoubtedly the most worthwhile that I ever undertook.

16

Blade Runner – Incept Date: 1979

Although my tenure at EMI proved a brief one, it had been a golden time for the film company. There was the usual chorus of moaners who attend every British success story: 'Spiky Dealings' was a popular epithet, as was 'Wheeley Deeley'. True, we used our negotiating skills to the full, but this was how we briefly turned the film division into the most profitable sector of Thorn-EMI or any other British film company – this, having come from British Lion, a meagre little outfit where we could barely meet the payroll at the end of each week.

After leaving EMI I headed east, back to my retreat in Cape Cod, to rethink my life. What was next? After all, I had briefly reached the top of the game, at the head of a studio. My professional life seemed to have regularly fallen into three- or seven-year cycles – seven years in the cutting rooms, three years at MCA-Universal, three at Avon Films, three at Woodfall . . . and so on. Now Spikings and I had been working together for seven years, and that seemed sufficient. I was ready to return to independent production.

My contract with EMI provided me with three years' income, profit shares from my three American films and, as a further part of my settlement, they wanted me to take over and produce for them two films they had in development. One was *The Nine Tiger Man*, a story set in the Indian mutiny of 1857. Alan Scott and Chris Bryant had written a very good script and the director was to be Graeme Clifford, whose editing skills had steered *Convoy* clear of Sam

Peckinpah's chemical-induced fog. But period films had fallen seriously out of fashion, especially those that dealt with British colonial history, and we couldn't find an actor who was right to play the romantic lead, a young Indian prince.

The second project was *The Chinese Bandit*, a rip-roaring adventure story based on a novel set in a Chinese province run by a warlord. But after concentrating on it a while I reached the conclusion that this book was in fact unfilmable. Its hero, captured early on by the warlord, would then spend half the film as a prisoner, and the capture itself was so demeaning and interminable that I couldn't see any movie star agreeing to subject himself to such on-screen abasement.

Still, once you've won an Oscar a lot of proposals come your way. One day I received a call from Las Vegas: it was Meshulam Riklis, a very successful corporate raider with a somewhat shadowy background. He had recently married Pia Zadora, once a child musical performer, still only in her early twenties – and he wanted my advice on how her career could best progress. As much out of curiosity as anything else, I agreed and was wafted to Vegas in his private jet. Riklis proved very seriously committed to the question of how his attractive young wife might graduate from frivolity to serious drama. We talked up and down this topic for hours and my final advice was that if she took the trouble to persevere in comedy she might in the long term develop the clout to take a shot at more serious work. This was not the instant magic solution that Riklis was seeking and back I went to LA. His wife did manage to win a Golden Globe for Best Newcomer in 1982, but also earned back-to-back 'Razzies' for Worst Actress in the following years. Mr and Mrs Riklis subsequently bought Pickfair, the incredible mansion built by Douglas Fairbanks Sr and Mary Pickford, and in 1988 they had it razed to the ground.

As for me, throughout 1979 I developed a handful of other projects in which I saw motion picture potential, but I didn't have any great enthusiasm for them. I couldn't find that one project, that one script or idea which had that extra sparkle – something which would provide me with the driving force to plot a course for a project and drive it into being through the illogical minefield of Hollywood. Then something arose that quite suddenly swept all else aside. I received an extraordinary piece of work: a screenplay based on Philip K. Dick's 1968 novel *Do Androids Dream of Electric Sheep?*, adapted by Hampton Fancher, a comparatively unknown actor and stage director now turned writer. This, however, was not my first acquaintance with the material.

At a certain point in the mid-1970s Hampton Fancher had come into $10,000, and decided to try to put it to good use by optioning a literary property that he thought could conceivably be the basis of a mainstream movie. He admired the legendary science-fiction writer Philip K. Dick and was encouraged to believe that this genre might be due a revival. Thus in 1975 he approached Dick about buying the rights to *Do Androids Dream of Electric Sheep?*, but at that time they weren't available.

Hampton and I happened to share a friend in the actor Brian Kelly, whom I had known since 1969, when he happened to visit his then-girlfriend Maggie Blye on the set of *The Italian Job* in Turin. Alas, in 1970 Brian was terribly injured in a motorcycle accident that left him partially paralysed. The timing of the catastrophe was particularly cruel in that he had only just begun work as the star of a major Columbia movie called *The Love Machine* which would likely have proved a great career springboard for him. As it was, he was forced to reconsider everything in his life and work, and turned his thoughts to producing. After receiving a settlement for his accident in the mid-1970s he asked if Hampton could help him option a film property, and Hampton suggested Dick's novel. Roughly a week later, much to Hampton's amazement, Brian had secured the option for a mere $2,000.

In due course Brian came to visit me at the EMI office in Beverly Hills, bearing a copy of the novel. It told of Rick Deckard, a twenty-first-century bounty hunter in a polluted San Francisco, regularly engaged by police to hunt and kill androids who have escaped to earth from slavery on an outer space colony. My initial reaction to it as a film project was negative. It was a wonderful piece of writing, and Dick's imagination was riveting, but as a whole it was maddeningly vague, and too ambiguous for me to see on the screen. At that time I was involved with a very commercial package of pictures – *The Deer Hunter*, *Convoy* and *The Driver*. My function as a corporate executive had narrowed my creative focus, certainly in the time since I had shared in Nic Roeg's visions on *The Man Who Fell to Earth*.

Kelly accepted the logic of my position but didn't give up. He went back to Fancher, relaying my response. Hampton had given the project a lot of thought, and composed a series of production notes that Kelly brought back to me. After reading them, I still had to give Brian the answer he didn't want to hear. Kelly, though, believed that Fancher had a writing talent nobody else had perceived; believed moreover that Fancher was the only man on the planet capable of transforming into a screenplay all the ideas that were racing around his head. Brian nagged and nagged but in the end it was Hampton's close friend, actress Barbara Hershey, who persuaded the reluctant writer to start typing.

Hampton and Brian made a deal to share equally all proceeds from any picture which resulted and to insist upon credits as joint executive producers. It took Fancher a murderously difficult year to craft his first feature-length script, but Kelly was delighted with the finished script and immediately pointed himself in the direction of my Brentwood office. I had been waiting a long time – not necessarily holding out much hope that a first-time scriptwriter could crack this difficult piece. Brian asked me to read it over the weekend and to give him an answer by Monday. He said he had a dozen other places that wanted it. I knew he was lying, and he knew that I knew that too. But I began reading it immediately and I have to say it was the most interesting and original piece of writing I had ever seen.

What Hampton had delivered was a marvellous blending of a thriller with a romance – the idea that Deckard, a sanctioned executioner, would become emotionally attracted to an android, Rachael, one of his supposed victims. I called Brian back on the Sunday and said, 'You've got a deal.' He had delivered me the goods and now it was my task to get the picture up and running. Early 1979 saw me and my assistant Katy Haber plunged into work.

First, there were a few rough edges of the script that I wanted Hampton to polish. His first draft was akin to Dick's book in that the Deckard character was in no sense a conventional movie hero: 'a Milquetoast, bureaucratic, Kafkaesque sort of guy', were Hampton's words for him. But then this draft was really the last time that the script would hew closely to its source. (Certain elements vital to Dick – such as Deckard's gnawing desire to own a live sheep in a society where non-artificial animals were rare commodities and status symbols – were also dear to Hampton, but over the life of this project such elements would be steadily reduced, distilled, or deleted.) In the short term we desperately needed a new title, one that sounded more like a movie than a sci-fi whimsy. There was no way that I could, with a straight face, try to sell a movie called *Do Androids Dream of Electric Sheep?* Nobody in the studio ranks would have heard of Dick's book and I would have been laughed out of the room.

Hampton came down from New York to my home on Cape Cod and we spent a couple of weeks shaping a second-draft screenplay. Deckard became a distinctively tough, world-weary cop. His wife in the novel, a depressed figure, was wholly excised in favour of Rachael, the android female for whom he falls. And the San Francisco location was switched to Los Angeles. Rather unimaginatively, the script was retitled *Android*, which at least got rid of those bloody sheep. But it still left me stuck with a title that nobody had ever heard of, let alone understood. Then Fancher saw a book entitled *Mechanismo*, which became the next title, until its publishers refused to let me use it. We settled on *Dangerous Days*, which I particularly liked because it expressed the script's romantic aspect.

I now started discreetly showing the second-draft script to selected friends, senior executives, at the major studios. We didn't have a package – we weren't zeroing in on a director or a star – but I wanted to test the water. The studios liked the script. We felt a serious futuristic film was about due. But they were nervous about the public's level of interest. It was plain to me that I hadn't been kicked out of the arena but I needed some heavy-hitting ingredients to make this dream come true.

One totally unexpected supporter came out of left field. Gregory Peck had somehow got hold of the script and read it. He called me and asked me to meet him at his home, a palatial house on an enormous spread in Bel Air. There he told me how important it was that I get this picture made. More practically, he wrote not only to the MPAA but to some of the studios emphasising the importance of the film. He sincerely felt that the script's themes of moral crisis and urban pollution were vitally important. Such a generous act is indeed rare in Hollywood.

But to turn the studio's moderate interest into something more useful, I had to pin down a director. Katy and I checked the availability of every A-class 'helmer' in the book. Initially, for no reason I can remember, we were fixated on non-American directors: Michael Apted (*Coal Miner's Daughter*, 1980) and Ridley Scott – but we figured that Ridley wouldn't really want to do another science-fiction picture so soon after *Alien* (1979). Fancher was very keen on Australian director Bruce Beresford after seeing *Breaker Morant* (1979), but Beresford was unavailable. The first director to become attached to the script was veteran Robert Mulligan, who had recently directed *Bloodbrothers* (1978), a movie which Fancher adored. Given that his better-known pictures were *To Kill a Mockingbird* (1962) and *Summer of '42* (1971), it is strange that Mulligan liked *Dangerous Days*. He had earned his reputation by making 'relationship movies', and I suppose, in retrospect, that the love affair between Deckard and Rachael was a lot gentler at this point in the film's development and it may have been a notion which attracted Mulligan to the script.

I saw a further advantage in attaching Mulligan to *Dangerous Days*, for the director had a longstanding relationship with Universal and this connection could serve a producer well – especially as I didn't yet have finance. Mulligan responded well to the script I sent him – particularly the romantic element. But soon after Mulligan came on board it dawned on me that I had misunderstood his interest in the project. We never made much progress in the three and a half months that we worked together. I also felt that his previous successes were encouraging him to seek more control of the project than I would be happy with, given I had $120,000 of my own money tied up in the endeavour and he had yet to form a clear vision of where the film was to go. Eventually, the whole team felt that we simply were not on the same planet as Mulligan. He left the project around Thanksgiving 1979.

Universal had been taking quite a close interest in the rewrites, but they wanted the film to have a happy ending if they were to become involved. Hampton reluctantly put together a walk-away-in-the-sunset finish, but with Mulligan off the picture Universal's interest in *Dangerous Days* quickly faded.

Throughout the Mulligan months, a lot of interest in *Dangerous Days* had been shown by Donald March of the CBS Television network. CBS had decided to diversify into a whole new business, CBS Films Inc., which was to make feature films with budgets up to $8 or $9 million. It was presumed that CBS's decision was in response to the increasing prices the networks were having to pay for feature product: now they would make their own films, with all the additional revenues that ownership should bring. At that stage our production based on Hampton's current script was budgeted at about $9 million. It was set in LA but with a look very similar to 1979. A few futuristic toys had been added but the script, essentially, didn't require complex exterior scenes and it could be shot on local locations at a modest budget. It looked as though CBS was to be my project's final home.

Ridley Scott had always been my ideal choice to direct *Dangerous Days*. I had met him and his brother Tony years before in London and I knew him well. It didn't hurt that he had just come off a huge hit, *Alien*, but I did think it an obstacle that I was trying to lure him back into the sci-fi genre.

Ridley created an environment for *Alien* which was unique and I felt that he had the absolute best eye in the business. No other director can touch him for the creation of detail as well as scope. Somebody once asked how the painter Seurat could possibly achieve magnificent effects by producing thousands of little dots? Ridley is a pointillist, too, and the effect can be magical. That's what I felt we needed for our picture. I loved the material that Hampton had delivered but I couldn't visualise the environment in which this should take place. I didn't want that environment to be created by an art director. I wanted it to be a visual package put together by the director who would be driving the movie's action through the landscape he had created.

Ridley had, in fact, been the first person I had spoken to when I first agreed to take on the Kelly/Fancher venture, but he had been too busy preparing Frank Herbert's novel *Dune*. This was an enormous project which he had been working on for several months with little probability of starting shooting for at least another year. He was unavailable – so I quickly accepted that there was no chance for us to get him.

It is true that his aide, Ivor Powell, had loved the *Android* draft and constantly reminded Ridley that it could be good back-up material if the *Dune* project fell through. I was back in the agent's offices now with CBS's money behind me and searching for a director when an awful event occurred. Ridley's older brother Frank died of skin cancer, and this was a hammer-blow to him.

Suddenly he was seriously depressed at the prospect of another year or so on *Dune* before any chance of shooting. Shooting film is what Ridley thrives on, then more than ever when he wanted to block out the tragedy of his brother's death.

He had to have a change of scene and there was Ivor holding a script financed and ready to go. Ridley later described *Dangerous Days* as an extraordinary piece of work with 'marvellous design possibilities'. Those last three words are the music to which Ridley set Hampton's story. That description describes the function that we needed Ridley to perform. It also signalled to me in my deeper consciousness that *Dangerous Days* might be about to develop into something beyond CBS Films' budget parameters.

Ridley signed on to the picture on 21 February 1980. By this time my project had clearly become too rich for CBS Film Inc., but the transfer to a new distribution company was immediate. Filmways stepped up with a budget of $12 million, delighted by the prospect of a serious project with a hot A-list director and a recently Oscar-winning producer. *Dangerous Days* at last had the green light.

Our team moved into the old Sunset-Gower Studios in Hollywood during May 1980 to begin pre-production. These unprepossessing quarters were economical and efficient as we got to grips with the nuts and bolts in endless meetings. The most critical matter was to lock down Hampton's script as Ridley visualised it. Ridley had to create a world, which we now decided should be Los Angeles in 2019. Some judgements (or presumptions) had to be settled about the general state of a city forty years hence (never mind what the motor cars would look like or how people may dress – these were details to be settled later). This was the time for the strategic decisions which would set the tone of the picture. What would the climate be like? Would the people be roughly the same mix as currently, or would immigration change the look of the population? How decayed would the urban landscape have become – or would it be modern and smarter? And would gene science, cloning, even 'biomechanics' have made great leaps forward? Ridley's designer mind was well ahead on the general look of the film, but as the future we were creating became clearer in his mind he became more concerned about the script.

Dangerous Days was tough material, but not yet tough enough for Ridley. He didn't see much kindness in the harsh world we were creating to accommodate a gang of murderous off-planet androids. What Hampton regarded as pretty much the final script was still a mile away from what was coming together in Ridley's imagination – and so Ridley and Hampton were in constant conference.

By his own admission Hampton was a reluctant rewriter who went about his work rather slowly. ('Happen Faster' was a nickname I coined for him, one he didn't seem to mind.) But Hampton, although fascinated by some of Ridley's concepts, was still fighting to retain his romantic elements. Hampton's narrative was of a man on a mission to kill, through which he discovered his conscience. It was also a tragic love story. The reader saw that Deckard, having been in some sense 'less human' than the androids he was hunting, fell in love with Rachael and was 'improved' by her. The tragedy was that she, like all these artificial beings, had no time to live. In the first draft she and Deckard escaped to a wintry landscape and there Rachael committed suicide. In Hampton's mind, the piece was to

The deliberate and none-too-speedy manner in which *Blade Runner* screenwriter Hampton Fancher went about his work earned him the affectionate nickname 'Happen Faster', and inspired Ridley Scott to draw this doodle on a Post-It note.

have the flavour of a Robert Mitchum film noir of the 1940s – indeed, I think Hampton would have loved to see Mitchum play Deckard – and this ending certainly had that doom-laden quality. It also borrowed a little from the murder in snowy woodland that forms the climax of Bernardo Bertolucci's much-admired *The Conformist* (1970). Ridley, though, spotted a further similarity to another European art-house hit, one that he wasn't happy with: it all reminded him rather too much of the Swedish director Bo Widerberg's *Elvira Madigan* (1967), wherein two lovers in a forbidden relationship elect finally to die together in a wood.

Ridley's mind had not yet finally settled: every day he was developing new ideas. While Fancher was enthusiastic, the director had often moved on before the new pages could be delivered. This intense creativity was wearing on the writer. Ridley wanted to make Deckard a more active protagonist in at least one vital respect: as he put it to Hampton, 'Deckard's a detective, right? But he doesn't do any *detecting* . . .' Another major advance Hampton had to cope with was the emergence of Ridley's vision *outside* the interior world in which *Dangerous Days* had been taking place. Feeling the script was in danger of being a chamber-piece, Ridley was keen to broaden the visual scope. 'What's outside the *window*, Hampton?' he asked at one point. 'That would be a good thing to think about, you know? *Exteriors* . . .' In this line Ridley introduced Hampton to the cult magazine *Heavy Metal*, which had been offering readers a futuristic brand of illustrated 'adult' fantasy since 1977.

Syd Mead had arrived on the picture while Fancher was struggling with the rewrites. Now the script had to cope with this new exterior cityscape in which so many scenes would have to be reset. I think Hampton was beginning to realise that his script was only a part of the film Ridley was planning – that the designed visual qualities would be an unusually important part of the event future filmgoers would experience. Hampton must have begun to realise that he was creating words while Ridley was creating pictures.

Syd Mead was not a member of the Art Directors Guild and I

had to find a suitable title for him which did not conflict with their membership regulations. Mead was finally credited as 'visual futurist' – a modest title which does not begin to reflect his impact on the film's look. Nor does it emphasise how useful he was to Ridley in locking down the picture's form. Ridley had first noticed Mead when he saw a book of his work entitled *Sentinel*. Mead was a hardcore science-fiction fan but after art school he had set up his own company designing for electrical manufacturers and, eventually, the Ford Motor Company. He had designed aeroplane interiors, including that of the supersonic Concorde airliner for British Airways and Air France. Mead's first Hollywood job was to design a giant space vehicle for Paramount's *Star Trek: The Motion Picture* (1979). He worked alongside John Dykstra and Doug Trumbull (who would work with him later on *Blade Runner*).

It was around this time that the *Dangerous Days* title bit the dust and the project's fourth and final title came into use. This happened at one of the meetings with Hampton when he and Ridley concluded that to have Deckard as a police detective was too old-fashioned for a world set forty years into the future. If there were androids prowling the streets there would be some special authority created to deal with disruptive elements. 'So what do we *call* this guy?' Ridley asked. Hampton was an avid fan of William Burroughs, author of the incredible *Naked Lunch*, and he now mentioned a little-known Burroughs work from 1979, a tiny paperback published by Blue Wind Press of Berkeley California entitled *Blade Runner: A Movie*. Coincidentally Burroughs' story was set in the future, and 'Blade Runner' struck me as precisely the label we needed for the profession of gunning down artificial humans. For a modest sum of money Mr Burroughs permitted me to buy his title.

Ridley and I originally engaged Mead solely to design the flying cars, or 'spinners', which law enforcers would use to patrol the skies and streets of the metropolis. Mead's car designs were fabulous. In his sketches, however, he was beginning to draw streets to frame his creations. These were generally based upon Ridley's thoughts, and a grungy, metro look began to emerge. Ordinary buildings would be covered with add-on cylinders and pipes, layer after layer, to create this used-up city environment.

As these drawings emerged, I had two concerns. Syd had now progressed well beyond his originally budgeted car-design function and we had not allowed for his $1,500-a-day fee to last beyond the design of the spinners. More importantly, I was becoming increasingly worried that these set drawings represented a scale for which we were not budgeted either.

Moreover, I still didn't have a leading man. Mike Fenton and Jane Feinberg were the most able casting directors in Hollywood at the time, vital for the general cast we needed, because we were determined not to use familiar faces for any of the supporting parts. The androids, particularly, had to be brand-new faces: after all, they weren't real people, but creations exclusively for use in *Blade Runner*. The only exception had to be Rick Deckard – the leading man. I had to have a star, if for no other reason than to satisfy our financiers at Filmways.

I gave a copy of Hampton Fancher's script to Dustin Hoffman, whom I had first met in New York when Peter Yates was directing him with Mia Farrow in *John and Mary* (1969). Dustin was intrigued – sufficiently so that Ridley Scott and I flew to New York to meet him. In a strangely unfurnished apartment, the three of us sat around a card table for hours, with Dustin doing most of the talking. (Ridley later said that the scene had the lonely look of an Edward Hopper painting, which was coincidental because Ridley had always kept in mind *Nighthawks*, the Hopper painting of the corner café, when he talked about the mood of *Blade Runner*.) Dustin was too intelligent to think he could play Deckard, the man of action, as written. He asked for suggestions as to how the script could be adapted to suit him physically, and Hampton once again was asked to come up with ideas.

This time, Deckard was to be a mean and embittered little man, dissatisfied, selfish and dangerous. Ridley and I figured that although this character sounded seriously unattractive, the nature of his enemies would make him comparatively sympathetic. We reckoned that Dustin could always pull off a sweet little twinkle if his character was too dark. And if we cast Rachael, the leading female character, cleverly enough, she could bring out a responsive softness in Dustin's Deckard.

Dustin was delighted with the opportunities this revised characterisation offered him and a number of lengthy story conferences took place in September. By then Dustin had buried himself in this character and came up with numerous suggestions of his own. For instance, in Hampton's script Dr Eldon Tyrell, the scientific/corporate mastermind behind the production of almost-human androids, was due to be cornered and killed in his palatial headquarters by Roy Batty, the leader of the renegade androids who have ventured to earth from an off-world colony, seeking from their maker an extension of their limited lifespans. In fact Batty then proceeded to go from room to room, murdering Tyrell's entire family and staff. Hampton certainly made the reader feel the wrath of Batty's vengeance, akin to that of Frankenstein's monster. So I think Ridley's enthusiasm palled for a moment when Dustin proposed that this potential bloodbath be modified simply to the killing of Tyrell.* (In fact Dustin's proposed script change did stay, although the way Ridley would finally shoot Batty's execution of Tyrell was probably ten times more gruesome than Dustin would have liked.)

But Dustin's enthusiasm for detail and insistence that every word of the script be micro-managed began to have a leaden effect. Out

---

* Hampton had also imagined that Tyrell kept a menagerie of exotic replicant animals and mythic beasts, designed by J. F. Sebastian – one of them a unicorn – and that Batty would gain admission to Tyrell's HQ by tagging along with one of Sebastian's deliveries. The menagerie idea was rather more than we could afford, but in the end the idea of a rolling chess game between Tyrell and Sebastian worked fine as a replacement.

of the blue we were suddenly discussing cryogenics and how exciting was the prospect of freezing people with terminal diseases just
before they expired, keeping them on ice until a cure could be
found, whereupon the lucky person would be defrosted. I felt it
was getting out of hand – the film seemed as though it was drifting
on an endless ocean. Our conversations were sounding like first-
year film-school debate instead of closing off casting for the immi-
nent production of a very expensive picture.

The discussions with Dustin finally fizzled out. By mid-October,
there were only three months until the scheduled start of principal
photography. This start date seemed crucial. There was a possible
strike to be called by the Directors Guild for July 1981 and I was
adamant that principal photography on *Blade Runner* had to be
completed before the strike began. Later, that threat abated and I
decided it would be safer to put principal photography back a few
weeks to a start date of 9 March 1981. We had wasted vital months
trying to adjust the script to Dustin or vice versa. We needed a real
leading man and they are hard to obtain at short notice. Ridley and
I put our heads together and came up with what proved to be a
lucky thought.

Harrison Ford was not on our original list of leading men. He
had been in the hugely successful *Star Wars* pictures, but as part of
an ensemble cast, and without the hard realism we needed for
Deckard. Still, when Ford's name came up, I was struck by the fact
that he was working on a big Steven Spielberg production in which
he played the sole lead, an action adventurer of the type only a
leading man could pull off. Spielberg was directing *Raiders of the
Lost Ark*, which had a tremendous buzz going for it. He kindly
offered to show us some rushes and Ridley and I flew to London to
Elstree Studios, where the movie was in full swing. In the few years
since *Star Wars* (1977) Harrison had developed a much more mature
screen presence. He had worked on *Force 10 from Navarone* (1978)
and *Hanover Street* (1979), his first solo lead, and *More American
Graffiti* (1979) as well as the second *Star Wars* picture, *The Empire*

214

Strikes Back (1980). We both believed that Harrison had more potential than any of these pictures had given him the opportunity to show.

After watching only a few minutes of the *Raiders* rushes, Ridley and I knew we wanted Harrison; he was exactly what we were looking for and perfect for *Blade Runner*. Literally only two weeks after finishing with Dustin we met Harrison one night after he had finished shooting. He strode into his hotel where we were waiting, still wearing his Indiana Jones outfit, a leather jacket and Indy's trademark brown fedora hat. Ridley told me later, 'Shit, I wanted that hat for Deckard!' 'Tough,' I responded. 'We lost a hat but we gained a star. Not a bad exchange.' That was it. Within no time we had Ford committed to the picture. And Ridley wound up giving Deckard an entirely un-Harrison Ford buzz haircut.

While Ridley and I were meeting with Harrison in London, Hampton Fancher remained in Hollywood continuing to tweak the screenplay. But his days were numbered. When Ridley saw Harrison in *Raiders* he saw a mature, hard-edged man, not the romantic hero who had always lurked on Hampton's pages. Shortly after arriving back in Hollywood, Ridley and Hampton started bickering. Hampton thought Ridley was being outlandish and Ridley thought Hampton was becoming recalcitrant, unproductively stubborn. Ridley hadn't fully cast in concrete the final style of his film, but he knew it wasn't either going to look or sound like *Dangerous Days*. Ford had triggered a sea change and Ridley needed another talent to help put this on the page.

Production was now only twelve weeks away and new, as yet unwritten, ideas were affecting the texture of the film. I think Hampton mistook the significance of his executive producer credit. He had been involved in all the processes, but not for any producing reason. He didn't at this point grasp that this was 'A Ridley Scott Film' and if he couldn't or wouldn't do what Ridley wanted his executive producer credit did not give him any additional clout.

One particularly harsh disagreement ended in an explosion. Hampton told us that if we didn't like what he was doing then we could just fire him. I don't think he meant this literally, it was more of a boyish bluff, but Ridley and I decided to take it at face value. Hampton Fancher, the writer, was now off the picture.

Hampton's original screenplay was glorious. I loved it. But a script is not like an architectural plan a builder works from when putting together the bricks and wood to construct an edifice. The script up until the beginning of production is a living creature, constantly undergoing change as the director defines for himself and his actors and crew more precisely what he wants. Ridley was so much further down the road towards his *Blade Runner* than Hampton was.

By mid-December 1980, pre-production was in full swing. Sets were being constructed and our office on Sunset-Gower was abuzz with action as we approached the starting line. By now, we had spent nearly $2.5 million of Filmways' money on *Blade Runner* and it was clear to Ridley and me that, the way the film was developing, we would certainly need to raise the budget substantially again. There was an ongoing negotiation with Filmways as we struggled to reach our new target of $20 million, a sharp increase over the $12 million they had originally agreed.

A major studio is used to the budget changes which can occur as a film grows. They can evaluate it at every change, usually anticipating an increase above the producer's original pitch – which he may have kept too low to entice the studio's interest. Their evaluation is a commercial judgement. If they think that much more elaborate sets, as we now required, would add to the picture's box office they could agree to raise the budget to whatever extent was necessary. But Filmways was a small independent without the experience of large-scale production or the financial flexibility to make the aforementioned judgements.

A rumour was circulating at this time that Filmways were negotiating to take on Brian De Palma's *Blow Out* (1981). De Palma was on a roll – *Dressed to Kill* (1980) was expecting to gross a bundle and perhaps Filmways were switching their interest from *Blade Runner* to *Blow Out*, or perhaps they only had enough to make *Blow Out* plus *Blade Runner* if our budget stayed around $12 million. (Filmways did make *Blow Out* on a budget of $18 million but it achieved a disappointing gross of only $12 million. It would seem that Filmways haven't engaged in any more production since 1981.)

Then the roof fell in. Katy Haber called me at seven in the morning. She had just picked up the trades and there in front of her was an announcement from Filmways. They weren't proceeding with *Blade Runner* but putting the film into turnaround, which meant that I was given the chance to take the project to another studio as long as Filmways were repaid their money. The reason for Filmways' abandonment of *Blade Runner* was less important to me than fighting to maintain the existence of my project. Bitterness and bad temper wouldn't win the day. I was determined to have Filmways leave their $2.5 million in the picture and continue paying salaries while I set the picture up elsewhere. I asked for a further month of payroll and they agreed to two weeks. That's how long I had to raise $20 million.

Miraculously, it took ten days. But I had a lot more to sell than when I was dealing with Universal or CBS Films. I now had a major star as well as a hot director along with advanced production plans and a full crew ready to shoot. I put on my racing shoes and ignored the usually delicate approach of submitting to only one company at a time. I bombarded all the majors and almost anybody else I knew who might help. I suspected the majors would not move fast enough to get a deal settled before the deadline, particularly since their recent experiences on Spielberg's costly failure *1941* and UA's crippled condition after *Heaven's Gate* had made all the studios cautious about big-budget productions.

So I reverted to the fragmented financing method which had worked so well during my British Lion and EMI days. Alan Ladd Jr, an old friend and a very successful studio head when he was at 20th Century Fox, was the first to respond. Laddie and Jay Kanter had set up a production house within Warner Brothers. Laddie had been in charge of Fox when it financed *Alien*; he admired Ridley and agreed to come in with $7.5 million from Warner Brothers. In turn they became the American and Canadian theatrical distributor.

Shaw Brothers was a well-established and highly successful Asian filmmaker and distributor: the company was owned by Sir Run Run Shaw, with his son Harold playing a major role in the company. I did a lot of business with Harold for Far Eastern rights on films which were very successful in his territories – for example *Convoy*. It took one phone call and a few telexes to obtain Shaw Brothers' commitment of $7.5 million advance for theatrical rights outside the USA and Canada.

So within a week I had $15 million from two solid sources and major studios distributing throughout the world. There remained all the ancillary rights – television, video cassette and 'any other mechanical contrivance designed for viewing which is in existence or yet to be invented', which soon meant DVDs. Laddie put me in touch with Jerry Perenchio, a former boxing promoter and talent agent, a man with a golden touch whose every project made him even more millions.

Perenchio and his partner Bud Yorkin invested through Tandem Productions, putting up the rest of the budget to give them a share of worldwide profits, if any, and first recoupment from the ancillary rights. They were also to provide a completion guarantee which meant that if the production cost exceeded $22 million they would provide such additional funds as were necessary to deliver the film for distribution to Warner Brothers and Shaw Brothers. In the hurried flurry of documentation which had to be achieved in the brief time we had, Tandem acquired certain rights of control as well as physical ownership of the negative. This did not bother the other financing parties who had received their distribution rights throughout the world unfettered by any concerns about budget overages or copyright ownership. Certainly Ridley and I would not have given in to all the demands expressed in the small print of the Tandem contract had we had any alternative source for the final chunk of money we had to have in order to make *Blade Runner*. But within the deadline set by Filmways, I had put together $22 million. Nobody in the pre-production crew had missed a day's pay and *Blade Runner* was now back on track with a more realistic budget.

Ridley and I both wanted to shoot *Blade Runner* on real streets, so we went to New York, London and even to a huge abandoned housing estate near Boston's Logan Airport. This might have worked, although we could have had trouble clearing out the 'homeless' occupants, but it would have taken an enormous amount to add the height and retro look that Ridley needed to create his metropolis. Two other problems would have been the difficulty of keeping the public completely away from such a large shooting area, and then night shooting in the winter in Boston was a horrendous thought. For example, if it snowed what would you shoot the next night? Ridley and I finally recognised that we needed to shoot in a completely controlled environment with a temperate climate.

This meant Los Angeles and a studio backlot, and the only backlot with the necessary scale was Warner Brothers' at Burbank, where several New York streets had been built and used for dozens of films. These were the streets which we could retro-fit to become Los Angeles in 2019.

This task fell on the able shoulders of Larry Paull, the production designer, and art director David Snyder, whose jobs were in many ways not made easier by Ridley's rigid control of every aspect of the film's appearance. His 'Ridleygrams' – sketches drawn by Scott – showered onto the art department like confetti. Sometimes one sketch would be followed two days later by an improved version. Larry and David did a brilliant job keeping up – so did Linda De Scenna, who, as set decorator, had to think forty years ahead about every detail that appeared on the set.

Construction began late in 1980 to transform the Burbank lot into what was later to be christened Ridleyville. Scott designed the architectural look of the city based on the principle that eventually it will become too cumbersome and expensive to simply tear down old buildings and replace them with the kind of new shiny structures seen in most futuristic films of the 1970s. Ridley wanted the old buildings to look retro-fitted with pipes, transformers and whatever other gear was needed to keep these relics going. Paull had taken dozens of pictures of the backlot and had begun to develop the new look by superimposing Mead's futuristic ideas over them. Immediately we started to see the world of *Blade Runner* come alive. Ridley's designs had cleverly adapted the worst characteristics of Hong Kong, New York's Times Square and London's Piccadilly Circus.

As the eight blocks were transformed the crew watched with

In his meticulous attention to the visual design of his pictures Ridley Scott is wont to shower his art department with scenic sketches known as 'Ridleygrams'. On these facing pages are two such sketches: the first (above), a sequence of frames depicting the brutal conditions in an 'off-world' slave colony; the second (right), unmistakably an early vision of *Blade Runner*'s muscular renegade replicant, Roy Batty.

amazement. After listening to and studying Ridley's detailed designs for months they were slowly seeing the reality. As we strolled down the set it was quite breathtaking to see the detail that was being built in. Pipes snaked down the facades, subways disappeared into the sidewalks and large pylons supporting huge video walls were being erected at the corner of each block. Obviously this huge revamp was scarily expensive – which is precisely why in the refinancing I had added a further $10 million to the Filmways budget. Although every inch of the frame would be filled with elaborate embellishment, not a penny was being wasted.

Writer David Peoples was working for Ridley's director brother Tony at Filmways, rewriting a script of his own for Tony to direct. Tony had come to the view that David could perhaps step into Hampton Fancher's shoes and provide the missing *Blade Runner* elements his brother was in need of. Ridley arranged a screening of George Miller's *Mad Max*, to which Tony and David showed up, and introductions were made. Previously David had been involved successfully with shorts and documentaries but now he was to be hurled into the madness of a major motion picture about to start

production. He handled it incredibly coolly. I gave him Hampton's draft to read, with one important caveat: 'Ridley has a few ideas . . .' Two hours later we went to the Château Marmont hotel on Sunset Strip for his reaction. He was bowled over by Hampton's work and said there was nothing he could do to improve it. This might

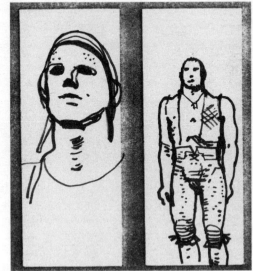

have cost him a job but we explained to him the need now was to make the big leap from what we had to what Ridley wanted. Ridley explained exactly where we had to go and David's response was spectacular. They were on the same wavelength instantly. Before Christmas, David came back with some amazing writing – in some cases outdoing even Ridley's imagination.

Peoples' new draft started at an off-world crematorium for the disposal of time-expired androids. Hidden among the corpses is Roy Batty, who saves a number of other androids who then escape with him to earth. As great an opening as this might have been, it was outdone by the one Ridley eventually decided upon, an epic visual introduction to the great metropolis.

David also started to include some of the detecting elements Ridley felt he needed, in order that the movie's central pursuit contain more of a puzzle. Ridley badly wanted Deckard to make use of an 'Esper' machine that permitted close analysis of the interior of a photographic image, so that it would lead him to a snake scale with a serial number on it, from which he could pursue the snake's owner, the android Zhora. The pay-off for all this would be an exciting foot chase through heavy traffic and Zhora's death as she smashes through glass windows. But that seemingly straightforward elaboration with the Esper required many more expository pages from David.

David also found a brilliant substitute in the script for the word 'android', which both Ridley and I were heartily sick of, as I continually nagged that it sounded to me like B-movie lingo. David's daughter was majoring in chemistry and microbiology at UCLA, and he had the smart idea of consulting her on some technical terms, in which she proved to be a mine of useful information. During one conversation about cloning she began talking about the replication of cells, and so gave David the idea of calling the androids 'replicants'.

I had thought Hampton was the chief romantic on this picture, but then David and Ridley too clearly shared some form of similar impulse, for David imported some lines from Shelley's famous poem 'Ozymandias' into the script, only for Ridley to rule, 'I think we need some Blake . . .' David duly went out and sourced a Penguin paperback collection of William Blake's poetry and found what he needed in the 1793 work *America: A Prophecy*. Slightly amended from the original, David allotted these lines to Roy Batty as he confronts Tyrell's eye-designer Chew in his freezing-cold laboratory: 'Fiery the angels fell / Deep thunder rolled around their shores / Burning with the fires of Orc . . .'

But with only ten weeks until filming began Ridley still didn't have everything he wanted. With Ivor and Katy we spent a week cutting and pasting scenes from Hampton's earlier drafts into David's 15 December screenplay. We didn't produce the final script but this effort focused us onto what was needed and Ridley's next briefing to David Peoples put us right on track for the script we finally shot.

Casting was in full swing when we moved the production HQ to *Blade Runner*'s home at Burbank. Katy Haber had packed up dozens of boxes containing the history and ongoing paper from the start of the show: all drafts of the screenplay, memos, sketches and contracts. But the filing cabinets which arrived at Burbank were empty. The removers had junked all the paperwork we had stored in cardboard boxes. This was seriously inconvenient at the time but historically disastrous when you are writing an account of what happened. At least all the records of our casting searches were safe at the offices of casting agents Fenton and Feinberg.

Our most important casting task now was to find for the role of Roy Batty an actor strong enough to put the fear of God into Harrison Ford's Deckard – and he had to be a first-class talent, not just a tough. A third requirement was that along with all the other replicants he must be unknown to mainstream US audiences. The Dutch star Rutger Hauer was the solution. Thirty-seven years old and at the height of his physical powers, he had an incredible presence. His early adult life had been spent knocking about the world as a sailor and he had had many other jobs before turning to acting. I had first seen him in *Soldier of Orange* (1977), in which he played a guerrilla fighting against the Nazis. Before that he had made a dozen or so pictures in Europe and he was used to the medium. Hauer brought to *Blade Runner* – his first big-time Hollywood role – a special intelligence. He smiled and seemed sweet-tempered until the moment of the kill arrived. Ridley was shocked when he first met Hauer, who turned up at his house wearing pink silk pants and a Kenzo sweater with a fox fur draped over his shoulder. He had bleached his hair and was wearing Elton John-style glasses. He was an astounding sight and Ridley paled. He had already been cast and after a slightly uncomfortable meeting Rutger left. Ridley was seriously upset, convinced that Katy Haber and I had foisted on him a gay activist to play the most aggressively masculine part in the picture.

The role of Rachael, meanwhile, was a tough one to cast. She was a replicant but had to be pensive and vulnerable in a way that the other female replicants could only pretend. Hampton was very keen for his friend Barbara Hershey to play Rachael. Without doubt she was an actress of such excellence that it would have been very easy for her to meet the demands of the part. It also would have had a justice to it, since Hershey had long ago been the driving force, along with Brian Kelly, who pushed Hampton Fancher into writing the original script, so kick-starting this whole adventure. In the end, we tested three actresses and Barbara was one of them. She was certainly the best actress of the three and it was with reluctance that Ridley and I decided that she failed our other test – she was simply too well known.

But I admit that the first time I saw Sean Young I knew she was perfect for Rachael. Twenty-one and utterly beautiful, there was some restraint in Sean, something held back, which, with a certain sadness, was the perfect image of a young woman with a terrible secret. (In the picture she learns that she is a replicant only after Dr Tyrell insists that Deckard test her with the Voight-Kampff analyser.)

Daryl Hannah was not yet twenty when we cast her as Pris, the third renegade replicant. She looked fourteen, but had already appeared in De Palma's *The Fury* (1978) as well a number of minor films. She certainly fulfilled our 'new face' requirement and Ridley and I liked the bonus of her being a niece of the great cinematographer Haskell Wexler.

The final two replicants were played by Joanna Cassidy and Brion James. The choice of Joanna was easy: we all knew her work but she was capable of completely changing her appearance. Beautiful and uncommonly athletic, she could perform the stunts which the character of Zhora had to do mostly without a double. Ridley and Katy Haber interviewed Brion James when he was sent over by the casting directors. He was experienced but not well known. The replicant Leon is none too bright – he is muscle, an enforcer. Brion had a menacing look which won him the job. When he went back to see Ridley later he had just had a horrifying motorcycle accident. His face and hands were cut to ribbons. Ridley told me he was delighted with this damaged look and that was that.

A curiosity among the supporting roles was that of Gaff, a side-kick to Deckard's former boss Bryant, seemingly resentful of Deckard's return to duty. Gaff was a character invented by Hampton who then slipped into abeyance over subsequent drafts. David revived Gaff and gave him more to do. But there were many different conceptions of where Gaff came from, what was his ethnicity and native tongue. David was well prepared for this sort of work, as he had attended high school in the Philippines and was familiar with the discrepancies between the national language of Filipino and the ethnic variant of Tagalog. David also had an interest in the Anglo-Spanish 'Spanglish' that was spoken in communities on either side of the US–Mexico border. At one stage Ridley decided Gaff should speak only Japanese, so David began writing in subtitles. But when Edward James Olmos came on board he seized the opportunity and greatly developed the character. Olmos had a bigger reputation as an actor than the part of Gaff really called for. A well-known figure in the Hispanic community, he had directed and acted in both Spanish and English. Ridley worked really hard with Olmos, developing a character who would stand out in all his brief moments. His blue contact lenses, natty clothes and gobbledegook metropolis gutter language, first heard when Deckard is arrested, actually had some scholarly linguistic basis, mainly in Hungarian. As such Olmos can be largely credited with the polyglot language referred to in the film as 'Cityspeak', though, as with many aspects of *Blade Runner*, the idea arose from much collaborative thinking.

Four weeks before shooting, any picture is a nightmare. All the loose ends should have been tied up but they never are, so the producer, director and all the crew are scuttling around concentrating on getting the first two days of shooting locked down. Wardrobe and make-up tests create friction between cast and crew, new script pages float in and locations get altered for some reason beyond anyone's control. Already the budget is causing anxiety as last-minute failures in special props need to be expensively replaced. We lost some of our custom-made vehicles in an arson attack on the workshop where they were being constructed; our brilliant wardrobe department had been let down by some of the suppliers; and so on. The good news is that this is quite usual and all of us who work on pictures expect that last month to be frantic. The hope is that on Day One, when the first line is spoken and the first frame of film is shot, everything will be okay and we will roll on week after week with no problems. That never happens. As Ridley famously said, every movie is like going into battle. But *Blade Runner* was World War I and II combined. I steeled myself for the biggest undertaking of my career.

17

Blade Runner: T-Shirt Wars

I was supposed to have a story meeting with Ridley at 10 a.m. one morning, shortly after Harrison Ford had signed on to the picture. I go in and there's Michael sitting at his desk. I say, 'Jeez, Michael, where's Ridley?' Michael looks up, brow knitted, and says, 'Ridley's going to be a little bit late this morning. He was up until God knows what hour with Harrison. Harrison wanted to "break down the barriers" . . . And Michael paused for a moment, then looked up at me again and said, 'You know, we British rather like the barriers.'

David Peoples

The majority of the *Blade Runner* shoot took place over long gruelling nights on the converted backlot that our art department had raced to finish as the time for principal photography loomed. As the sun went down over the hills behind Warner Brothers, and darkness fell over Ridleyville, you really did feel yourself transported into a new world; that backlot certainly didn't feel like your average movie set. Moreover, the massive proportion of night shooting concealed the backlot's limitations. By day one could clearly see the hills behind the studio, so limiting the camera's scope. At night one was wholly immersed in an imagined urban environment. Futuristic newsstands were dotted along the streets, selling specially designed twenty-first-century publications mocked up by the art department. We had built huge neon signs advertising TDK, Atari and suchlike, and they featured with sufficient prominence for the companies themselves to meet the cost.

But *Blade Runner*'s street sets had to be completely re-dressed almost constantly, because that lot was required to represent many different corners of LA. As we turned up for work each night and the lot came alive, it even started to smell differently: odours of burning coffee, garbage and boiling food created a realistic, squalid, rundown city atmosphere.

Three of the prophetic themes running through the film's narrative were mass immigration, urban decay and climate deterioration. *Blade Runner*'s city sets (retro-fitted to the existing 'New York' street buildings on the lot) really conveyed the sense of a physical cityscape in decline. Our extras thronging the streets were predominantly Asian, as was much of the decor: these were not your typical Los Angelinos of 1981. As for the weather we created, this was brilliantly effective, but, in working terms, a nightmare. We needed a climate deluged in acid rain. A prop man with a garden hose squirting a few extras was the usual solution – but not for Ridley. *Blade Runner* had an elaborate overhead sprinkler system, like a giant fire retardant device in a huge office space. These rapidly spinning sprinklers produced the downpour Ridley demanded, but from time to time shooting would stop while all the rain effects were recharged. And even when we shot indoors, we had smoke effects to contend with. So the eventual seventeen and a half weeks of principal photography (stretching from March to July) were hard on everybody, even though the results promised to be visually astounding.

On 9 March Ridley's cameras began rolling on Stage Four, capturing Deckard's first encounter with Rachael in Tyrell's office. Finally, it was happening. After all the ups and downs, Ridley's vision of Hampton's dream was coming to life. Tyrell's office was massive, symbolising his enormous power. Here was a man who could produce almost perfect counterfeits of humans: the grandeur of his surroundings had to match his achievement. The design did indeed have a Mayan splendour to it, and the floors gleamed. For Ridley there was but one problem, namely that the stone columns he had sketched at design stage had been installed upside down. He would not be content until these were the right way up, but the remedial work consumed all of a morning. For an actress as young and inexperienced as Sean Young it was bad luck to be thrust into this setting on Day One. Ridley spent a lot of time with her, but wasn't really satisfied when the sequence was cut together later that week. There were lighting problems too, and Ridley wisely bit the bullet to reshoot this vital opening scene. Ridley's perfectionism is not extravagant: he was right to redo this work, and the decision set a tone of quality and precision which this film demanded.

A further adjustment to this scene came in post-production. As Rachael enters, a beautiful tawny owl flaps across the set and lands on a perch, from where it observes Rachael and Deckard. Deckard asks, 'Is that owl artificial?' When the scene was shot, Sean Young followed the script and answered, 'Of course not.' Later in the picture, when Batty murders Tyrell, that same owl is watching: as Tyrell dies, a cut to the owl shows its unnaturally gleaming eyes, a characteristic that we have come to see as the tell-tale mark of a replicant. The owl shot was an afterthought, yet it meant that for the sake of form we had to go back to the dubbing theatre and change Rachael's line to 'Of course it is.' The emendation was worthwhile, though: that fake owl further displayed the terrifying skill of the Tyrell Corporation.

The image of Sean Young smoking a French Boyard cigarette would become one of *Blade Runner*'s visual signatures. Her 1940s hair, make-up and clothes combined to make a striking picture of a beautiful young woman, calm and collected. Sean was amazingly cool about having to smoke these disgusting cigarettes, which Ridley had picked for their 'look' without much consideration of the acrid smoke that had made for generations of emphysemic Frenchmen. I wondered at the time if we were breaching our insurance in Sean's case.

The casting of Tyrell had presented some difficulties. Ridley had seen Joseph Turkel as the supernatural bartender in Stanley Kubrick's *The Shining* (1980), and was rightly impressed by his presence. The problem with Joe was that he found it hard to remember dialogue, which meant that we had to resort to the traditional but inconvenient device of painting his lines on giant white cardboard cue-cards which were placed strategically around the set. This consumed a little extra time, because Joe's movements had then to be thoroughly rehearsed so that he could pick up his lines without the appearance of reading them. I would have the same problem on a later project with Maximilian Schell; and yet, interestingly, both actors could put over a seamless performance without betraying any sign of their off-camera assistance.

The Voight-Kampff analyser – integral to the film's narrative – also makes an appearance in this scene, as Tyrell challenges Deckard to test Rachael. Syd Mead designed the VK machine as a retinal scan, focusing on the human eye and measuring its response to a series of apparently innocuous questions: the ominous bellows on the side of the VK is sucking in evidence of nervous sweating. This threatening device turns Rachael's world upside down when she duly learns that she is in fact a replicant. This leads her to question Deckard: 'Have you ever taken a Voight-Kampff test?' Thus one of Ridley's favourite ideas is planted in the audience's mind: is Deckard, too, a replicant – a sort of class/species-traitor hunting down his own kind? I cannot say for sure at what point this notion was seeded in Ridley's own mind, but without doubt it germinated as work on the picture went along. David Peoples certainly wasn't thinking that Deckard was himself an artificial life form, but inadvertently he may have helped to fire Ridley's imagination on this point. The story is probably best told by David himself, as follows:

I had written an ending much the same as Hampton's, kind of bittersweet. I had it that Deckard and Rachael went off into the snowy countryside, then Deckard was alone, and we heard his voiceover: 'She didn't know what her date was, but she wanted a choice.' Then you heard a shot off-screen and you knew she'd *made* that choice – rather than just dying on the date she'd been told to because she was some manufactured thing. Then Deckard said something like, 'I was thinking – what's the difference between me and Roy Batty? Difference is, I can't go confront my maker and ask him what my date is . . .' Now, there I was referring to *God* – we all have a maker, we all have a date. Well, subsequent to this draft Ridley started telling me I was a genius and I had such a wonderful *Heavy Metal* mind – and I didn't know what he was talking about, but I was glad of the compliment . . . Then it would come up in Ridley's conversation that Deckard was a replicant, and somehow he seemed to credit *me* with that. It wasn't until years later that I looked at that draft and realised it could be read in another way . . .

The first few days of filming interiors were considerably more civilised before the unit began the gruelling night shoots. The police-station scenes were shot in LA's downtown Union Station. Deckard's boss Bryant has hauled the Blade Runner in to brief him on the escape of the murderous renegade replicants. Union Station, one of the most beautiful buildings in Los Angeles, was our most comfortable night location on the picture. Working conditions got tougher the next night when we started shooting the sequences in the abandoned building that is home to Tyrell employee J. F. Sebastian, a genetic designer suffering from 'accelerated decrepitude'. Our chosen location was the landmark Bradbury Building, originally constructed in 1893 in the 'commercial Romanesque' style of the time. The first shot was of the ornate exterior as replicant Pris 'picks up' Sebastian and persuades him to take her up to his apartment. The building was essentially an office block, and every night after the workers went home the art department transformed this elegant architectural site into a nightmarish slum.

Then, after ten days out and about, the unit shot its first night on the Warner Brothers backlot. The opening sequence in which Deckard is arrested at the Sushi bar was our first sight of Ridleyville at its seediest. It was also the first time the audience saw the street level of 2019 LA as a milieu dominated by Orientals.

After a few days on the lot came a further week of relief from night shoots, including the sequence of Chew being murdered by Batty and Leon in his laboratory (actually a functional freezer room). When the replicants visit Chew to discover a way into Tyrell's private home, they rip out his body-heating air hoses and leave him to freeze to death. Because of delays and reshooting I was determined to make up a few days here, so we cut the schedule from four days to two and excised (on cost grounds) a wonderful visual moment from the script. It was intended that Deckard follow the replicant trail to the laboratory and there find Chew standing frozen solid: given a small push, the cadaver topples to the ground, smashing up into tiny glistening particles like a statue of pure ice. This would have been wonderful to see, but it really didn't have anything to do with keeping our story moving and we had never worked out how to do it economically. But as for my desire to catch up on the schedule, the freezer room proved a mixed blessing. It was a considerable hardship shooting in that temperature: cameras froze, so wasting time, and we needed to break every hour to give people a chance to warm up. This was adding to what was slowly becoming a considerably pressured unit.

The following week the Burbank night shoot began in earnest – three weeks of it. We couldn't roll until nightfall but Ridley's floor crew would arrive at least an hour before to set up the equipment and block out the first shots, walking the actors through their movements in the scene. Ridley, Katy, Ivor Powell and I would normally be in the studio from about 3 p.m., particularly in the early days when there were refinements still being made to the script and a million other details Ridley had to sign off.

Shooting start times varied a bit according to the weather, but if the skies were overcast we would gain another half-hour of 'night'. We needed every moment we could get, particularly to rehearse the crowds of extras we used in such scenes as the Sushi bar sequence. We provided some of the extras with illuminated umbrellas, ostensibly to shield themselves from the continuous rain and light their way through the cluttered streets but really, from a practical point of view, they were vital to cinematographer Jordan Cronenweth since the fluorescent neon handles allowed the camera to see the extras' faces, otherwise hidden in shadows. Our make-up chief Marvin Westmore had a department of at least three dozen to provide the variety of looks Ridley wanted. He was very tough about inspecting them all before shooting to make sure there was sufficient variation in hair, make-up and costumes to create the sense of a polyglot crowd.

Daybreak always signalled the end of our shooting. A couple of close shots might be snatched before the sun came up but usually by 5:30 everybody was on their way home. Flora, my Scottish terrier, who would spend the night snoozing in my trailer, would then hop into my car and we would drive west along Hollywood Boulevard, which would still have a smattering of exhausted looking street-walkers looking for a trick or two before they quit after a long hard night. I would grab a few hours' sleep and then the whole process began all over again.

Gradually I began to sense that an unhappy relationship was developing between star and director. In due course much would be said by others of this so-called 'schism' between Harrison and Ridley. A certain coldness did arise between them, but it must be said that this wasn't one-sided. Both men were under considerable pressure, from the physical difficulties of the shoot alone. Interminable nights, wet exteriors and stiflingly smoke-filled sets were all aggravations. Harrison could at least retire to his trailer while Ridley was preparing the next set-up, but that seemed only to afford him time to brood.

I have referred already to Ridley's method as a kind of pointillism: every pixel on Ridley's screen is painted in by him. This takes time and total concentration. So when the second assistant director would call Harrison onto the set for his next scene, it was as likely as not that Ridley would be thirty feet up in the air on a crane looking through the viewfinder and adjusting the last tiny details within the frame, leaving not much time to confer with his star.

Still, I truly believe that Ridley expected Harrison to know what to do without being coddled and directed down to the smallest aspect. Ridley did concentrate more on the performances of the supporting actors, because he considered this necessary, whereas in Ridley's eyes Harrison was a seasoned professional who had come off many big pictures made by big-name directors. Perhaps where Ridley got it wrong was that those same directors had usually spent a lot of time on Harrison, and he was accustomed to serious conversations with his directors, not only about the required action of the scene but about the character's interior thoughts. So, as the weeks wore on, the gap between Ridley and Harrison grew. Ridley felt that he had a Herculean task to get the picture right and no time for unnecessary chit-chat. He did try at one point to explain to Harrison that it was the high level of confidence he had in the actor that led him to entrust Harrison's performance largely to Harrison. The star probably didn't buy this, and continued to feel that he had been neglected. Sadly, neither Ridley nor Harrison found an opportunity during the shoot to reconcile the other's attitude. For twenty-four years Harrison chose to remain silent about his experience on *Blade Runner*, whether out of professional courtesy to Ridley, or perhaps because he didn't want to recall what for him was an unhappy experience. (Only in 2007, with the release of *Blade Runner: The Final Cut*, did Harrison speak out – contributing an interview to a documentary released with the DVD.)

Gossip and rumour abound in Hollywood and *Blade Runner* was certainly not immune to these insidious forces. The transformation of the familiar Warner 'New York' lot into the colossus of Ridleyville drew sightseers from all over the studio. People had heard that *Blade Runner* was an unusually tough shoot with a demanding director at the helm. I had a sign posted on the massive gate of the stage where we were shooting, specifically forbidding entry to anybody but crew members unless they had written authority. The last thing I as producer could risk was unauthorised photos of such an extraordinary-looking movie leaking to the press. Nowadays the greatest fear is of unauthorised Internet exposure.

My trailer, where all the phone calls and meetings took place, was parked seventy-five feet away from the stage entrance. One day I looked out of the window and saw a couple of people I didn't know opening the stage door. The red light wasn't on, which meant cameras weren't actually turning, though they might do so at any moment. I shouted out to the two people and ran out of my trailer to the stage door. One of them said, 'Hi, I'm a friend of Harrison's.' Politely I asked them to wait while I checked his availability.

On the edge of the set which was being relit for the next shot, Ridley and Harrison were in earnest conversation: this I was pleased to see, since Ridley was usually too busy for verbal conference. So I didn't interrupt them but went back out and told Harrison's friends that I would let them know as soon as he was available, and then returned to the stage. Ten minutes later Harrison and Ridley finished their conversation and I went back outside. But Harrison's friends had departed.

The following day Harrison said peevishly to me, 'Why did you insult Steven Spielberg?' At first I was puzzled, then realised that one of yesterday's visitors was vaguely familiar to me, although I had only met him briefly once in London. I told Harrison that Spielberg and friend were walking onto a closed set and that, whoever they were, they shouldn't do that. Moreover, it was a discourtesy for one director to go onto another's set except by permission or invitation. Harrison grumbled a bit but seemed to understand my point, although he possibly felt that the Prince of Hollywood merited the red-carpet treatment, even if it risked offending *Blade Runner*'s director. Spielberg had been one of the key contributors to Harrison's stardom and I'm sure was a close friend too – but that was beside the point. Obviously Spielberg had even then developed a very high opinion of himself and his importance, because being treated like a regular person, however politely, had annoyed him.

I had this much confirmed to me a while later, when I also realised that I had lost a valued old friendship. Calling his office one day, I couldn't get through to Quincy Jones and he didn't return my call, which was unusual. We had been friends since he had come to London with his wife and baby thirteen years earlier to write the music for *The Italian Job*. Not only did he produce a spectacular score but we spent a lot of time together and later I stayed at his house while visiting Hollywood. Assuming he was busy, I sent him a script I wanted him to look at. I heard nothing but finally collared him on the phone. His tone was uncharacteristically hostile and almost his first words were, 'Why did you insult my friend Steven Spielberg?' Whatever Spielberg had said to him was sufficiently heavy-hitting that my account of what actually happened didn't interest him and we didn't speak again. Quincy clearly knew upon which side his bread was buttered.

It was some years later before I woke up to a possible explanation for Spielberg's sensitivity. Our enormous science-fiction picture was released that same summer of 1982 as Spielberg's sci-fi opus *E.T.* It seems reasonable to imagine that Spielberg, through his personal relationship with Harrison, might have hoped to sneak onto the *Blade Runner* set to see what, if any, threat our picture might be to his. In the event *E.T.* was a completely different piece of work, with no relevance to *Blade Runner* and vice versa.

One of the more dangerous sequences that Ridley needed to capture was the foot chase through a traffic-jammed Ridleyville as Deckard pursues Zhora in his attempt to retire (*Blade Runner* lingo for 'kill') her. Having tracked Zhora to her place of work as an exotic dancer, Deckard has decided she may well be a replicant, but this is not a situation for the VK machine. He cannot arrest her without evidence. And his sneaky questioning is transparent enough to arouse the suspicion of a highly tuned 'Nexus 6'. Even though Zhora is naked with a seven-foot python on her shoulders, Deckard continues to question her: pretty suspicious behaviour if a man can ignore such a body as Joanna Cassidy's.

The joy of this scene is that both artists are very athletic – Joanna especially. From the moment Zhora lashes out and sends Deckard crashing to the floor, this is a serious hell-for-leather foot chase. By the time Deckard struggles to his feet, Zhora has donned a see-through plastic raincoat and is halfway down the traffic-choked street, wriggling between the cars, seeking to hide in the teeming crowd. Deckard jumps onto the roof of a car and skids across half a dozen other vehicles, attempting to cut her off. I should say that having to watch your million-dollar movie star, upon whom the entire production depends, performing a dangerous stunt is one of the nastier aspects of being a producer. Had Harrison slipped and broken a leg, or worse, the insurance company might well have refused payment on the grounds that allowing an actor to do something so dangerous was prohibited under the insurance contract. Harrison pooh-poohed this concern and went ahead, doing, as usual, his own stunts. I admired this devotion to duty; it was pleasing evidence of Harrison's commitment that he was prepared to take risks. Then again, I had to smile ruefully when the production manager, John Rogers, told me that Harrison had put in an invoice for services rendered as a stuntman. We paid him this modest sum without comment and I hope he enjoyed his little windfall.

The stunt coordinator on *Blade Runner*, Gary Combs, is a fine person and a very experienced stuntman. I had worked with him a few years before on *Convoy*, when he had patiently endured the vagaries of a Peckinpah film. Stuntmen have to be meticulous, calculating the risks and building in any fail-safe devices they can hide off screen. A stuntman falling off a roof knows just how many cardboard boxes he has to go through to break his fall. In Gary's case, doubling for Pris's somersault attack on Deckard was not a dangerous stunt but did require great athletic ability, as well as willingness to wear revealing female clothing. More seriously, parts of Zhora's terrifying run through the plate-glass windows had to be performed by stuntwoman Lee Pulford, who walked away from a very dangerous scene with minor cuts.

Soon it wasn't only Ridley who found himself scribbled off Harrison Ford's Christmas-card list. Almost from the start of shooting, Sean Young was trying the patience of the star and vice versa.

Ridley had a deeper sense of the material than Harrison, and he cast Sean Young as a replicant not merely because she was another pretty ingénue. Of course a replicant female would be beautiful: such would be the natural instinct of a male creator like Tyrell. But Sean had a special withdrawn quality, a vulnerability that was not unworldly.

I know Sean disliked Harrison because he showed her no respect, making life hard for a young actress appearing in only her third feature film. I never found out why Harrison felt the way he did: perhaps it was her youth and inexperience that irked him. He managed to put up with Julia Ormond on the ill-fated remake of *Sabrina* (a task I would consider from personal experience to be considerable), so dealing with Sean ought not to have been too hard. After all, he wasn't James Woods . . .

But disconcerting evidence of the schism between the star and his leading lady was all too clear in the one 'love scene' between them. This famous scene (in which Deckard seems to force Rachael both physically and verbally to respond to his advances) does have a strong element of sexual excitement, because we witness a struggle between attraction and revulsion. The Blade Runner is attracted to this beautiful woman who should be his prey: he is about to make love to an arch-enemy, and seen in this light the conflicted Deckard's violence makes absolute sense. What, though, of the feelings attributable to the sensitive female replicant? Feminist film critics would have much to say on this matter in due course. And as for the two performers enacting the controversial scene, those of us who witnessed it being shot (and it was longer and more erotic in an earlier cut) were uncomfortably conscious that there was too much personal truth in this violent encounter.

By the end of May we were two-thirds of the way through our schedule. The entire crew were tired, beginning to resent the tough days and Ridley's meticulous expectations. Scenes could run up to fifteen or more takes, which wasn't unreasonable for a picture of *Blade Runner*'s complexity, but it was something that many actors and technicians were no longer accustomed to in 1981. The volume of television films and series being shot on tight budgets, often with simple themes, had accustomed people to two, three, four takes maximum. One of our financiers, Bud Yorkin, certainly couldn't come to terms with Ridley's 'extravagant' number of takes. Then again, Yorkin had never worked on a picture of this complexity, and this was true of some of the crew members too. Yorkin would probably have preferred Ridley just to print the first take – which I suspect was Bud's own practice when he was directing. In the end, though, Ridley's insistence on precision is one of the reasons that *Blade Runner* looks so great a quarter of a century later.

It was becoming clear that there were other prices to be paid besides money. Actors and crew members were ragged and quick-tempered. Ridley might come on a set which had taken thirty-six non-stop hours to build and it might not be exactly what he wanted. Ridley never gave up on the standard of detail he demanded: he just wouldn't settle for less. Some crew members began to regard Ridley as unreasonable, because no other director in their recent experience had cracked the whip as unremittingly.

Ridley had to cope with the increasing distance between Harrison Ford and himself, while I was receiving daily complaints from some of the more hard-pressed departments. I would always try to be soothing: 'Only another couple of weeks . . .' or 'I agree, it's hard work, but you're doing a great job . . .' But they knew that

Ridley, Katy, Ivor, and I were unquestionably on the same team. It certainly didn't help that we were four British aliens in a sea of Americans, some of whom probably thought their civil rights were being abused. A fact overlooked by the complainants was that Ridley was getting less sleep than anybody. He had rushes to see, he had the next night's work to plan – and that wasn't just planning the shooting but covering every department's contribution to the sets. That supervisory role was one of the main areas of conflict: Ridley's view of 'ready to shoot' was different from everybody else's. Some people just couldn't accept his perfectionism, and they didn't last long. One or two people from the art department didn't get past the first week of shooting.

As the end of June approached, tension on the set reached boiling point – further aggravated by the fact that the Directors Guild strike scheduled for 1 July still looked likely. If it wasn't settled, we would have to break off the shoot and reconvene some time later to shoot the final scenes between Deckard and Batty. Then something happened which, although maliciously intended, perhaps did perform the service of blowing off a little steam.

Ridley had given an interview to a UK journalist from the *Guardian*. Asked to compare working in England on *Alien* with his current experience on his first big American picture, Ridley said that he felt handicapped by the US union's refusal to let him operate the camera himself, as he had always done in the past. The British union deals elegantly with the problem by permitting a director to operate provided he is paying an operator to stand by, thus not depriving a technician of his livelihood. Ridley, when asked which crew he preferred, diplomatically responded to the British reporter that he favoured the British model. It was perhaps a little guilelessly that he went on to say that he got a better response from British technicians: 'Yes, Guv' would be the stock reply, and he would get what he needed.

A copy of this interview was in Ridley's trailer but somebody stole it, though nobody had the guts to own up. The next morning copies had been left in a pile next to the coffee machine for every-one's enjoyment. One of the department heads, who should have known better, had his illiterate revenge: he had made sixty T-shirts, emblazoned on the front with '"Yes, Guv" – MY ASS' and, on the back of some of them, 'You soar with eagles when you fly with turkeys' – a sentence which didn't offend us because we had no idea what it meant. Other versions had on the back 'Will Rogers never met Ridley Scott'. When Ridley discreetly asked Katy what this meant, she was obliged to tell him that it was Will Rogers who coined the phrase, 'I never met a man I didn't like.'

These shirts appeared on the backs of certain crew members towards the end of the day. Ridley simply smiled and carried on as usual. Next morning Ridley, Katy and I appeared on the set wear-ing our own T-shirts, stating in bold letters: 'Xenophobia Sucks' (which probably sent the designer of the 'Yes, Guv' shirts scurrying off to a dictionary, if indeed he owned one).

In the end the incident didn't prove harmful. A degree of ten-sion was relieved. These were mutterings rather than full-scale mutiny, and we responded moderately and without anger. People today are proud to have worked on *Blade Runner*, and could hardly have assumed during production that they were at work on what would prove to be a durable masterpiece.

The long chase sequence between Deckard and Batty was the last and probably hardest sequence of the entire movie – particularly for Harrison Ford, who was required to fall off rooftops and be knocked about while Rutger Hauer enjoyed the physically easier task of strolling through the sequence, taunting Deckard as he tries to escape. We had planned originally to shoot this sequence on location in Los Angeles, but though the interior scenes might have been managed, to get the full proportions of height would have been impossibly dangerous, particularly with Harrison doing his own stunts. He insisted on doing all jumps other than his final failed leap between two buildings, where he saves his own neck only by grabbing on to a projecting piece of metal. This trick was engineered by Gary Combs. To pull off the scenes on the rooftop and on the side of the building as Deckard clings on for dear life, the art department constructed a huge twenty-five-foot mobile set. It could be turned and even pushed into a stage if weather or light considerations hampered shooting.

Another tower, some thirty feet high, acted as the camera plat-form, though sometimes Ridley used a crane from which to shoot. These elaborate and innovative devices pretty much eliminated all the hazards location shooting might have created. We were still on the backlot with all the amenities Warner Brothers offered.

The threatened Directors Guild strike was averted, but we were behind schedule with still another ten days needed to finish. Naturally the completion guarantors were anxious and ominous mutterings were coming from the financier's office.

The interior chase scenes were completed in the few days after the T-shirt War. Mercifully, we were shooting by day up until the 4 July holiday. Perenchio and Yorkin understandably hated the fact they we were spending the money they had pledged as guarantors of completion, and they had been sending daily threats to fire the entire unit and have another director knock off an ending to the film. This pressure had already affected the work but there was no way this film could be finished without the final scene between the two principals. Rutger was devoted to Ridley, sensing how power-ful his performance was becoming. I think he would have refused to work with any jobbing director if Ridley was kicked off. But the threat had to be considered.

The last two days of shooting were as nightmarish as you would expect, given the atmosphere. Ridley had to shoot the moment when Deckard's fingers give out and the hero starts to plunge six hundred feet to his death. For this, Harrison was hanging on to the side of our rolling roof, held in place with a line around his waist and an air bag below him in case the line snapped. The physical effort required of an actor in his forties at the end of a long and arduous shoot is huge, but Harrison was stalwart and professional to the end. Secretly I thought to myself, *He would do anything to get off this picture . . .*

The last night was the toughest for the crew. Many of us had been up for thirty-six hours straight and there was still a ton of work to be done, particularly Rutger's death scene. Everybody was scurrying about, desperate to finish before dawn, but when the second assistant went to call Rutger, the actor asked to speak with Ridley. Our director, though, didn't necessarily have time to climb all the way down the ladder from his shooting platform just because Rutger had come up with a piece of dialogue which had not been mentioned before. Ordinarily, this is the last thing a director wants to think about when he is in a hurry. But Rutger had offered a lot of ideas and many of them were extremely good, so Ridley wisely paid him this courtesy. In fact, Rutger had rewritten his closing lines. Much of the final soliloquy was as written by David Peoples. One telling line ('I've seen things you people wouldn't believe . . .') was reapportioned from an earlier draft where Batty had thrown it at Chew. But Rutger had a special image in mind to end as a valediction. As Batty walks through the derelict building he picks up a roosting dove, and it is this dove he cradles in his hand as he utters his final words:

> 'I've seen things you people wouldn't believe. Attack ships on fire off the shoulder of Orion. I watched c-beams glitter in the dark near the Tannhauser Gate. All those . . . moments will be lost . . . in time. Like . . . tears . . . in rain. Time . . . to die.'

As Rutger's head fell forward in death his hand opened to release the dove, whom we confidently expected to take flight. There weren't many laughs in the making of *Blade Runner*, and yet this solemn moment unexpectedly proved to be one of them. The dove, looking slightly surprised, paused and then hopped out of Rutger's hand and toddled away. What none of us had realised was that doves won't fly in the rain – and we sure had rain that night, the same as every other night. We didn't have time to find a dry pigeon, so the necessary insert was shot later, rather inadequately, in England.

Otherwise, the night was passing fast. As Gaff's spinner rose into frame behind Batty's body the sky was beginning to turn blue. We still had several hours to shoot – for example, we needed Harrison's close-ups as he watches Rutger die. We rolled the roof set into a sound stage and re-dressed it and went on shooting. Harrison's face wore a wonderful world-weary expression that was truly moving – in fact, he was exhausted, barely able to stay awake. We finally wrapped at 1 p.m. on 9 July – the longest night shoot any of us had ever done.

My last job that day was to issue instructions that all the 'retro-fitting' to the New York street set should be destroyed immediately after we had checked the final rushes to make sure that nothing had to be reshot. Not only was I contracted to restore the Warner Brothers backlot to the state in which we found it, we also didn't want anybody else shooting anything in Ridleyville. We further destroyed the specially built cars and spinners so that they wouldn't show up in other movies or TV shows ahead of *Blade Runner*'s release. We did preserve two full-scale spinners and two Deckard sedans for promotional purposes, although I don't know what finally became of them. (They were scheduled to be destroyed in due course, and until one of them turns up for sale on eBay I have to assume they met their fate.)

My Scottish terrier, Flora, and I drove home in broad daylight – for a change. The work wasn't over, we still had a mass of special-effects shots to finish, but now it was completely in the hands of Ridley in the cutting rooms. I imagined it ought to be smooth sailing through a long but vital post-production process until the film was ready for its release in a year's time. But, in typical *Blade Runner* fashion, a nasty surprise lay lurking in the wings for Ridley and me.

18

Blade Runner – Waiting for Vangelis

All film productions involve risk and risk requires insurance. Obviously third-party liability cover is required, as with any other business, but because films involve stunts, car chases and other more or less dangerous activities the risk is somewhat greater, and so is the insurance premium. In addition the entire crew is insured against accident, and key personnel – the director, principal actors – are heavily insured, since the death or incapacitation of one of these crucially important people certainly would cause serious delay, or even abandonment of a film in mid-course.

Among the most significant forms on insurance on a picture is the completion bond. This, simply put, is a policy that provides for an insurance company to pay the cost of shooting a film if it goes sufficiently over the intended budget. Take a picture budgeted at $20 million. A contingency is added of ten per cent ($2 million), which is not allocated to any particular part of the budget but is used as an emergency fund – a cushion to cover the many unforeseen events that might occur. The completion bond has always been used in Britain, where films have historically been financed by more than one investor – often by means of a letter of credit against which a bank would lend money to a producer. If the film were not finished the letter of credit would not kick in and the bank would be out of pocket to the extent of their loan to the producer. So banks insist on a guarantee of completion from a reputable specialist insurer.

In the case of *Blade Runner*, there were initially two financiers:

Sir Run Run Shaw and Alan Ladd Jr with Warner Brothers. Each of these financiers paid a fixed amount with no responsibility for overruns on the cost. Each delivered a letter of credit which, when borrowed against, created the demand for a guarantee that whatever happened on the movie they would get delivery.

The third financier to come aboard *Blade Runner* was Tandem Productions – Jerry Perenchio and Bud Yorkin, who contributed cash and also provided a completion bond to the satisfaction of the other financiers. They could quite easily have laid off this obligation to one of the many experienced professional completion bond underwriters but they chose not to, preferring to take the risk, and the completion bond fee – at three per cent of the budget, some $700,000 – themselves. Later, when *Blade Runner* went over budget as so many films do, Tandem must have bitterly regretted their decision.

The guarantor of completion does have some power to limit the overage. Once a picture is ten per cent over its budget, including the contingency, the completion bond holder can take over control of the production. Obviously, in the process attempts will be made to cut corners to reduce the payout. The bond holder will definitely handle the chequebook, and may even fire the director and/or producer to replace them with faster and perhaps less talented substitutes. Sometimes the very threat of such action is sufficient to encourage the financiers to put up more money rather than risk their picture being ruined by a hack whose only ability is to knock off scenes quickly. Imagine firing Ridley Scott in the middle of *Blade Runner*! No director in the world could replace him. Tellingly, the powerful Directors Guild of America also severely discourages its members from taking over another director's work in such circumstances, and no reputable director would have anything to do with such a situation.

So here is *Blade Runner* finishing its marathon shoot on 9 July 1981. Principal photography is over but there is still a year's work to do – special and optical effects, editing, insert shots, music, the whole post-production process. What do Perenchio and Yorkin do? They instruct their lawyers on 11 July to deliver to Ridley and me a notice that they are taking over the picture under the terms of the completion bond agreement. In other words, we were fired.

Tandem's takeover had no practical effect: nobody but Ridley could oversee the rest of the work that had to be done and Yorkin had been hanging around the production on and off since it had started – as was his right – so what was different? The formal letter had been written and we had been notified, but obviously our services were still required. We had come this far and weren't going to abandon our picture. Ridley and I figured that the letter of notice was a manifestation of frustration. Had Ridley taken it seriously and quit, Tandem would have had a lot more to worry about than their investment.

Ridley went off to London to spend a few days shooting inserts – like the famous white dove which had been too wet to fly on the last night of shooting. While he was away there was a rather impertinent visit to our cutting rooms by one of the Tandem executives. Editor Terry Rawlings is a respected figure in his field and, as one would expect, he was completely loyal to his director, appalled at any suggestion that the film now be recut by Tandem. Rawlings procrastinated in a technical way until either the Tandem person was reminded of the Directors Guild of America regulations or he was warned off by wiser heads at Warner Brothers or in Alan Ladd Jr's company. The director has the absolute right under guild regulations to cut the film as he wishes without any outside interference until a certain amount of time has elapsed. Since the inserts were still being shot and special effects wouldn't be complete until 19 December, the clock hadn't even started on Ridley's right to the first cut.

Blade Runner, as far as special effects are concerned, would be a very different movie if it had been shot at any time after the millennium. Computer-generated images are now the norm. CGI can create huge crowds – look at Ridley's *Gladiator* (2000) and all the current mega pictures ranging from *Spider-Man* (2002) to *Troy* (2004). These techniques did not exist in 1982 and Ridley's visual imagination had to be brought to the screen in a different way. I had spoken to George Lucas's company, Industrial Light and Magic, but in the end we decided to put together our own team drawn from the best proven talents in Hollywood.

The names are legendary – Douglas Trumball, Dick Yuricich and David Dryer headed our team. Stimulated by Ridley's exciting ideas, their first costing for special effects was over $5 million – which we certainly didn't have. Some compromises were made, some shots cut, and we ended up with a budget nearer $2 million, which was already a great deal more than we would have spent if we had shot Hampton's first draft which didn't explore the world outside Deckard's window.

Although Trumball's crew was now working flat out embellishing *Blade Runner* with a host of optical, visual and special effects, they had in fact been preparing for this task since August 1980, seven months before the cameras had even turned a foot of film. The team used matte paintings, hundreds of miniatures and sophisticated optical effects to turn into substance Ridley's vision. It must be said that one of the most impressive sequences is the opening shot of the picture, when we are presented with a colossal metropolis. This panoramic shot of fire belching from oil refineries and factory smokestacks in a dystopian overgrowth perfectly seduces the audience into Ridley's vision of LA circa 2019, and it showcases the brilliance of Trumball and his team.

I have to admit that special effects is the technical area in which I am least versed. From time to time I would drive down to Maxella, Trumball's studio, and stare goggled-eyed at the proceedings – individual bits which would mean nothing until half a dozen or more shots were layered with minute precision one atop the other. What Ridley didn't know about the process, which wasn't much, he seemed to pick up very quickly. After months of working with him the confidence I already had increased every day.

Blade Runner is, in retrospect, the first picture of its kind to rely so heavily on effects to enhance the quality of the film. The movie emerged at the dawn of this new and exciting medium which has become part and parcel of most action-adventure Hollywood productions. None of *Blade Runner*'s effects have dated, but the same challenge today would be considered much less daunting. Many of the ideas which were incorporated into *Blade Runner*'s effects had never been achieved before, although on some occasions money was spent on an experimental shot which might not even come off. The movie was highly innovative and represented an important moment in the evolution of special effects.

Ridley went into the cutting rooms with Terry Rawlings to put together his director's cut. A few scenes were dropped and some moved out of script order with a view to clarifying the narrative. A hectic weekend was spent at Elstree Studios near London doing a rough dub of the picture – re-recording dialogue and sound effects with a borrowed music track because *Blade Runner*'s composer Vangelis hadn't delivered his music yet.

On 15 September 1981 we screened the working print for Tandem – their first exposure to the assembled film. Perenchio and Yorkin loathed it. Their comments included the words 'dull' and 'pointless'. They also found it confusing and asked us to put a voiceover commentary to explain things to the audience.

By December, the cut was much more refined and Ridley and I were able to show it to Vangelis – the talented but idiosyncratic composer whose score for *Chariots of Fire* (1981) was, in the opinion of many, the reason it won a Best Picture Oscar. Evangelos O. Papathanassiou, brought up in Athens, taught himself music and played in a Greek rock group until moving to Paris where he had a band with Demis Roussos, a singer popular throughout Europe. By the time he started scoring for movies, he had developed a considerable talent as a keyboard player and was soon into synthesised music.

Vangelis is literally a one-man band. He writes the score and records it himself, instrument by instrument, layering one sound upon the other to create his highly original music. The problem is that this meticulous process (to some degree a parallel to Ridley's directing style) can take a very long time. An orchestral score for a film can be recorded in days and then dropped into a work print in its predetermined locations. Not so with Vangelis.

We signed him up in December and didn't get the finished music until April. After a few weeks with no action from the composer I was beginning to get the feeling that he was either too busy finishing up other jobs or couldn't make up his mind how to treat the music for *Blade Runner*. The picture was a far cry from his last great success on *Chariots*. His mellifluous score for that film was quite different from the discordant feeling of our metropolis. Ridley's choice of this composer was perfect but the length of time the music took was a cause for anxiety.

Meanwhile, the screening of 15 September had thrown up suggestions for a number of improvements and finishing touches which Ridley felt would make a significant difference to the picture. I wrote to Tandem with half a dozen requests for additional shots varying from an inexpensive view from the top of a New York skyscraper to add to Deckard's jeopardy when he is holding on for dear life at the end of the picture, to a scene showing Zhora's night-club dance, which would have been expensive. Tandem turned down all these requests. They might have been in agreement that these ideas could improve the picture but the suggestions added up to further expenditure approaching $500,000, and they had spent enough.

At the end of January we screened the latest cut for Bud Yorkin and Robin French, an experienced television executive who had joined Tandem. The reaction was even worse than that to our first screening: their response this time included condemnation of Harrison Ford's voiceover, which we had recorded against our own instincts and at their request. They described Harrison as sounding 'drugged', which was impertinent, although, in truth, Harrison hated the idea of a voiceover, just as Ridley did, and his lack of enthusiasm may have affected his performance. One of the Tandems – whether it was Yorkin or Perenchio I cannot recall – came up with a classic line: 'This movie gets worse with every screening.' But apart from some inserts, the biggest difference since the first screening was the Tandem voiceover.

Warner Brothers were cranking up publicity for the picture and as early as January 1982 the first trailer went into theatres. A general obsession in Hollywood is the search for an 'event movie'. The auteur school of directorship as practised by Coppola, Bogdanovich, Scorsese et al. was showing signs of decline, perhaps due to the catastrophe Michael Cimino had caused with *Heaven's Gate*. The industry was now hooked on finding the next *Star Wars* or the next *Jaws*. These pictures needed to have size and be action-packed with effects and big set pieces. *Raiders of the Lost Ark* had been the summer blockbuster of 1981 and with the summer of 1982 now approaching Warners was hoping that *Blade Runner* would be the next 'event'. It certainly had size; moreover, it had the hottest star in Hollywood above the title.

This promotion seemed very early, since the film wouldn't be released for at least six months. Even the sneak previews weren't yet scheduled. Sneaks are a time-honoured device which Hollywood regards as serious research. It is true that no original film can be fully judged before the audience gets its hands on it. Film critics' opinions vary wildly, and studio executives are no more unanimous about the future prospects of an unreleased film. Previews are intended to cut through some of the uncertainty, helping filmmakers to spot the *longueurs* in their dramas.

There was certainly an ambivalence about *Blade Runner*'s prospects, and it was hoped that sneak previews would feed back valuable information. Because the film was unique, there were no

TANDEM PRODUCTIONS INC.

BLADE RUNNER

1901 Avenue of the Stars
Suite 666
Los Angeles, CA 90067
Telephone (213) 553-3600
TWX: TANDEM · TAT · LSA

Jerry Perenchio + Bud Yorkin Note.

SCREENING NOTES JANUARY 21st 1981

1982!

J.P.	1.	"Where's the Vangelis music ?"
	2.	Opening too choppy. Voice over dry and monotone.
J.P.	3.	"This voice over is terrible, the audience will fall aslepp".
B.Y	4.	"We need the line about the 100 questions" (Rachael interrogation).
B.Y.	5.	Leon flashback dialogue confusing. "Is he listening to a tape?"
B.Y.	6.	"I thought we decided to lose the stick figures".
J.P.	7.	"This movie gets worse every screening".
J.P.	8.	"Why is this voice over track so terrible, hopefully this is not being dubbed in. He sounds drugged, were they all on drugs when they did this?".
B.Y	9.	Too many shots of Pris getting into Sebastian's building.
J.P.	10.	This picture gets duller every time we see it... it can't just be that it is black and white and undubbed (I tried to explain!)
J.P/BY	11.	Deckard at the piano is interminable.
R.F	12.	The synagogue music is awful on the street, we must use Vangelis.
B.Y	13.	Why did they put in more slow motion in Zhora's death ?
.A.L	14.	They have put back more tits into the Zhora dressing room scene.
A.L.	15.	We still don't go back to Rachael fast enough, therefore Leon death doesn't work.
B.Y	16.	"Deckard/Rachael in the apartment is far too long enough". (I explained that you put it back the way it was because J.P felt there was not enough emotion)..."Yes, we know, but now it's too long !" (This is Deckard washing his face, getting changed, her walk to the bedroom, the glass in hand etc).
B.Y	17.	"Why do we need the third cut to the eggs (Seb,Batty, Pris). They liked the addition at the front of the scene.
B.Y	18.	"Is he good, your opponent" This is confusing!
J.P.	19.	"Deckard takes forever to come into the building" (Robin told him that with music this would be OK!)
A.L.	20.	Second shot of the nail should be out, and Pris death too long.
J.P.	21.	Pris' tongue is sticking out in the wide shot after Batty has kissed her.

GENERAL COMMENTS.

Up to Zhora's death the picture is deadly dull.

Voice over is an insult.

Stub dub now and bring the picture over with Terry and have LADD/TANDEM pool their notes and have Bud cut the picture. This was vetoed due to the amount of film that would have to be brought over.

Alternative Bud and Robin go to London and cut the picture with just Terry.

Ridley and crew have had three cuts and still have not done what was agreed now they should do it themselves.

These January 1982 screening notes from the Tandem team of Bud Yorkin and Jerry Perenchio indicate clearly their dissatisfaction with the state *Blade Runner* was in, even as the movie's first trailers were playing in theatres.

comparisons available: we had to go to the public to get a reaction. Sneaks tend to be held as distant from Hollywood as practical. There is no point in having a theatre full of film-industry insiders who have already heard whatever local gossip has circulated, and on *Blade Runner* there had been plenty of that. Generally distributors like to go to a substantial city with a good-sized college-student population, because undergraduates are thought to typify younger cinemagoers. Moreover, they are presumed to have sufficient education to fill out legibly and intelligently the questionnaire cards which are distributed at the end of the show.

Warners and Alan Ladd Jr selected Denver for a *Blade Runner* sneak on Friday 5 March 1982. Whichever film was due to screen at eight o'clock that night got bumped for a showing that was advertised locally as a Harrison Ford thriller from the director of *Alien.* The presentation was pretty rough. The last two reels were missing and, of course, Vangelis's music was still being created. Even so there were some favourable responses. I don't see how the audiences could have understood what was going on, but an astonishing forty-four per cent found the picture 'Excellent' or 'Extremely good'.

I had sat at the back of the theatre with Alan Ladd Jr having a secret chuckle, remembering the famous story of the preview in 1977 of *Rolling Thunder* which had been produced by Larry Gordon for 20th Century Fox when Laddie was president. This picture contained an infamous scene of a gang of robbers trying to steal a hoard of silver, invading William Devane's house and killing his wife and family – which was bad enough. Then one of the crooks grabbed Devane's arm and thrust his hand into a waste disposal unit. The gout of blood and crunching fingers, coming so soon after the brutal murders, was too much for the audience. Seconds later, Laddie and his venerable deputy, Jay Kanter, were to be seen fleeing down San Jose's main street pursued by a raging mob. For *Blade Runner* Ridley had shot a similarly graphic scene of Batty crushing an unsettlingly lifelike model of Tyrell's head. Thank God we cut this shot – I wanted to be in one piece when I left Denver and I'm sure Laddie did too.

The next day Ridley, Katy and I went on Warners' Gulf Stream jet to Dallas for the second sneak. The cinema was packed, though I was worried by the general youth of much of the audience, which had probably been expecting *Raiders of the Lost Ark 2* in response to the local press ads. Reaction to *Blade Runner*'s glorious cityscape opening was rapturous. But as the action proceeded the mood of the audience grew darker and darker. Many among them seemed depressed, and later commented negatively on the pessimism and confusion in the film's narrative. It was a disheartening event. The response cards majored on the difficulty of following the story, and some complained about the violence of Tyrell's murder. A frequently asked question was: 'Why was the world so grim with constant rain?' We thought that by signalling 2019 we were stating as flatly as possible that this was a prophecy of where the world was heading if it did not clean up its environmental act. But now we were panicking – all of us, not merely Tandem as usual, but Ridley and me too. It was bad enough that we had gone over budget, but now we were looking at a nearly finished work which, though beautiful, was clearly 'difficult' for its first audiences.

With twenty years of hindsight I can see that *Blade Runner* was initially problematic as a big sci-fi film just because of where the action took place. *Star Wars*, *2001: A Space Odyssey* and *Alien* were set in outer space, a clearly defined and readily identifiable convention. *Blade Runner* unfolded in Los Angeles, a city we know but cannot recognise without projecting ourselves forty years into the future.

In spite of the stunned silence that concluded the Dallas sneak, the figures weren't terrible – forty-two per cent were 'Excellent' or 'Extremely good' – but this was not enough to ensure success for a picture as expensive as *Blade Runner*. We certainly could not go back to the drawing board, but we had to come up with some good ideas as quickly as possible if this grand production wasn't to prove a costly flop.

★ ★ ★

Among half the preview audiences the most solid 'negative' cited was confusion. Filmmakers who have spent anything from three months to three years grappling with a physical production usually have done so with a pretty complete knowledge of the story and its nuances. After all, they have read the script, the director has told them what they are doing and the actors have done what the script has told them to do. The difference with *Blade Runner* was that it was to some degree a work in progress. The transition from Hampton Fancher's script to the harder, less romantic style of David Peoples took place over quite a short period, and when shooting started Ridley had not yet entirely settled his own vision. Certain half-formed or half-expressed concepts such as the point (if you will excuse the pun) of a briefly seen unicorn and the issue of Deckard's identity – is he human or is he a replicant? – weren't fully explored before Ridley's 'Director's Cut' was created for release a decade later. Perhaps shooting the picture before these ambiguities were resolved in the script added a level of confusion. In any event we weren't about to go back and reshoot; moreover Ridley had made us all aware of his contempt for 'Irving the Explainer' – the sort of character gratuitously wheeled into a movie to offer verbal prompts and exposition for a half-asleep audience.

So now the great controversy – voiceover! – reared its ugly head again. There had been voiceover in the script from day one. Hampton's *Dangerous Days* included voiceover and so did David Peoples' draft. The atmosphere of the 1940s noir detective movie had always been hovering over the project, and voiceover is a time-honoured device of that genre. But Ridley had wanted it for its atmospheric contribution – not as a stopgap to cover structural or story defects.

Ridley and I were in London with Terry Rawlings for re-recording after the sneak previews when we received a note to the effect that a friend of Yorkin's, a television writer, had produced a new voiceover that Harrison was to record under

Yorkin's direction. Another writer, Roland Kibbee, was also involved in this Yorkin narration. A lot of narration was attempted and written by various people but the final work was knocked out in a rather amateurish way by Ridley, Ivor Powell, Katy and me in a bar one night. It was what you might call a 'collaborative effort'. We just worked it out between us, trying to cover the holes in the story.

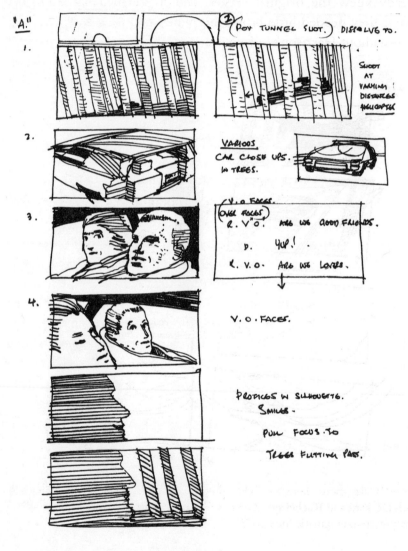

Two of the aspects of *Blade Runner* which are still argued over to this day are the voiceover and the 'happy ending'. The voiceover was occasioned by the audience's response to the sneaks: when those previews said 'Confused', we had to do something about it. When Ridley's 'Director's Cut' came out in 1992 many reviewers said (I paraphrase), 'Gosh, this is terrific. We didn't need that awful explanatory voiceover.' But these were the views of people who already knew the original version and its detailed narration: of course they needed little prompting when revisiting the material, even without Harrison's voiceover.

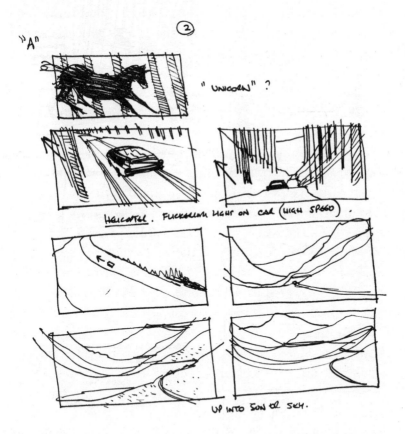

More 'Ridleygrams': here, a storyboarding of a possible *Blade Runner* ending, with Deckard and Rachel speeding out into the countryside by car, and a glimpse of an enigmatic 'unicorn'?

The 'happy ending' issue is more muddled, perhaps because of the sea change the script went through. *Dangerous Days* was essentially a romantic picture, never mind its darker side. Ridley's *Blade Runner* was much bleaker, and this metamorphosis didn't happen overnight. The addition of David Peoples' style was the first 'hardening' of the story and Ridley seized upon this evolution keenly. As the conclusion of shooting had approached it was clear that a harder-edged ending was appropriate. Apart from anything else, we had run out of money and Ridley was very keen to finish the film on the ambiguous note of the elevator doors closing on Deckard and Rachael with Gaff's enigmatic line over: 'It's too bad she won't live. But then again, who does?' This was a late contribution from Hampton Fancher, whom we had summoned to look at some dailies, and it was to remind the audience that Rachael is a replicant – and that Deckard might be too. However, after the Denver and Dallas previews, with the hounds of panic snapping at our heels, Ridley and I easily persuaded ourselves that something joyous had to be found. Of course, we were wrong: we weren't making *It's a Wonderful Life*. Our special-effects people did conceive a rather gorgeous and costly happy ending, but 'costly' was a word no longer on Tandem or Brighton Productions' approved list.

Then Ivor Powell had a canny idea and he suggested to us that we call Stanley Kubrick to ask if Ridley could borrow a short piece of film from *The Shining* (1980). This rare courtesy from one director to another provided us with the footage that depicted Deckard and Rachael driving through an extraordinary landscape toward their happy future together. One day of shooting in northern California with Harrison Ford and Sean Young provided sufficient close shots to splice into Kubrick's footage. Terry Rawlings, back in the cutting rooms, came up with an ingenious way of reformatting the yellow Volkswagen which appeared in *The Shining* so that it looked like some completely futuristic vehicle. *The Shining* had been paid for by Warner Brothers, who gave Stanley Kubrick an unprecedented amount of financial and creative freedom. No money passed between Brighton Films and Warner Brothers for this material, which was achieved by a mere wave of Kubrick's hand. He did, quite reasonably, require only that no material be used if it had appeared in the final version of *The Shining*.

In May 1982 the third preview took place in San Diego. It seems that the studios' later previews always take place nearer to Hollywood, because it's less expensive to set up and limos rather than jet planes can ship the glitterati to the event. Once again the theatre was full and once again there was a conflicting mix of serious film buffs and young girls who thought they were seeing a *Star Wars* film – a reaction confirmed when Harrison came into the theatre and was ecstatically cheered. Alan Ladd Jr was representing our US distributors. On the whole, the audience reaction cards were much more upbeat than those we had received in the two previous previews. Perhaps the voiceover had broken the curse?

The changes since the San Diego sneak had been modest. Now the most pressing decision was exactly when Warner Brothers should release *Blade Runner*. That summer there was a spate of movies opening that might conflict with it. Paramount had *Star Trek II: The Wrath of Khan*, Universal was releasing *Conan the Barbarian* and John Carpenter's remake of *The Thing*. But my biggest concern was *E.T.*

Distributors have different views about the perfect release date for a picture. Obviously it's unlikely that a picture called *Father Christmas* will be released in July, but the summer has historically been the time to open each studio's biggest product. In the US, school is out and air-conditioned theatres are a very pleasant place to be. Big-money pictures therefore tend to play summer and awards prospects go for a late-year release. *Blade Runner* probably would have been better qualified as a serious Oscar-attractive project – distancing itself from the hoi polloi of *Conan the Barbarian*, *E.T.* and other young people's fare.

But we thought we had a formula. We would give *E.T.* as much as six weeks of exposure before releasing *Blade Runner*. Our woefully misjudged presumption was that after a few weeks of this sentimental movie, young and mature audiences would be ready for something harder. *E.T.* was charming and relatively lightweight but, as we failed to realise, this was the essence of its appeal.

Almost a decade after Hampton Fancher first tried to visualise Philip K. Dick's novel, its cinematic manifestation opened in 1,300 theatres across the USA. The date was 25 June 1982. We picked up a reasonable opening weekend, exceeding $6 million, but we weren't making any headway outside the intelligent hardcore sci-fi cognoscenti. The critics didn't know what to make of *Blade Runner*. It showed an amazing vision of the near future that had

bud yorkin

March 9, 1981

Dear Michael:

I know that we are embarking upon a project that you have worked a long time on and that it is going to be everything you have dreamed of. You have my best thoughts all the way.

Regards,

/d

Mr. Michael Deeley
The Blade Runner
Burbank, Ca.

Bud Yorkin's good wishes to me at the outset of our shared *Blade Runner* adventure in March 1981 . . .

never before been seen on screen. It was sci-fi but it didn't obey the traditional sci-fi rules and this baffled many reviewers. The people who made *Blade Runner* – writers, director, production team – didn't even see the picture as sci-fi: we saw it as future history. We seriously believed that we were making a picture about what life could be like forty years hence. We believed Syd Mead's picture of our world a few years forward. We believed Philip Dick's theories, and Fancher and Peoples' interpretation. Most of all, we believed in Ridley's vision of how the world would look.

The critics' ambivalent bafflement, combined with robust competition, assured *Blade Runner* only a modest financial success. Had the picture's substantial budget not itself demanded an early release to recoup as soon as possible it may be that we all would have calmly acknowledged the summer threat and held off for a November or December opening. The high-quality look of the picture was recognised. *Blade Runner* was nominated for two

---

INTER-OFFICE COMMUNICATION

TO: Steve Warner DATE May 10, 1982

FROM: Bud Yorkin RE: "THE BLADE RUNNER"

Jerry and I spoke over the weekend and we both agreed that everyone should be off THE BLADE RUNNER payroll by Friday, May 14th. Of course this doesn't include you or Jack Smith; if there is still work to be done in London.

To quote Mr. Perenchio, he used the term "BASTA" which literally translated means -- "get off my back," "enough," and "I've had it!"

If anyone has a problem with the above, have them call me.

/d B.Y.

cc: Charles Weber
    Robin French

. . . and the unhappy end, with Bud Yorkin's communication (to production controller Steve Warner in May 1982) that he and Jerry Perenchio were putting the stoppers on *Blade Runner*'s post-production.

Academy Awards in the categories of Art Direction and Visual Effects, eight BAFTA awards, of which it won three, and a Golden Globe nomination for Vangelis. In 1993 it would be listed on the US National Film Registry by the National Film Preservation Board.

But the financial disappointment of *Blade Runner* was tough for all of us who had spent years developing our dream. It had been such a hard labour – firstly to get it made, and secondly to *keep* it being made. I've done a lot of controversial pictures: some have come off and some haven't. You get used to your dreams not always coming quite true, but the money side of it is just one part of the equation. I'm immensely proud to have produced a picture which, over the years of recuts and reissues, has travelled from being more or less a flop to becoming a cast-iron cult, and today, it seems fair to say, a classic.

19

A Form of Retirement

After the release of *Blade Runner* I was ready for a break, so I returned to my home on the ocean in Cape Cod and took stock of my position. I had now overseen some thirty movies, and I had been working continuously for the last twelve years without respite. *Blade Runner* had been extremely hard, and I wasn't in the mood to make another picture of that size again. Nor did I want to hang around Hollywood – a disposition that I knew would be a problem if I wished to carry on making serious movies, which would call for the upkeep of all the compulsory courtships and dances with the industry's power brokers. I'd had enough of all that.

I sold my house in Los Angeles. Ruth and I had bought the Cape Cod home chiefly as a stopover to ease the burden of frequent commuting between London and LA, but I had grown to love the Cape. Sailing had become a passion of mine, particularly racing, which for me meant that every couple of years a new boat had to be found: preferably one sufficiently innovative as to bamboozle the handicappers. I bought a thirty-three-foot Halsey Herreshoff design, which was moored on my dock alongside a gaff-rigged sixteen-footer designed by Halsey's grandfather, Nat.

I was having a great time. By 1984 I was sure I was retired from all filmmaking activities. Then, out of the blue – at a Christmas drinks party in the English countryside – I was invited to head up production for Consolidated, a TV company seeking to expand further into US network television after some early forays. I'd had no contact with the made-for-TV sector since my selling days at

MCA in the late 1950s, so there was a lot for me to catch up on. But what very quickly got me excited about TV-movie production is that it is entirely producer driven – particularly in the US, where success depends on the efficient shooting and delivering of a quality product as contracted, without spending a cent over the budget. Unlike the movies – where ever-changing estimates of a picture's box-office potential can lead to urgent reshoots and extra spending – there is no use in a TV director saying, 'Give me more money.' He has to work to budget or face the sack. So, for a producer, television is a very different business. You're not serving a director. Frankly, he's serving you – and to my mind this made for a rather pleasant change from the awful days with Pekinpah and Cimino.

Amid my early endeavours at Consolidated the one of which I was most proud was *A Gathering of Old Men* (1987), which I co-produced with Gower Frost. Based on a book by Ernest J. Gaines, it was a powerful drama set in a bigoted backwater of Louisiana (where, indeed, the film was shot). Gower secured the brilliant German director Volker Schlöndorff, best known for *The Tin Drum* (1979), which won both the Palme d'Or at Cannes and the Oscar for Best Foreign Film. Volker was keen to try his hand shooting in America, and his presence alone attracted a great cast: Lou Gossett Jr, Richard Widmark, Woody Strode and the young stage actress Holly Hunter, about whom CBS's casting department were initially unsure, failing to see in her the talent that soon carried her to her own Oscar triumph in *The Piano* (1993).

I also kept an eye on any theatrical film opportunities that came up. American director Irvin Kershner was high on the success of *The Empire Strikes Back* (1980) and *Never Say Never Again* (1983), Sean Connery's (admittedly troubled) comeback as James Bond. Irvin called me up and took me to the White Elephant to propose a new project, *Redcoat*, which would tell the story of a young English country boy tricked into the military and shipped with his regiment to America to fight the rebels in 1775. The idea promised what seemed to me a wining combination of action and romance, and there was a cracking part for a young leading man. Consolidated was not in a position to hire a top-drawer American screenwriter, but I knew that if the idea first found the form of a published novel then it would be a much easier pitch to a studio. Thus I engaged a young writer, Bernard Cornwell, to write a novel based on Irvin's story. My scheme was developing very promisingly – until we were blindsided. In 1985 director Hugh Hudson, he of *Chariots of Fire* fame, came out with *Revolution*, and despite a mighty cast including Al Pacino and Donald Sutherland, the film was a disaster. Since it was set in a similar period and context to *Redcoat*, its failure killed our project too. The sole beneficiary of this affair, happily, was Bernard Cornwell: his book was published by Michael Joseph, and he marched on to huge success with a series of novels set during the Napoleonic Wars, later turned into the TV series *Sharpe*, starring Sean Bean.

By the end of the 1980s Consolidated was still producing around forty hours of television a year. Chris Bryant, a friend of mine since he co-scripted Nic Roeg's *Don't Look Now,* came to me with a great idea for making a four-hour mini-series on the life of Catherine the Great, the ruthless Russian empress famous for her sexual exploits, who rose from being a demure provincial princess to become the dictator of Russia, even conniving at the murder of her husband on the way. Marlene Dietrich had made a good fist of this role in *The Scarlet Empress* back in 1935, under the direction of Josef von Sternberg. But the time seemed ripe for a fresh take, and I really wanted to produce *Young Catherine* myself. Chris and I decided to hone in on the years between Catherine's engagement to the future emperor and her coronation. A mini-series was a big wager for a US network: it needed stars, production values and a gripping story that could deliver a big share of the available audience. It was Ted Turner's Turner Network Television that came on board with us.

Clearly we had to shoot in Russia, but the Soviet Union remained dauntingly obstructive to foreigners. I travelled to St

Petersburg and found to my delight that the Soviets had spent four decades restoring the imperial palaces to the kind of brand-new condition that would greatly abet the shooting of a period piece. I then called upon Harold Wilson, who wrote on my behalf to someone high up in the Kremlin, so repeating the kindness he had shown me when he contacted the prime minister of India while we were planning to shoot *Flashman*.

I secured Michael Anderson as director, knowing from our work together on *Conduct Unbecoming* that he had the right blend of charm and efficiency to helm this production. Our cast needed names in order to satisfy a smorgasbord of co-production partners

F

```
The Rt. Hon. The Lord Wilson of Rievaulx KT OBE FRS
```

```
                                        31 January, 1990


Dear Michael,

            Thank you for your kind note.

            I did receive replies from all
those to whom I wrote, though the Soviet
side was quicker and I think more effective
from your point of view.  I shall be
interested to know how it all works out for
you now, and I hope you will let me know.
It would appear the British have been
experiencing some difficulties their own
officially with the telephone system, so it
may well be that you have been instrumental
in helping them, in view of the Soviet
response to my approach !

            With kind regards,

            Yours sincerely,

            Wilson of Rievaulx
```

This 1990 letter from Harold Wilson's office in the House of Lords illustrates the kindness he showed me in assisting my production of *Young Catherine* in the USSR.

(Canada, Italy and Germany). We drafted in Christopher Plummer as the urbane British ambassador to Russia, Vanessa Redgrave as Catherine's mother-in-law (even though this veteran of the Workers Revolutionary Party might seem an unlikely Russian aristocrat) and Maximilian Schell as King Frederick of Prussia. Marthe Keller played Catherine's mother, replacing my dear friend Lee Remick, who sadly was now in the advanced stages of the cancer to which she would succumb.

For our eponymous heroine, we sought an unknown. Michael Anderson and I interviewed more than twenty prospective Catherines and screen-tested five. The best was Julia Ormond, who had done almost nothing since leaving Webber Douglas Drama School two years earlier. She photographed like a dream and seemed responsive to Michael's direction. So we cast her.

Although the film was budgeted at $7 million, I planned to bring it in for much less, not least after I discovered that the Russian crew thought it infinitely preferable to be paid in US dollars than the absurdly inflated ruble. This strategy did put me in a risky position, since whenever I made runs to London I would bring back with me a bag stuffed full of US banknotes – sometimes as much as $50,000. This required me to keep a cool head when coming through airport customs. But the result was that the Russian crew was kept happy, and soon became great mates with their British colleagues on the production.

Unfortunately, this *entente cordiale* did not extend to relations with our leading lady. It is not uncommon to run into problems with cranky veteran movie stars who might feel demeaned by having to hurry their way through TV shooting schedules. Certainly Max Schell would get impatient with his inability to handle dialogue without cue cards. However, we imagined that young, inexperienced Julia Ormond would be a lamb. But about two-thirds of the way through the shoot, her arrival on set would be accompanied by the frequent request that she sit down with the director to review the pages of that day's work, the question being whether the script couldn't be 'improved' by some new ideas of hers. We were working to a template, and in any case Chris Bryant's script was characteristically elegant. Michael Anderson did not refuse to listen to Ormond's ideas but he did ask her to have any major discussions out of shooting hours, explaining that they simply couldn't afford to stop for script meetings.

Still, the final scene of the picture, when Catherine is triumphantly crowned empress, became a big problem over a small matter. Michael asked Ormond to show the faintest smile of satisfaction as her dreams were realised and the crown finally rested upon her head. 'No,' she said. 'Why on earth would I smile? I don't see it that way.' Reasonably, the director suggested that they try the scene both ways, with and without the smile, then decide which was best in the edit. Ormond stood her ground: 'No, you'll just use your version.' Michael assured Ormond that he would do what was best for the film. Finally, he proposed they try a rehearsal in his way, and then if she agreed they would shoot it. This rehearsal ran smoothly, through that final, faint-smiling close-up – and then Michael called 'Cut!' and Ormond shouted angrily. Of course Michael had quietly instructed the crew to shoot the 'rehearsal' but without a clapperboard. Once Ormond had calmed down he then shot her version too, but there was no doubt that the gentle smile on the Empress's face was the culminating moment of the movie.

Ormond's dissatisfaction with the script began to escalate alarmingly, though, and Michael and I started to hear mutterings about our leading actress walking from the picture. With only four-fifths of what we needed already in the can, we were somewhat at Ormond's mercy, though she surely had to realise that such a walkout would only lead to a massive lawsuit and a probable career suicide. Still, hastily but discreetly, Michael and I rearranged the schedule to get through Ormond's close-ups, so that, if she did quit, we could just about manage to shoot around her with a double and a few additional days. The crisis passed, but thereafter I found it difficult to look at Julia Ormond without distaste. In the mid-1990s she was cast as the female lead in several big Hollywood releases, some that performed (*Legends of the Fall*), others that nose-dived (*Sabrina*, *Smilla's Sense of Snow*). When *Young Catherine* reached screens in 1991 it became the highest rated mini-series that Turner Network Television had ever broadcast. But it was my last production. Consolidated was wound up shortly afterwards, and we all went our separate ways.

This newspaper advert for the cable premiere of *Young Catherine* showcases the formidable cast we had put together.

Coda

I remain very much in touch with the business as Deputy Chairman of the British Screen Advisory Council, which works with the British government and the European Commission on a wide range of media issues. What started in 1975 as the Prime Minister's Working Party on the Future of the British Film Industry has kept up to date, and now covers pretty much anything that can be seen on screen.

I am no longer responsible, however, for putting motion pictures onto aforementioned screens. That said, the steadily increasing tendency of the film business to cannibalise or revisit former glories has meant that several of my old productions have enjoyed peculiar second lives.

Sometime around 2002 it came to my attention that the successful British producers Eric Fellner and Tim Bevan of Working Title had reminded Paramount of their ownership of *The Italian Job*. I heard a rumour that an attempt was being made to remake the picture. I asked Sherry Lansing, then head of the studio, about it and she referred me to another studio executive who told me they were 'trying to develop a script'. I later heard that at least two sets of writers had been involved – even that someone was contemplating using the new VW Bug which had just come on the market, instead of Minis. This suggested to me that the remakers had no interest in the driving theme of the original movie – a conflict between Britons (in British cars) and Italians.

I was told that the first script was too much like the original and the second script was too different from the original. Since the final script was slightly like the original and very different then I guess they went for a happy medium. In the British version nobody was shot. In the American version Donald Sutherland was riddled with bullets – a fate which did not befall Noël Coward. They also moved the car chase to Hollywood because they felt that this would give the film broader appeal. Rumour has it that the new movie cost $75 million. Ours cost a little over $3 million, but if I had had a bunch of free Minis it would have been less. I certainly envied the remake's producer Donald De Line when BMW had the brains to see the advertising value for their new Mini Coopers and provided massive support.

But how often do remakes (as opposed to sequels) really succeed, commercially and/or creatively? The 1960s and 1970s are now seen as something of a golden age in cinema, but retooling the iconic pictures of the era has rarely yielded dividends. For example, nobody seemed to profit from the Sylvester Stallone remake of Mike Hodges' *Get Carter* in which Michael Caine had made a riveting anti-hero. The craziest of all recent remakes, surely, was *The Wicker Man* (2006): a flop shot in Canada at a cost of $40 million. Its subsequent recognition included a rare five 'Razzie' nominations – Worst Picture, Worst Actor, Worst Screenplay, Worst Screen Couple (for Nicolas Cage and his bear-suit) and – wait for it – Worst Remake. (Christopher Lee's character, Lord Summerisle, didn't even feature in the new version, which may have caused him further pain.) Now, as I write, it seems that after thirty-five years Peter Snell and Christopher Lee are once again working with Robin Hardy on a film written by Hardy entitled *Cowboys for Christ*, and reported to have strong echos of *The Wicker Man*. To top it all, pre-production has been announced on a remake of Nic Roeg's masterpiece *Don't Look Now*.

I'm perfectly aware that studios must make money by whatever means they can, but I believe there are enough good writers with original ideas who, if nurtured by producers, can turn out something fresher than the average remake. Generally, remakes feel like yesterday's newspaper – worthy at best, but diminished by time.

Blade Runner too was to be resurrected, but in a form that only honoured and enhanced the original production. In 1992 Ridley Scott approved a 'Director's Cut' of the film for theatrical re-release, one that got rid of Deckard's voiceover but drafted in his strange dream of a unicorn which – taken in tandem with the little origami unicorn left for him at his apartment by Gaff – would suggest that Deckard's own memories are 'implants'. This version also took that enigmatic moment on which to close the picture, so excising the previous fantastical ending of Deckard and Rachael driving off into a happy sun-kissed future.

Cut to 2007, and in the new world of super-enhanced DVD Ridley seized the chance to completely oversee a 'Final Cut' or 'Twenty-fifth Anniversary Edition' of the movie. When I sat down to view Ridley's handiwork I hadn't seen the picture for a long time, but I found the Final Cut fabulous, and hugely improved. The changes were not substantial. There were a couple of new shots. Zhora's final moments as she shatters her way through successive glass windows were performed by the lovely and evergreen Joanna Cassidy, so replacing the original stunt double in her wig – an extravagant activity, but one that took care of a fairly blatant 'blooper' from the original release. And the dying Batty's release of the dove into the air was reshot, so that the creature made off into an appropriately blackened sky.

A few of the film's violent elements were made just a little more wince-inducingly graphic: the crushing of Tyrell's head by Batty, the shooting of Pris, and Batty's gouging of his own palm with a rusty nail so as to stay awake and alive for just a little longer. One of the film's most oft-cited lines, of which Hampton Fancher was particularly proud – namely 'I want more life, fucker' – was subtly swapped for a version as revoiced for US television, which proposed a yet more intriguing subtext: 'I want more life, Father.'

Elsewhere the picture quality and Vangelis's music was more pin-sharp and precise. One comment from an early excited viewer seemed especially apt to me: 'It feels not like a newly cut film but a screening of a restored classic.' One thing that certainly did my own heart the world of good was the ending, as the elevator doors close upon Deckard and Rachael and the screen cuts to black, whereupon up comes the first credit:

A MICHAEL DEELEY/RIDLEY SCOTT PRODUCTION

Credits are the currency of the movie business, and so it is a very satisfying thing to have one's name lodged in a prime spot on a major picture, not least one that has entered the canon of cinema history on top of having proved to be one's happiest creative experience in motion-picture making. It was my pleasure to have played this part in bringing Ridley Scott's vision to its proper projection onto cinema screens.

As to what the future holds for the medium of film, I am less sure of what can be said. Movies are made for different motivations and for different audiences than when I was in the prime of my career. Back at the start, of course, I was handling and cutting film every day in the editing rooms. Now cinema projection itself is changing, as is the mode of distribution, in tandem with the increasingly digital nature of shooting and editing. I don't know how many years celluloid has left. Who does? But movies have given me extraordinary highs and delights, albeit with umpteen headaches along the way. I have seen things some people wouldn't believe – and in writing my reminiscences, I realise now that none of these moments have been lost. Moreover, whatever were the travails in their making, those movies that were built properly to last have indeed done so and, I suspect, will continue to be viewed with pleasure by future movie-lovers – until such time as our planet chokes on its own fumes, or we are all of us replaced by replicants . . .

Acknowledgements

I am grateful to these good friends who shared their memories. Some told me things I never knew. Some helped in other ways. Without their input this book would never have happened.

Michael Anderson, Steven Bach, Peter Bart, Sir Michael Caine, John Chambers, Graeme Clifford, Hampton Fancher, Gower Frost, Katy Haber, Terry Illott, David Kleeman, Alan Ladd Jr, Paul Lazarus, Syd Mead, Sir Alan Parker, David Peoples, Paul Prischman, Lord Puttnam, Quinn Redeker, Nic Roeg, Paul Sammon, Sir Ridley Scott – and a special thanks to a special editor, Richard T. Kelly.